The
Little
QuicKeys
Book

The Little QuicKeys Book

Steve Roth
Don Sellers

An Open House Book

Peachpit Press

The Little QuicKeys Book
Steve Roth and Don Sellers

Peachpit Press, Inc.
2414 Sixth St.
Berkeley, CA 94710
(510) 548-4393
(510) 548-5991 (fax)

ISBN 0-938151-59-2

0 9 8 7 6 5 4 3 2 1

Printed and bound in the United States of America

A Book About QuicKeys?

By Donald Brown, CE Software, Inc. Author of QuicKeys 2

When Dave Loverink, QuicKeys product manager, first mentioned the idea of someone doing a book about QuicKeys, I was confused. "A book about QuicKeys? What would they have to say? QuicKeys is so intuitive, so simple, and so well documented. What use could anyone get out of a book?"

After Dave stopped laughing, he pointed out some of the subtle nuances of the package that our manual doesn't cover. He then pointed out some of the creative things people have done with QuicKeys that others haven't stumbled across. He finally had started to list parts of QuicKeys that are less than crystal-clear, when I cut him off and told him what a great idea it was.

You now hold that book in your hands. Steve Roth and Don Sellers have done a marvelous job walking you step by step into QuicKeys, and then giving you ideas and strategies to get the most out of the program. Even I managed to pick up a few new ideas from this book.

One of the most marvelous discoveries I've made over the years is that QuicKeys gives people the chance to really customize their Macs. No two heavy-duty QuicKeys users will have exactly the same keys. Steve and Don let their personalities show in this book. I don't agree with everything they've said (I think they were a little rough on Real Time recording), but everything they said was thought-provoking and entertaining. Hang on to your hats. You're in for some fun!

Contents

Chapter 14: QuicKey Strategies   187

Deceptive Simplicity

"Who would want a book about QuicKeys? What's to say?"

"There are actually a lot of nooks and crannies to the program, you know."

"Well, yeah, you know the other day I was building this big Sequence…"

So we started talking. And then we talked some more. And the more we talked, the more we realized that QUICKEYS is a deep, deep program masquerading as an easy-to-use utility (it's that, also, of course). There are hidden treasures in the program that we didn't find until we were writing the last chapter of this book (and making pages for the second-to-last). QUICKEYS is deceptively simple, but when you start exploring it, you discover that it just keeps on going.

QUICKEYS is one other thing: It is the best program available for increasing your across-the-board efficiency on a Mac. So we are always surprised when we meet someone who owns a Mac but doesn't know about QUICKEYS. We're doubly surprised when we meet someone who owns QUICKEYS, but who doesn't take full advantage of it.

Why We Wrote This Book

We wrote this book because we're crazy about QUICKEYS; it's integral to our day-to-day poundings on the keyboard. When we happen to sit down at a Mac that doesn't have QUICKEYS (or *our* QuicKeys) installed on it, we fumble around, grumble imprecations, and generally make annoyances of ourselves. QUICKEYS has become so integral to how we work that we can't seem to use our Macs anymore without it.

But you have to set up and use QUICKEYS correctly to make it worthwhile. Although the QUICKEYS manual is very good, it doesn't tell you the tactics and strategies that result from years of working with the program. The manual doesn't mention the foibles and inconsistencies that you may encounter (that's right, we're in love but we're not blind). The manual doesn't include passels of application-specific QuicKeys that expert users have developed and refined.

That's what this book is about. We designed it to be both a teaching tool and reference guide. It is our hope that after reading it your efficiency will have improved so much that you wish someone had written it years before. (We wish someone had, so we didn't have to.)

How to Use This Book

We've tried to make this book as transparent as possible. You don't need a reference to little icons to figure out what's going on, nor do you need to use the book in any order. You can get at the information in several ways.

- Read it from beginning to end.
- Browse through.
- Refer to it in times of crisis.

Reading the book from beginning to end is our favorite recommendation, but we're not fooling ourselves. Browsing is another great method, and we've tried to provide a lot of ways into the book through browsing. Peruse the heads, jump into the figures, and jump from them to the figure references in the text (the references always precede the figures).

For those seeking a point of reference, we offer three methods.

Table of Contents. It includes chapter titles, and first- and second-level heads.

Index. This is the tool if you have a specific question.

Chapter 4: Thinking About QuicKeys. Starting on page 54, we list (nearly) every QuicKey in existence as of this writing, and give page references where you can find in-depth discussion. You may want to supplement this method with a look in the index, since the page references in Chapter 4 refer only to the main discussion of each type. There may be some peripheral discussion in another part of the book.

Acknowledgments

Many people helped create this book. We'd like to start by thanking the folks at Peachpit, who are always such a pleasure to work with and who do such a great job. Ted, Gaen, Keasley, Gregor, and all the rest, thanks.

CE Software

We could never have attempted a project like this without the support of CE Software.

Dave Loverink, the QUICKEYS development manager, was a constant source of information and enlightenment. His responses were always immediate, thorough, and expert. His reading of the manuscript was extraordinarily helpful and gracious—he could have been dogmatic about his own beliefs (like us), but instead he only tried to improve our work. CE is lucky to have him.

Don Brown, QUICKEYS creator, willingly gave time out of his busy schedule to diffuse the mist that sometimes obscured our understanding of his program. His insights on the ramifications of QUICKEYS were especially fascinating, and his foreword graces the front of this book.

Dave Reed, the hardworking head of CE Tech Support, always lobbed back the right answer when we served up a question—and we served up a bunch of them.

Sue Nail was the first person we met at CE, and it was a fortuitous meeting. She's been instrumental in steering us to the people who can help us, and getting us the things we need.

Despite the support from CE, any errors or omissions in this book are ours, not theirs.

Contributors

Three people contributed their words to this book. Howard Hansen of The Oasis Group in Seattle wrote the chapter on Excel. Joe Kroeger, editor of *The FileMaker Report*, wrote the chapter on (you guessed it) FileMaker. Don Munsil, programmer *extraordinaire* at ElseWare, wrote the section on Apple Events.

We'd like to offer great thanks to these three writers. They contributed a great deal more than their time.

Others   **Simeon Leifer.** No one has done more to move QUICKEYS beyond the simple-macro world than Simeon Leifer. Simeon wrote the great QUICKEYS extensions WindowDecision, WindowWait, CursorDecision, MenuWait, and MenuDecision ('zat all, Simeon?), which have done more to empower our QuicKeys strategies than any other tools. And he makes these babies available on a PWYTIW (pay what you think it's worth) basis. Thanks, Simeon.

A few people answered our requests for interesting keysets. Thanks to David Siegler, and to Jon Shulman of The Shulman Consultancy. John Trevor Wolff sent the idea about opening up Word windows.

Also, David Blatner, always helpful, kept bugging us to add good stuff. Ole gives great design. Seattle ImageSetting—above and beyond, other usual praise. Susie Hammond and Cindy Bell worked at meticulous editing, and Mike Arst entered all those changes (we'll write it better next time).

Finally, thanks to Susie Hammond for giving us Jesse and doing without Steve, and to Lucy, Sam, and Speedy for stoically surviving many evenings alone while Don was hard-a-working.

Steve Roth
Don Sellers

The Gateway to QuicKeys Knowledge

If you don't have much experience with QUICKEYS, this is the place to start. This chapter explains the basics—how the program works, where you'll most likely use it, and what you ought to know before you begin. Begin here if you are just tearing off the shrink wrap, or if you've had QUICKEYS installed for a long time but have never really bothered to learn how to use it.

Those devotees already familiar with QUICKEYS may want to jump over this chapter completely or perhaps jog by the headings to see if anything looks new. There might even be a few disciples who will want to race past the next few chapters to Chapter 4, *Thinking About QUICKEYS*. You QuicKeys monsters know who you are. (However, we would suggest you stay right here if you don't have over five keysets in your QuicKeys folder, and you don't nod sagely when we say, "I can't wait until CE builds some conditional branching into this program!")

The rest of you shouldn't worry—you're in exactly the right place. This first chapter will familiarize you with some of the sights and sounds you'll encounter on your ever-accelerating journey to QuicKeys nirvana.

QuicKeys Nirvana

What is QuicKeys nirvana? It's increasing your efficiency, going home early, mesmerizing your boss with flying fingers and flashing screens, feeling the heady pride of capturing the potential speed that's been lying dormant within your Mac. Ultimately, like any good nirvana, what you find when you achieve it all depends on what you're after. QUICKEYS, like any computer tool, only provides you with help in accomplishing something—how wisely and creatively you use QUICKEYS as a tool is up to you. Luckily, you sought the right help (us), and we're going to make it easy for you to maximize your relationship with QUICKEYS and minimize the pain.

Introduction to Macros

QUICKEYS makes macros. A macro is a little program that performs for you a task that otherwise you would have to do yourself. Macros happen to be particularly useful solutions for repetitive tasks. Like a task, a macro can be so small as to contain just one operation (a micro-macro), or be large enough to handle hundreds of operations (a macro-macro).

Macros are often thought of as "automators," which is a reasonably accurate description. You can also think of them as "abbreviators," something small representing something big. QUICKEYS abbreviates standard mouse movements, screen manipulations, dialog box responses, menu choices, keyboard strokes, and a variety of special routines. You include one or more operations in a QUICKEYS macro and designate a keystroke combination which activates it. Then, whenever you want to invoke that macro, you type in your keystroke combination, and QUICKEYS takes over. If you built your macro correctly, it does what you want it to; if not, QUICKEYS makes it easy for you to return to the drawing board and correct your errors.

Some macros are application-specific—they work only within and for a particular application program. For example, Excel has macro language built into it. Others, like QuicKeys, work within nearly the entire Mac environment.

Why Macros Anyway?

Why macros? We generally don't like to answer such profound questions so early in your training, so instead we'll ask you a question. Would you like your life to be easier? If you answer yes, then look onward to how macros can help (if you answer no—put the shrink wrap, with tape, back on the package, return ASAP). Here are some standard QUICKEYS tricks.

Opening Files. You start your computer and tap a few keystrokes. In seconds, all the files you need open are open.

Moving Between Applications, Desk Accessories, etc. As you work in your desktop-publishing program, you need to get to your calendar (Chooser, drawing program, whatever). With a keystroke, you're there.

Standardizing. Do some of your programs use Command-W to close the window? Does one use Command-W to reduce the size of the window? Do others entirely lack a keystroke short-cut for window closing? QuicKeys can make Command-W the universal keystroke to close windows in all applications.

Housekeeping. Want to empty the Trash? Keystroke, it's done. Restart your Mac? Another keystroke, and it happens. Change printers? Zap!

Customizing. Want to search for a key word in your word-processing application, copy that paragraph, open a new document, paste that paragraph into the document, save the document (even taking the time to fill in a new file name), then return to the mother document and continue this process again and again? QuicKeys can do it faster than we can describe it.

QuicKeys Basics

The work-saving benefits of QuicKeys are obvious, but how easy is it to operate? QuicKeys is a simple program—but it's possible to be waylaid by some of its quirks.

The best way into QuicKeys is to get grounded in the basics. Please pick up an appropriate item from your desk—an old bullet will do—bite on it and we'll pound through the stuff you need to know.

Management Window

The most common way to manipulate the QuicKeys program is through the QuicKeys management window (see Figure 1-1). CE Software calls this the "QuicKeys window" but we don't find that either a distinctive or descriptive enough name for such a fundamental component of the program. The management window acts as the main QuicKeys control panel—which would be the perfect name for it except that there already is a QuicKeys control panel in the Control

Panel section of the Mac system (accessible from the Apple menu). Although we don't want to say "windows" so many times that you think we're getting kickbacks from Microsoft, we've found that "management window" works well.

Figure 1-1
THE QUICKEYS
management window

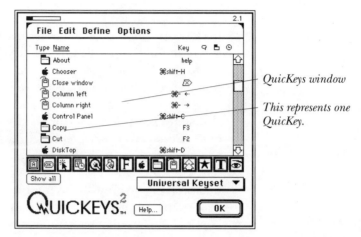

QuicKeys window

This represents one QuicKey.

QuicKey

A QuicKey is one macro written in the QUICKEYS program. You usually create a QuicKey yourself, but you can also use those that CE Software has included in the package. Most QuicKeys that you use are permanent—they are stored by the QUICKEYS program. Sometimes you will make a temporary QuicKey for a specific job, and then get rid of it. We have described a whole bunch of incredibly useful and creative QuicKeys in this book; all you have to do is enter them into the program and you'll be ready to go. Other QuicKeys are available from online services such as CompuServe and America Online (see Appendix, *Resources*).

QuicKey Attributes

Every QuicKey has a few standard attributes. Some of these attributes are integral to how the program works; some of these attributes we created so we could discuss logically delineated program components. We found that getting a firm footing in the standard attributes helped us to learn other aspects of the program.

Name. Each QuicKey usually has a unique name. What you name a QuicKey is up to you (in most cases). The name should be easy to recall, so it helps to make the name short (it must be less than 16 characters) and descriptive. Sometimes you'll find that naming a temporary QuicKey is a waste of your time, but it never causes problems to name your QuicKeys. Get in the habit of doing so, at least as a novitiate. Later on, it will be obvious when you won't want to bother.

Type. Each QuicKey is also of a specific type. Each QuicKey type is a functionally distinct tool. We have listed the QuicKey types we discuss in this book in Table 1-1. You may not have all these types available to you (some are not supplied with the program), but you'll have most of them. All the types that you do have available are displayed in the Define menu and submenus of your management window. Chapter 4, *Thinking About QUICKEYS*, discusses all of the different types and refers you to the chapter where we investigate each in detail.

Table 1-1
QuicKey types

Alias	Location	Select rear window
Balloon Help Off	Menu/DA	Select second window
Balloon Help On	MenuDecision	Sequence
Buttons	MenuWait	Show
Choosy	Message	Show Clipboard
Click	Mounty	Shut Down
Close window	Next Application	Sleep
Column left	Open	Sound
Column right	Page down	Speaker Changer
CursorWait	Page left	Start FileSharing
Date/Time	Page right	Start/Stop Real Time
DisMounty	Page up	Start/Stop Sequence
Display	Panels	Stop FileSharing
Double QuickQuotes	Paste Ease	Stuff
End	Pause	Text
File	Print	Toggle Balloon Help
FKEYs	QuicKeys 2	Toggle QuicKeys on/off
Get Info	QuickQuotes	Transfer
Grab Ease	QuickReference Card	Type Ease
Home	Real Time	UnStuff
Last Appliation	Repeat	Wait
Line down	Restart	WindowDecision
Line up	Screen Ease	WindowWait
		Zoom window

Categories. Some QuicKey types are also grouped together into what we call categories. The categories are what you see on the Define menu of the management window (see Figure 1-2). As you may notice, some of the categories are also types. This occurs when the category comprises only one type. For those items that are just categories, their submenus list their types.

Figure 1-2
The Define menu
in the QUICKEYS
management
window

Define

Alias...
Buttons...
Click
Date/Time ▶
Extensions ▶
File...
FKEYs ▶
Menu/DA...
Mousies ▶
Sequence...
Specials ▶
Text...
Real Time

Both the historical evolution of the program and its inner workings influenced the composition of the Define menu (that is, the categories), with the result that the distinction between some categories is obscure. For example, Specials and Extensions seem to be functionally indistinguishable categories to many people (even though they are very different to a QUICKEYS programmer).

We believe that the types should be categorized by *function*. Doing so helps you choose the right QuicKey for your job. Our recategorization of the categories is in Chapter 4, *Thinking About QUICKEYS*.

Icon. Each QuicKey category has its own little icon associated with it. There's a little mouse for the Mousies QuicKey category, a little OK button for the Buttons QuicKey category, and so on. These icons show up in the QUICKEYS management window (see Figure 1-1) and on the Define menu (see Figure 1-2).

Adding a little fertilizer to this jungle of iconography is the fact that all the categories have icons but *some* of the types have icons, too. For example, Extensions (as a category) has an icon, and each different Extension QuicKey has a different icon. The Mousies category has an icon, but the types that comprise the Mousies submenu don't have icons. But as Steve says, "Who cares?" It may not be the perfect paradigm, but the little icons are all very cute—and, in a practical sense, any visual aid to categorization helps keep QuicKey functions separate in your thinking.

Influence. Some QuicKey types only influence one target. For example, a File QuicKey opens one specific file. So it is likely you will have lot's of File QuicKeys—different ones to open each of your important applications and documents.

Some other QuicKey types are untargeted—they often display a dialog box which allows you to select the target-of-the-moment. Usually, you will only need one representative of an untargeted QuicKey in your keysets. The Transfer Extension is a good example of an untargeted QuicKey type. When you invoke a Transfer QuicKey a dialog box is displayed asking you what file you wish to open. We sometimes call these untargeted QuicKey types *generalists.*

Keysets

Different QuicKeys are bunched together as sets in QUICKEYS. Each of these sets is called a keyset. QUICKEYS automatically creates a keyset for each application as you open it, and maintains a keyset for each application for which you create a QuicKey. For example, if you are working in Microsoft Word and you create a QuicKey that enters some specific text, that QuicKey is saved in the Microsoft Word keyset which QUICKEYS automatically created, ready for you to use.

Universal Keyset. QUICKEYS also has a special keyset which is open whenever QUICKEYS is open. This is the all-powerful and appropriately named "Universal Keyset." It contains the QuicKeys that you might want to invoke from *any* application. For example, if you want to standardize Command-S as the Save command for all your applications (some of them aren't designed that way; we don't know why), you include that QuicKey in the Universal Keyset.

Achieving Nirvana

That's all you need to know for now. There are a few other QUICKEYS quirks, but those will have to wait until later (see Chapter 3, *QUICKEYS Doctrine*).

Now that we've decided where we're going (QuicKeys nirvana, of course), in the next chapter we'll check out the resources available to succor the pilgrim (that's you, pilgrim) on the way.

The Old Kit Bag

It's best to start on any journey fully prepared, and the path to QuicKeys nirvana is no exception. CE Software has outfitted you with two jam-packed disks, a traveller's kit bag that's chock full of items—so many items that, in some cases, you might question their reason for being included. In this chapter, we check out the QuicKeys package. We investigate what you need to know about installing QuicKeys on your Mac. We describe how QuicKeys lives inside your machine by revealing the crannies and corners in which you can find QuicKeys. And we dump out the entire contents of the QuicKeys kit bag and sort through what's inside.

Inside Your QuicKeys Package

If you have one of the more recent versions of QuicKeys (2.x), then the bulk of this chapter—in which we describe the QuicKeys package—will make sense to you. If you have some older version, you should seriously consider springing for an upgrade. The newest QuicKeys performs all sorts of tricks that previous versions can't, and CE offers a variety of upgrade plans depending on how old your copy of QuicKeys is. So far the company has supported perpetual sanctuary (it's always possible to get an upgrade rather than buy a whole new program), but that can't be guaranteed to go on forever. If you have version 2.01 or earlier, give CE Customer Service a call (see Appendix, *Resources*) and a rep will tell you how to come in from the old.

Both QuicKeys disks that come in your package are packed with applications, folders, and files. On first glance, you might wonder what all this stuff is doing there: some of it you didn't know you were getting, and there's some stuff in there you won't find reference to in the manual.

This bounty is due to CE's "be prepared" corporate policy. The wizards at CE constantly upgrade their product, and include changes on their disks more quickly than they can publish requisite support literature. Instead of the literature, they include Read Me files within different folders to explain what's what. It's great to have the most advanced features, but most of us don't relish trudging through the mire of Read Me files; we want to jump right in and get to work. To do that, you must first install QUICKEYS.

QUICKEYS Installation

QK2Install is a small application that places the QUICKEYS elements you need in the places you need them.

QK2Install. QK2Install arrives on your main QUICKEYS disk. When working with any master disk like this, the cardinal rule is: Don't. Lock the master and then make a copy of it. Forever after, work with the copy. You'll need to enter your program's serial number on its first activation. The number is on the back of the master disk.

Insert the copy of your master disk and double-click on the QK2Install icon. A dialog box appears that is self-explanatory, especially since it has its own Help box on the right. Pointing to different areas in the dialog box elicits illuminating messages in this Help box.

At the bottom-left corner of the dialog box, some of you (Mac Plus and 512Ke owners) have the additional option of choosing the keyboard you use. This option exists because these machines don't know how to handle function keys on third-party extended keyboards. This section is only active when installing QUICKEYS on a Mac Plus or 512Ke; it is grayed out for everyone else.

What options you install depend on whether you are in System 6 or 7 (see Figure 2-1). In System 6 you want the three basic options: QUICKEYS, Extensions, and DialogKeys. CEIAC and QK.Help (Balloon Help) are for System 7 only.

To activate QK2Install, press the Install button. (QK2Install might be more aptly named QK2Install/Remove, because you can set it to remove the same categories it can install.) QK2Install checks to see if you have an old copy of QuicKeys already in residence. If so, it updates the old QuicKeys application and related files to the present configuration and then places them in the proper folders.

Figure 2-1
QK2Install options

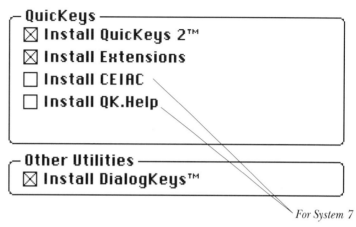

┌─ **QuicKeys** ─────────────────────────
☒ **Install QuicKeys 2**™
☒ **Install Extensions**
☐ **Install CEIAC**
☐ **Install QK.Help**

┌─ **Other Utilities** ──────────────────
☒ **Install DialogKeys**™

For System 7

QuicKeys 2.1 requires that you use QK2Install—don't drag the files into their folders. QK2Install lets the System know how much memory QuicKeys needs.

Confirming the Installation. After you install QuicKeys on your Mac and restart, you might notice something—there isn't much to notice. QuicKeys sits invisibly in the background of your computing environment. However, there are a few ways in which you can reveal that QuicKeys actually lurks inside your computer, waiting to do your bidding.

- **Check the Apple menu.** You can verify that QuicKeys is installed and active on your machine by pulling down the Apple menu and seeing if "QuicKeys 2" (or something similar) is on it.
- **Activate a QuicKey.** Type in an activating keystroke combination for a QuicKey. If you have none available yet, see next chapter, *QuicKeys Doctrine*.
- **Notice the startup icon.** If QuicKeys is loaded, its icon will appear while your System is loading after startup.

Inside the Installation
QK2Install does different things depending on whether you are in System 6 or System 7. Here's a quick rundown of

where everything goes. You will find a complete description of each installed item in "The Necessary" and "The Helpful," later in this chapter.

System 6

- **System folder.** The System folder, or "blessed" folder, is where your Mac looks for programs like QUICKEYS. The installer places the file QuicKeys 2 here. An accompanying INIT, CEToolbox, also goes here.
- **Preferences folder.** QK2Install creates this folder if you haven't already got one in your System folder. Inside the Preferences folder, the installer places the QuicKeys folder.
- **QuicKeys folder.** The QuicKeys folder contains the KeySets and Sequences folders, two repositories of different QuicKeys. The QuicKeys folder also contains the Extensions folder for your QuicKey Extensions, small auxiliary enhancements of the main program.

System 7

- **System folder.** The System folder in System 7 contains an Extensions folder, a Control Panels folder, and a Preferences folder.
- **Extensions folder.** The installer places CEToolbox, an accessory program for QuicKeys and some other CE programs, into this folder.
- **Control Panels folder.** The installer places the QuicKeys 2™ cdev into this folder.
- **Preferences folder.** The QuicKeys folder goes here. The QuicKeys folder holds the Keysets, Sequences, and Macros (Real Time recordings) folders, all repositories of different QuicKeys. The QuicKeys folder also contains the Extensions folder (identically named to, but different from, the System's Extensions folder). This Extensions folder contains small auxiliary enhancements of the main program, Extensions. And last, but not least, the QUICKEYS preferences file also dwells in the QuicKeys folder.

Disk Contents

You may notice that QK2Install doesn't use many of the items that come on your disk. Some of the items included in your QUICKEYS package are necessary, some are merely helpful, and some are only required for specialized applications. Here's a rundown on what you paid for.

The Necessary   These files are necessary to make QuicKeys function. Be sure to check out "The Helpful" to ensure you have everything that allows QUICKEYS to work at its best within your configuration.

QUICKEYS. The main QUICKEYS program comes in the form of "QuicKeys 2™". This is what you thought you were buying. QUICKEYS is a cdev—a piece of code that adds itself to the Control Panel (you can select the Control Panel from the Apple menu). You have to restart your Mac after installing QUICKEYS, because the Mac loads cdevs only during startup.

QK2Install. QK2Install is a small but powerful application that does the major housekeeping tasks associated with putting QUICKEYS on your hard disk.

Think of this installer as a QUICKEYS installation demigod that CE packages with your program. In previous incarnations, you could install QUICKEYS and the Extensions by dragging them into their appropriate folders. This is no longer the case. You must now use QK2Install because it makes System memory adjustments. It does reserve some work for you. If you want the Printing Templates, Sample Keysets, and Examples that might be included in the package, you need to copy these into an appropriate folder on your hard disk yourself.

CEToolbox. CEToolbox is an INIT (it used to be a cdev), a little program which loads on startup. As with the QUICKEYS cdev, you have to restart your Mac after it's installed. Several CE programs can take advantage of CEToolbox; it handles the following tasks.

- Makes QUICKEYS show up on the Apple menu in a variety of configurations (see Figure 2-2).
- Enables any File QuicKeys to work (so you can launch programs and open documents with QUICKEYS).
- Enables keystrokes to be displayed and edited in the QUICKEYS management window.
- Enables you to bring up a CEToolbox floating menu in which you can access QUICKEYS (and a variety of other CE programs, if you've got them).

Figure 2-2
QuicKeys on the
Apple menu

*You have your choice of
where QuicKeys appears
on the Apple menu.*

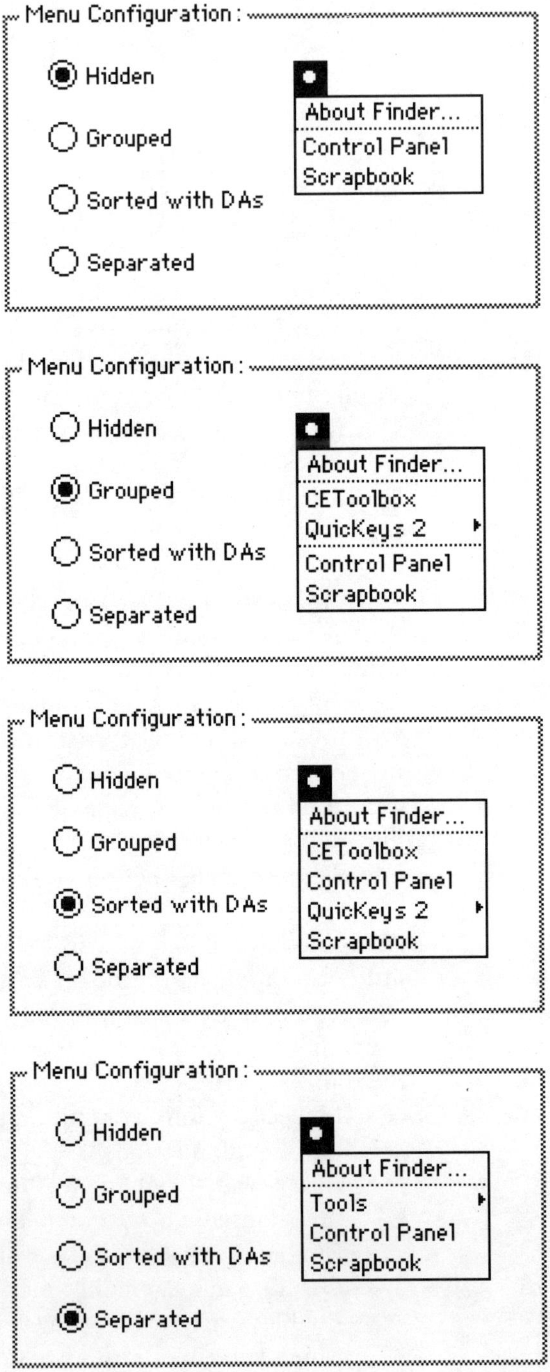

Menu Configuration:

- ● Hidden
- ○ Grouped
- ○ Sorted with DAs
- ○ Separated

About Finder...
Control Panel
Scrapbook

Nowhere…

Menu Configuration:

- ○ Hidden
- ● Grouped
- ○ Sorted with DAs
- ○ Separated

About Finder...
CEToolbox
QuicKeys 2   ▶
Control Panel
Scrapbook

at the top…

Menu Configuration:

- ○ Hidden
- ○ Grouped
- ● Sorted with DAs
- ○ Separated

About Finder...
CEToolbox
Control Panel
QuicKeys 2   ▶
Scrapbook

*in among
the DAs…*

Menu Configuration:

- ○ Hidden
- ○ Grouped
- ○ Sorted with DAs
- ● Separated

About Finder...
Tools   ▶
Control Panel
Scrapbook

*or on its
own submenu.*

QK2Install can place CEToolbox into your System folder for you. In System 7, it goes in the System's Extensions folder. If for some reason it isn't in your System folder, you'll get a message when you boot up (see Figure 2-3).

Figure 2-3
The warning displayed
when CEToolbox is
not installed

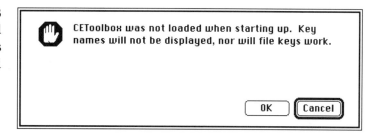

CEToolbox was not loaded when starting up. Key names will not be displayed, nor will file keys work.

OK   Cancel

You can still operate QUICKEYS in a crippled form without CEToolbox, but there is no reason to do so. That puts it on our necessities list.

Extensions and More Extensions folders. Extensions are additions to the QUICKEYS program that perform various specialized functions. You can think of Extensions as the citrus juicer or the dough blade attachments for your Cuisinart (or the hole cutter, circular sander, or grinding wheel attachments for your electric drill, if you're of that persuasion). They're extras that work with the same mother machine to make it more versatile. The sublime aspect of Extensions is that CE and outside programmers produce more of them all the time, and (so far) they are inexpensive or free.

Extensions should reside in the Extensions folder in the QuicKeys folder in the Preferences folder in your System folder. QUICKEYS can only access Extensions that are in the Extensions folder.

Inside the More Extensions folder of your QUICKEYS package you should find the Extension Manager, a little application CE built that lets you install and control your Extensions. QK2Install only installs some of the available Extensions; you need to use the Extensions Manager to install the rest.

Read Me files. These files contain the latest information on the particular version of QUICKEYS that you received, so they're worth glancing through to see if there's anything important that pertains to your system configuration. You never know what earth-shaking item will show up on a Read Me file. So you should definitely take a look at the main one—"Read Me (QuicKeys v2.1)" which is on your primary disk.

The Helpful

These items aren't absolutely critical to make QUICKEYS function. But you probably will want to use some of them, especially to take advantage of all the capabilities of QUICKEYS 2.1 and System 7.

DialogKeys. DialogKeys is a natural accompaniment to QUICKEYS: it puts keystroke control into dialog boxes—just dialog boxes. When DialogKeys is active you can tab through the buttons in the dialog box and choose the one you want—a function that usually requires the mouse.

DialogKeys comes with three keystrokes preset for its four functions (Click performs two functions: starts DialogKeys and presses the blinking button). You can change these presets through the Control Panel (see Figure 2-4).

Figure 2-4
DialogKeys

Moves backward through buttons

Moves forward through buttons

Invokes DialogKeys and picks whatever button is blinking

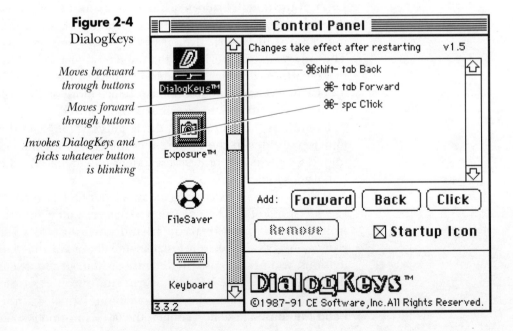

Because QUICKEYS can accomplish many of the same

things DialogKeys does, Don only uses DialogKeys in special circumstances. Steve uses it frequently, and there is no doubt that DialogKeys works well as "generic Button-like QuicKeys" for those who want to be able to press buttons without resorting to a mouse.

CEIAC. We're going to get a lot of flak on this one. A lot of QUICKEYS users will say this should be included in "The Necessary." Why? Because IAC (interapplication communication) is probably one of the *big* evolutions in the Mac, and QUICKEYS is positioned to take advantage of it. CEIAC (CE Software's IAC application) is an INIT-invoked application and is copied into the appropriate folder when you check the Install CEIAC option in the QK2Install dialog box.

CE Software created CEIAC to facilitate interapplication communication in System 7. Apple standardized a bunch of messages that could be sent between applications (Apple Events). CEIAC is the *medium* through which the Apple Event *messages* are sent. So far there are only a handful of Apple Event messages. But there are other messages that can use the CEIAC medium (Finder Events Extensions and Frontier Extensions). Expect to see more happening with CEIAC in the future.

For System 6 ONLY folder. Inside this folder is HeapFixer and its companion Read Me file. HeapFixer is a little application that helps your Mac solve a problem that sometimes occurs in System 6—your System file gets bigger than the amount of space allotted for it. Confusing? Not surprising! That's why many people bought Macs—so they wouldn't have to deal with obscure nonsense like this.

The explanation is actually pretty simple to understand: QUICKEYS is a program that loads itself on startup. Programs with this feature (such as INITs, cdevs, fonts installed in your system folder, and desk accessories) will sometimes grab memory that might be needed by the System. If you make demands on the System later, it can run out of available memory. Lack of memory is the number one cause of an unhappy and confused computer. Signs of this can be subtle: things slow down, and a general malaise embraces your machine. Or your Mac can just freeze.

The best method of diagnosis: in the Finder, choose "About the Finder" from the Apple menu. If the System bar is more than about three-fourths dark, you need to expand your System Heap.

Back in the early Mac days, this situation didn't show up too often—most folks had only a few things which loaded on startup. Lately, however, there has been a proliferation (some say a pestilence) of programs that load with the system. Unfortunately, Apple needed to get to System 7 to intelligently deal with the problem; in previous incarnations, you have to do it yourself. That's what the HeapFixer is for.

QK.Help. QK.Help is the Balloon Help file for System 7 users. If you click the Install QK.Help option in QK2Install, then QK.Help is copied into the QuicKeys folder (in the Preferences folder, in the system folder). Balloon Help isn't too helpful for us, but CE views it as providing hints, and it does that well. If you are just learning QUICKEYS, it may untangle some of your conundrums.

Printing Templates folder. Inside the Printing Templates folder is a little application and some associated files, which print out a schematic of your keyboard with the names of your QuicKeys located right on top of their appropriate activation keys. You can format the typeface differently for each modifier key (Control, Option, Command, etc.) so you can discern at a glance which goes with a particular QuicKey.

This you definitely don't need to have, but it can come in handy if you want to look at your QuicKeys keystroke distribution patterns (ours seem to bunch up on the left and right sides of the keyboard).

By the way, the Template Printer contains a surprise. Open it, choose "About Template Printer" from the Apple menu, then don't use your mouse or keyboard for 30 seconds, and you'll see what we mean. During the surprise, press Command-Option-Shift to drop in a ready-made visual critique.

Sample Keysets folder. CE has provided a potpourri of keyset examples that you may want to incorporate into your own QUICKEYS environment. Our version included the following bunch of keysets.

- **Alias.** The Alias keyset is simply a set of keystrokes that maps every key on the keyboard to itself. So A equals A, F1 equals F1. This keyset is useful if you're using a terminal emulation or computer emulation program; since the Alias keys override any QuicKeys you may have set up in the Universal keyset, those QuicKeys don't interfere with special keys used by the emulation program.
- **Dvorak.** This handy little package of Alias QuicKeys makes your keyboard think it has a Dvorak layout—an ergonomically friendly alternative to the traditional QWERTY keyboard layout. Dvorak puts the most commonly used keys close to your fingers where they belong (see Figure 2-5).

Figure 2-5
Dvorak and
QWERTY
keyboards

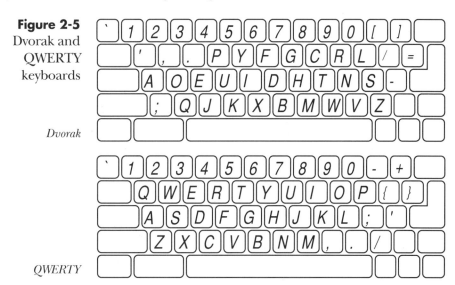

Dvorak

QWERTY

- **More Universal Keys.** There's nothing "more" about it. This keyset is CE's group of suggested universal keys. You can copy those you want into your Universal Keyset and you'll instantly have a starter set of QuicKeys. The best of these invoke common applications and standardize program-to-program keystroke functions (see Figure 2-6).
- **Screen Ease Keys.** These keys give you a plethora of screen display settings (for example, the number of colors or grays you are displaying). We can't think of any

application where you would want all of these loaded, but you might want to avail yourself of some of them.

Figure 2-6
Some of the
QuicKeys from
"More Universal
Keys"

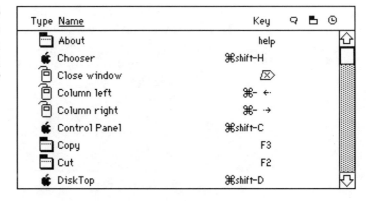

TeachText. TeachText is a ubiquitous little application that reads the basic type of word-processing file—the ASCII text file. You can open all of the Read Me files that CE includes in the QUICKEYS package with TeachText (undoubtedly, your own word-processing program can also open them). Because it is a small, simple program and many other software companies include files in the TeachText format, it is good to have one copy of it on your hard drive. However, when you drag whole disks and folders to your hard disk, you find that the little thing (19K) starts to proliferate. Don just searched through his hard disk and found four of the little buggers. After a brief and brutal session with DiskTop (another CE program we highly recommend) only one was left.

TAA. When we first saw this, we had some fun creating possible meanings for this acronym, but we never came close to the real root—Technical Assistance Assistant. TAA (rhymes with F.A.A.) inspects your entire Mac system from head to toe. It checks out certain important system files, memory, INITs, cdevs, fonts, drivers, and more.

Why would you need it? Most people don't. CE includes it as an aid for its technical assistance staff. If you experience a problem with QUICKEYS and petition CE technical support personnel for aid, they will sometimes ask you to send them a TAA report. Its information, most of it impossible for the average user to easily discover, is critical to the analysis of many problems. The TAA saves its report in text format (TeachText), retrievable by any word processor. After you set TAA loose, you can watch as it displays pages of technical (and often exceptionally boring) information.

One advantage of CE's foresight is that any sophisticated users can employ TAA to analyze their Mac setup. But be forewarned—if your configuration is fairly complex and dense (especially if you have lots of fonts loaded), the TAA readout will go on for pages and pages and pages. TAA versions 2.1 and later have a Configure button which allows you to select what areas you want tested. But, if the TAA output starts to run on too long, pressing Command-Period will make it heel (except while printing its cover sheet).

Vapor folders. According to our manual, there are two other folders included on our disks—Examples and Other Stuff. However, they aren't there. CE is updating the manual, so you may not have anything missing, but just in case Scotty beams these folders into your package, here's a rundown on their alleged contents.

- **Examples folder.** This folder contains a bunch of sample sequences included mainly to demonstrate how the Sequence QuicKey is the preferred (and, often, the only) solution in many situations. It is worth a look. Our Chapter 13, *Sequence QuicKeys,* covers the subject in detail.
- **Other Stuff folder.** Other Stuff acts as the grab bag for additional stuff that CE likes to send along. It might include Vaccine, a small (12K) cdev that helps keep nasty worms and viruses out of your system. While not as powerful as other, more sophisticated antiviral programs, it is better than nothing. And these days everyone should practice "safe computing." To install Vaccine, just put it into your system folder, and the next time you start up you'll find its controls and help available through your Control Panel.

The Specialized

Well, aren't you special? If so, you might need one of these.

Macintosh Plus extended keyboard drivers. The interfacement of extended keyboards with the Mac Plus is to technology what this sentence is to clarity. In other words, the Mac Plus wasn't designed to be used with extended keyboards, and it takes some work to make it function. For those of you who face this prospect, CE has included special keyboard drivers—for DataDesk and Tangent keyboards, along with their companion INITs (the newer DataDesk keyboards don't need this special INIT, and function strangely when it is included). See "QK2Install," earlier in this chapter.

For Programmers Only folder. One of the cool things about QUICKEYS is that it constantly evolves—not only through the efforts of the people at CE, but also through the work of independent programmers. These programmers create new Extensions, and so far, have generously made them available to CE to distribute to QUICKEYS owners.

To promote and support this arrangement, CE includes the For Programmers Only folder. If you weren't, aren't, and never intend to be a QUICKEYS programmer, you can ignore this folder. It contains source code in both C and Pascal for an Extension that is described in the Read Me documentation.

QUICKEYS XCMD folder. This folder contains an XCMD and its companion Read Me file. An XCMD is a small HyperCard extension that you can copy into your HyperCard application (using a resource editing or copying program). It will give your HyperCard program the ability to access QUICKEYS directly from its scripts. If you don't program in HyperCard, you won't need this; your usual QuicKeys will work in Hyper-Card with normal keyboard activation.

HyperCard programmers note: at the time of this writing (September, 1991), there is a bug within the Play QuicKey XCMD when it's calling a sequence—the XCMD passes control back to HyperCard before the QuicKey Sequence finishes. CE is aware of the problem and is working on it. One solution (possible in System 7 and HyperCard 2.1 or later) is to send an Apple Event to QUICKEYS telling it to play the Sequence. Control won't be passed back to HyperCard until QUICKEYS is finished. Another, albeit ugly, workaround is to make the XCMD the last item in the HyperCard script.

QuicKeys Doctrine

In this chapter, we reveal the fundamentals of QUICKEYS doctrine—the universal rites and objects necessary to create QuicKeys macros. We'll start by building, invoking, and editing a sample QuicKey—one that invokes the QUICKEYS management window. Then we'll discuss some of the foundations of QuicKey construction and the QUICKEYS program—including the QUICKEYS management window, keysets, Apple menu items, the QuickReference Card, the generic QuicKeys edit dialog box, and high-level QUICKEYS control.

A Useful QuicKey

In keeping with the convolutions of operating a computer, the QuicKey we'll create will open QUICKEYS. More specifically, our QuicKey will open the QUICKEYS management window. Once you have built this QuicKey and included it in your QuicKeys arsenal, you'll probably use it a lot; you can invoke this QuicKey as the first step when you create or edit any subsequent QuicKeys.

Creating and Invoking a Sample QuicKey

Let's pretend we're in the Army Corps of Engineers—we'll create the QuicKey first and then go back and figure out what we did.

1. Choose QuicKeys 2 from the Apple menu. The QUICKEYS management window, similar to that shown in Figure 3-1, appears.
2. Make sure that "Universal Keyset" is displayed in the Keyset pop-up menu. If it isn't, click on the menu and choose it.
3. Click on the Define menu and drag down until you

choose "QuicKeys 2" from the "Specials" submenu (see Figure 3-2).

Figure 3-1
QUICKEYS management window

Define menu

QuicKeys window

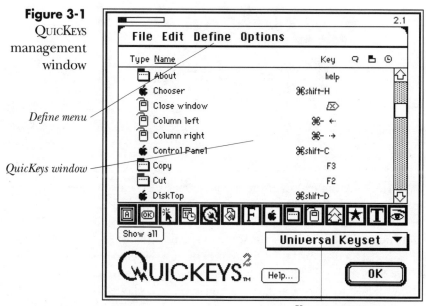

Keyset pop-up menu

Figure 3-2
QUICKEYS 2 in the Define Menu

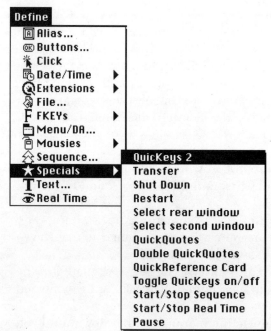

4. The edit dialog box for this QuicKey appears (see Figure 3-3). "QuicKeys 2" is already entered in the pop-up menu.

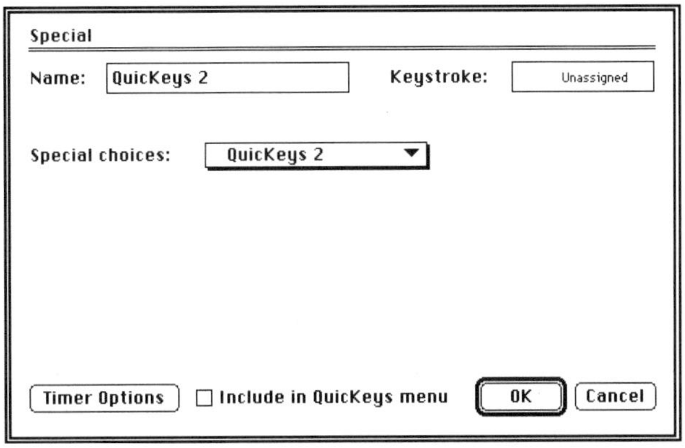

Figure 3-3
QUICKEYS 2 edit
dialog box

Special

Name: QuicKeys 2   Keystroke: Unassigned

Special choices: QuicKeys 2   ▼

Timer Options   ☐ Include in QuicKeys menu   OK   Cancel

5. Enter a keystroke in the Keystroke box. Don uses Control-Option-Q; Steve uses Control-Q.
6. Click on the Include in QuicKeys menu check box if you want to access this QuicKey from the Apple menu.
7. Click OK. The QUICKEYS management window returns with your new QuicKey inside. Click OK again, and you've finished.

That's all there is to creating a simple and useful QuicKey. Most of the rest of this chapter we devote to investigating what you've just done. We explain the different mechanisms and controls that are fundamental to the QuicKey manufacturing process.

Now that you've created a QuicKey, there are three ways to invoke it.

• Press the invoking keystroke that you typed in Step 4, above.
• If you clicked the Include in QuicKeys menu check box in Step 5, you can choose your QuicKey from the QuicKeys submenu on the Apple menu. We discuss the QuicKeys submenu in more detail in "QuicKeys on the Apple Menu," later in this chapter.
• Open the QuickReference Card (again, from the QuicKeys menu off the Apple menu) and click on the

QuicKey. We discuss the QuickReference Card in more detail in "The QuickReference Card," later in this chapter.

The QuicKeys Management Window

The QuicKey you've just created opens the management window—and you used the management window to create it. That's not surprising because nothing is more fundamental to building a QuicKey than the QuicKeys management window. Some of its features you use frequently, others seldom. Some of its controls are intuitive, others…well, we'll explain how they work.

A Stroll Through the QuicKeys Management Window

Let's take a look at the management window (see Figure 3-4). The middle area is blank if you haven't got any QuicKeys in the keyset it is displaying.

Figure 3-4
QuicKeys management window

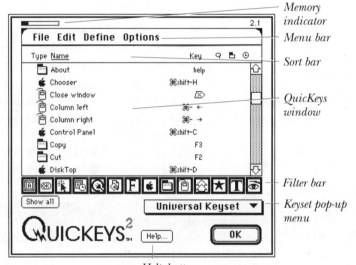

Help button

When the QuicKeys management window is open, you can't do much except work within the QuicKeys environment. The management window is a modal window; it essentially deactivates everything else on your desktop. Many of the management window's areas are active—by clicking on them you can perform some operation.

It looks pretty straightforward, but the QuicKeys management window's simple appearance belies its complexity.

Here are the main features of the QuicKeys management window.

Menu bar. The Menu bar is functionally similar to that used in most Mac applications, although this menu bar is at the top of the management window rather than at the top of your screen.

Memory indicator. The Memory indicator displays how much of the allocated memory your keysets occupy. The version number of your QuicKeys program is to the right.

Sort bar. The Sort bar primarily controls the display configuration of the large QuicKeys window that's right below it. The Sort bar gives you three ways to display your QuicKeys.

- **By Type.** This displays QuicKeys in the order shown along the filter bar.
- **By Name.** This displays them in alphabetical order. Numerals and special characters are sorted in the usual ASCII manner. QuicKeys without names are listed last.
- **By Key.** This displays them with function keys first, then most extended keyboard keys (except keypad keys), then numerals and keypad keys, and finally alphabetic characters.

On the right of the Sort bar are two or three symbols that can also appear in a QuicKey listing. Here is what they specify.

- ⬚ The QuicKey contains a comment (QuicKeys 2.1 and beyond).
- ⬚ You can activate the QuicKey by choosing it from the QuicKeys submenu under the Apple menu.
- ⬚ The QuicKey will automatically activate at a preset time.

We usually sort by key because that is how we delineate the different keys in our heads. When we want to sort by one of the other ways, we can choose it from the Sort bar or use a keystroke combination listed in the Options menu (see "Options," later in this chapter).

QuicKeys window. The QuicKeys window displays the QuicKeys in the keyset that is showing in the Keyset pop-up menu. You can edit QuicKeys quickly by clicking on different parts of this window.

- Double-click on the type icon or the name of the QuicKey to bring up its edit dialog box.
- Click on the keyboard shortcut and press a different keystroke combination to change the shortcut.
- Click in the comment column (⟨🗨⟩) to add a message to the QuicKey.
- Click in the menu column (📂) to add the QuicKey to the QuicKeys menu.
- Click in the timer column (🕒) to set up the QuicKey for automatic activation at a preset time.

Filter bar (and its Show all button). The Filter bar causes the QuicKeys window to display specific subsets of QuicKeys. Clicking on any of the Filter bar icons will show the QuicKeys for that particular type. By holding down Shift, you can select multiple types from the bar. Clicking the Show all button returns you to the default mode that lists all of the QuicKeys in the chosen keyset. You can display a subset of QuicKeys when you are searching for a particular QuicKey in a large keyset. Choosing the appropriate type for the bar cuts down your listing, and your search time, appreciably.

Help button. Clicking the Help button calls up a simple help window (see Figure 3-5).

Figure 3-5
The QuicKeys
Help window

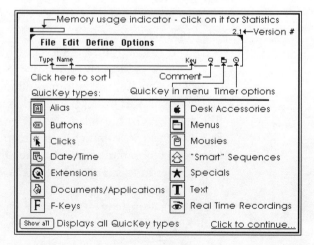

The Keyset pop-up menu. On the bottom-right of the QUICKEYS management window is the Keyset pop-up menu (Figure 3-6). Here you can choose the keyset in which the QuicKey you're building will reside. You can click the pop-up menu, and it opens to display a list of all open keysets. When you choose a keyset, the QuicKeys it contains appear in the QuicKeys window.

Figure 3-6
Keyset
pop-up menu

Keyset Clarity

When you build a QuicKey, one of the first things you determine is what keyset the QuicKey will reside in. Every QuicKey resides in a host keyset. Keysets can be confusing because QUICKEYS handles some of them in different ways—ways that influence how a keyset's resident QuicKeys function. It's important to become familiar with the properties of keysets so you can decide what kind of keyset you want your QuicKey to reside in. We provide some keyset clarity rules here and later in the chapter to help you master keysets.

Keyset Clarity Rule One

At any one time there are always only two keysets available from which you can invoke QuicKeys.

- **The Universal Keyset.** This keyset is always open and always has its QuicKeys available for activation. The Universal Keyset is the sidekick of keysets. Ever present and humble, its QuicKeys always defer to any QuicKeys of the active application keyset that have identical activating keystrokes.
- **An application keyset.** This keyset opens and closes automatically when you open and close an application of the same name. Each application keyset is a specialist, targeted to a specific application—which introduces the next rule.

Keyset Clarity Rule Two *An application keyset's QuicKeys are only available for activation while its companion application is active.*

When you open an application like Microsoft Word, QUICKEYS automatically opens its Microsoft Word keyset. If you build some QuicKeys and put them in this keyset, they are available to be invoked whenever you are working in Microsoft Word. When you close Word, QUICKEYS closes its keyset. When you open Word again, that keyset will again be available. QUICKEYS takes care of all this housekeeping in the background.

Keyset Names QUICKEYS finds an application keyset for each application as you open it because QUICKEYS names the keyset with *exactly the same name* as that application and then puts it into a folder labeled KeySets (the path to this folder is System:Prefer-ences:QuicKeys:KeySets).

You can name any keyset in the KeySets folder with exactly the same name as an application, and it will act as that application's specific keyset. But don't let two applications or two keysets have identical names, because QUICKEYS won't be able to distinguish between them.

One implication of this exact-naming convention: if you upgrade to a new version of a program, or change the name of the file (from "Microsoft Word" to "Word," for instance), QUICKEYS won't open that application's keyset anymore. The names are different, so it creates a new, empty keyset with the new application's name. There are two simple ways to solve this problem.

- In the QUICKEYS management window, open the old keyset. Select all the keys (hold down Shift and drag across all of them), copy them, switch to the new keyset, and paste them.
- Rename the old keyset so its name matches the new application name exactly.

Choosing a Keyset So where do you put your new QuicKey? If you want to be able to access it from any application, put it into the Universal Keyset. If it is application-specific (designed to work only with a specific application), put it into that application's keyset.

Our QuicKey which invokes the QUICKEYS management window went into the Universal Keyset because we might access it at any time. If the keyset you want to store a QuicKey in isn't currently displayed on the Keyset pop-up menu, you can choose it from the menu. Then the QuicKey you build will automatically be saved into that keyset when you eventually click OK on the QUICKEYS management window.

Open Keysets

CE Software has included some sample QuicKey keysets in your package (see "Sample Keysets Folder," in Chapter 2, *The Old Kit Bag*). One of them, "More Universal Keys," is a good example of a robust keyset. You can open it from the QUICKEYS management window by selecting Open from the File menu (or pressing Command-O). A standard Open dialog box will appear. Choose and open the More Universal Keys keyset in the KeySets folder. "More Universal Keys" appears in the Keyset pop-up menu, and the main window fills with a listing of its QuicKeys.

What does the concept of "open" mean? Does it mean the QuicKeys inside can be invoked? Possibly...but not necessarily. In fact, the QuicKeys contained in this More Universal Keys keyset *can't* be invoked from it. Why not?

Think of this as a corollary to Keyset Clarity Rules One and Two. Since only two keysets can have their QuicKeys activated, where one is always the Universal Keyset and the other always has the name identical to the application you are working with, then More Universal Keys can't have its QuicKeys invoked.

So what good is it? It's good—hell, it's great—because you can copy QuicKeys out of the More Universal Keys keyset into keysets that can have their QuicKeys activated. This keyset and all keysets that don't have an application's name are used as storehouses for QuicKeys. We call these storage keysets. Let's wrap this up in another rule.

Keyset Clarity Rule Three

QuicKeys cannot be invoked directly from storage keysets. But they can be transferred to keysets from which they can be activated.

So what does "open" mean? Keysets that are open can be viewed and edited in the QUICKEYS management window.

The state of being an "open keyset" should be reserved for those keysets you see listed under the Keyset pop-up menu. All other keysets are closed.

Manually opened keysets. Open the More Universal Keys keyset and click on the pop-up menu. You'll see "More Universal Keys" displayed above a dotted line (see Figure 3-7). Keysets that you open yourself are always displayed above this dotted line, and automatically opened keysets are displayed below it. This is QuicKeys letting you know that the keysets displayed above the line will only stay open as long as you have the QuicKeys management window open. When you are finished working with the management window and you click OK, the keysets that were displayed above the line close automatically.

Figure 3-7
Manually and automatically opened keysets displayed in the pop-up menu

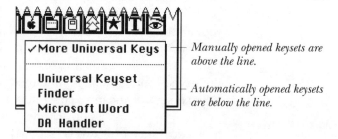

✓ More Universal Keys

Universal Keyset
Finder
Microsoft Word
DA Handler

Manually opened keysets are above the line.

Automatically opened keysets are below the line.

It's not just a storage keyset that can open above the line. If you want to open an application-specific keyset when its application is closed you can do so; that keyset shows up above the line, and you can view and edit its QuicKeys. For example, if you have made some QuicKeys for QuarkXPress, you can open them without having QuarkXPress open by going through the process of opening a keyset described above in "Open Keysets." The keyset for QuarkXPress shows above the line (see Figure 3-8).

Keyset Summary   Here are the few main points to keeping keysets straight.
- You can invoke QuicKeys from a maximum of two keysets (Universal and application) at any one time.
- You can copy and paste QuicKeys between keysets.
- If you open a keyset manually, it will automatically close when you close the QuicKeys management window.

Figure 3-8
The QuarkXPress
keyset is open while its
application is closed.

That's all for keysets now. We explain more advanced key-stroke theology in Chapter 15, *Keystroke Strategies*.

The Main Menu of the Management Window

Now that we've beaten keysets around, let's get back to con-sidering our management window controls. Many of the management window's controls are used in the display and editing of QuicKeys in different keysets.

We used the management window Define menu when we built our QuicKey. The first two categories of the menu, File and Edit, are familiar to anyone who has had any experience with a Mac. The third menu item, Define, is the primary con-trol for creating a QuicKey. The fourth category, Options, holds display and configuration controls.

File Most of this menu (see Figure 3-9) allows you to control keysets. Its operation is self-evident, except for a few areas.

Figure 3-9
The QUICKEYS
File menu

File	
New Keyset...	
Open...	⌘O
Close	⌘W
Save	⌘S
Save a Copy...	
Save Selection...	
Page Setup...	
Print...	⌘P
Quit	⌘Q

• "Save Selection" allows you to save highlighted

QuicKeys in the QuicKeys window into their own keyset.

- "Page Setup" can define the specifications of a page you might print your keyset on by utilizing the Print command.
- "Quit" is redundant, given the OK button in the QUICKEYS management window.

Edit   The Edit menu (see Figure 3-10) follows Mac interface standards, so it doesn't have many surprises.

Figure 3-10
The QUICKEYS
Edit menu

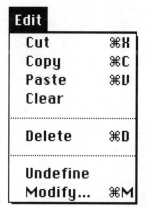

Edit	
Cut	⌘X
Copy	⌘C
Paste	⌘U
Clear	
Delete	⌘D
Undefine	
Modify...	⌘M

- "Delete" is active when at least one QuicKey is highlighted in the main window.
- "Undefine" and "Modify" are both redundant with operations that can be effected with the mouse in the QUICKEYS window. "Undefine" deletes a keystroke combination from a highlighted QuicKey. You can accomplish the same result by clicking on the keystroke and pressing Delete. "Modify" opens the edit dialog box of a highlighted QuicKey; double-clicking on the QuicKey in the main QUICKEYS window opens the edit window, too.
- Note there is no "Undo" in this menu. Since that is so, and since QUICKEYS has an automatic save feature when it's closed, when a QuicKey is deleted, it is gone forever.

Define   Here's something different—the Define menu (see Figure 3-11). We used the Define menu to make our QuicKey. The first objects that probably catch your eye when you open the menu are the peculiar little icons that precede the names of the QuicKeys. Many of the same icons are repeated in the Filter bar (below the main, scrolling window). Each icon (sort of) represents a different *type* of QuicKey. We discuss each QuicKey type extensively later on in the book (see Chapter 4, *Thinking About QuicKeys,* and subsequent chapters).

The distinction between different QuicKey types is sometimes obscure. They are more or less delineated by function,

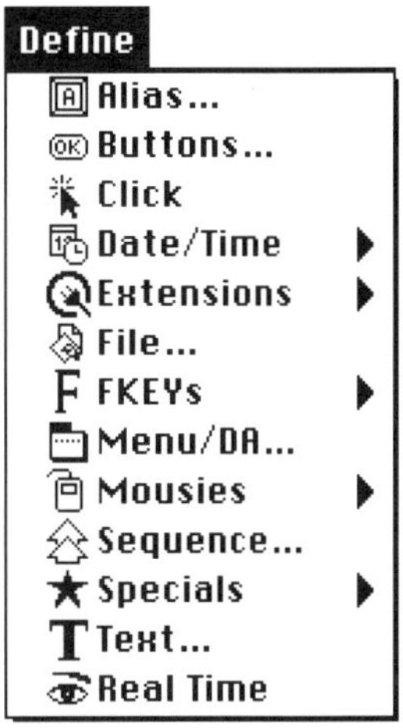

Figure 3-11
The QUICKEYS
Define menu

Define
- 🄰 Alias...
- ⊛ Buttons...
- ✳ Click
- 🗒 Date/Time ▶
- Ⓠ Extensions ▶
- 🖹 File...
- F FKEYs ▶
- 🖳 Menu/DA...
- 🗐 Mousies ▶
- ⌂ Sequence...
- ★ Specials ▶
- T Text...
- 👁 Real Time

but not completely. Making things even less explicit is the fact that many times you can achieve the same result in a number of different ways, using different types of QuicKeys. Both of these factors can create confusion in choosing which type to use for a job.

Our sample QuicKey is a good illustration of this. You can build it by starting with any one of five different QuicKey types from the Define menu! Plus, there are a few other, more complicated ways to achieve the same result. Luckily for you, we aren't about to describe them all because then we wouldn't be able to call this *The* Little *QuicKeys Book*. As you become more acquainted with the program, you can test your expertise by seeing how many ways you can come up with.

But there usually is a "best" QuicKey for your job. So figure out the way that you would go about doing something as efficiently as possible, and then see if there's a QuicKey type that's designed to do just that. We discuss this more in Chapter 4, *Thinking About QuicKeys.*

Options

The Options menu (see Figure 3-12) houses the redundant, lackluster, and obscure paraphernalia that couldn't be categorized anywhere else. Steve and Don use their desks (and the floors around them) for a similar purpose.

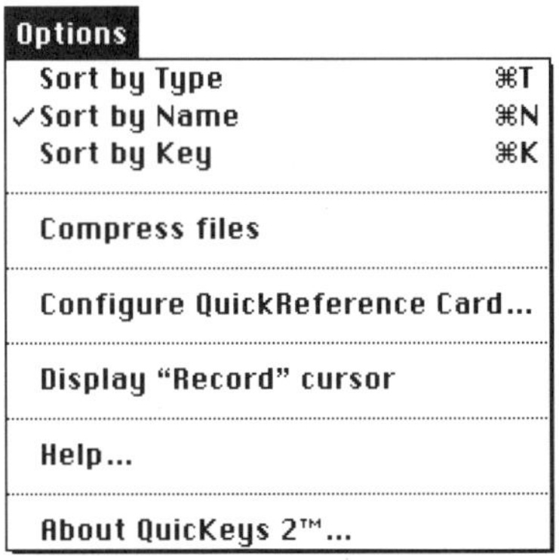

Figure 3-12
The QUICKEYS
Options menu

Options
Sort by Type	⌘T
✓Sort by Name	⌘N
Sort by Key	⌘K
Compress files	
Configure QuickReference Card...	
Display "Record" cursor	
Help...	
About QuicKeys 2™...	

The first three items on the Options menu mimic the Sort bar, but include keystroke combinations you can sort with. Other items on this menu are self-evident, except, perhaps, these three.

• **Compress files.** The Compress files item compacts new

QuicKeys you've written and confirms that all File QuicKeys (which can launch a document or application) have their target files where QUICKEYS was last told they were. It works on all the keysets in the KeySets folder, not just open keysets. System 7 doesn't need this help since File QuicKeys are located with the System's Alias Manager.

- **Configure QuickReference Card.** This card (a display that lets you view and activate your active QuicKeys) can be invoked from the QuicKeys 2 submenu on the Apple menu or through a "Special" QuicKey. We discuss the QuickReference Card in more detail in "The QuickReference Card," later in this chapter.
- **Display "Record" cursor.** Choosing this option causes a small microphone icon to be displayed when you record a QuicKey using the "Sequence" or "Real Time" QuicKey types.

QuicKeys on the Apple Menu

There's another place in your Mac system where you can manipulate, control, and invoke QuicKeys: the Apple menu. In the discusssion of CEToolbox in "The Necessary," in Chapter 2, *The Old Kit Bag*, we talked about how you can configure the QuicKeys menu in several ways on the Apple menu. When you get QUICKEYS, the QuicKeys menu is configured as you see it in Figure 3-13.

Figure 3-13
QuicKeys on the Apple menu

No matter which option you choose in CEToolbox for QUICKEYS' placement, you're faced with dealing with unwieldy hierarchical menus. That problem is at its worst, though, when you use CEToolbox's Separated option (see Figure 3-14), which makes you

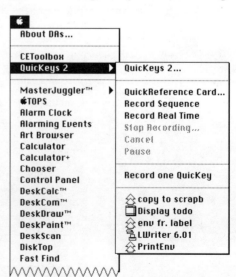

Figure 3-14
QuicKeys on the Apple
menu configured as
"Separated"

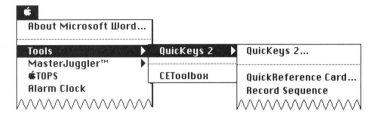

navigate through two levels of tricky submenus. We recommend the default option shown above.

**What's on the
QuicKeys 2 Menu**

Now that we've positioned the QuicKeys menu on the Apple menu, here's a rundown of the options available.

QuicKeys 2. The first option is simple; it brings up the QUICKEYS management window. You can avoid the submenus by simply choosing "QuicKeys 2." The submenu pops out, but you don't have to travel out to that submenu. Just let go of the mouse button, and the QUICKEYS management window pops up. Of course, we find it easier to use our keystroke shortcut (that invokes the QuicKeys 2 Special QuicKey) to achieve the same result.

QuickReference Card. The QuickReference card, discussed in more detail later in this chapter, lets you view your open keysets and invoke QuicKeys from those keysets.

Record Sequence. This is the easy way to create a Sequence. Choose "Record Sequence," perform the actions you want included in the Sequence, and then choose "Stop Recording." Up comes the Sequence edit dialog box, where you can fine-tune the Sequence. If you mess up while you're going through the Sequence steps, choose Cancel instead of "Stop Recording."

Record Real Time. This menu option lets you create a special kind of QuicKey: a Real Time QuicKey. Choose "Record Real Time," then perform the actions you want included in the recording. QUICKEYS includes all your actions in the Real Time Quickey, including any pauses and stray mouse movements. When you've finished, choose "Stop Recording" to bring up the Real Time edit dialog box. As with Sequence, you can get out of the recording if you mess up by choosing Cancel instead of "Stop Recording." For more on Real Time QuicKeys, see "Start/Stop Real Time" in Chapter 11, *QuicKeys Control.*

Pause. This command lets you pause in the middle of recording a Sequence or a Real Time QuicKey. You can start recording, then pause, and do other things without including those things in the recording. Select "Pause" again to uncheck it and continue recording.

Record one QuicKey. To record a single keystroke or mouse click/drag, select "Record one QuicKey." Press the keystroke or click/drag the mouse, and the appropriate QuicKey edit dialog box comes up. We wish this command were smart enough to know when we're clicking on buttons, scroll bars, and the like, but it isn't. It just understands clicks and keystrokes. Nevertheless, this feature is powerful enough that you might want to assign a Menu QuicKey to trigger it; then you can record a Click or Text QuicKey nearly instantly.

Your QuicKeys. Beneath the bottom line on the QuicKeys menu you'll see any QuicKeys you've created and chosen to put on the menu. You can put your QuicKeys on the menu in either of two ways.
- In the edit dialog box for the QuicKey, turn on the Include in QuicKeys menu option.
- In the QuicKeys management window, click next to the QuicKey's keystroke in the menu (🖿) column. This turns on the menu icon.

If you're including a QuicKey on the menu, you may not even need to assign it a keystroke. Just call it from the menu when you need it. Since your QuicKeys are listed on the menu alphabetically, you can customize the menu with different functional QuicKeys by naming members of a group with the same initial letter (all your printer Choosy QuicKeys could start with "P").

The Quick-Reference Card

We mentioned the QuickReference Card a few paragraphs back. Select it from the QuicKeys menu and up it comes (see

Figure 3-15). Our QuickReference Cards are set up to display all the QuicKeys in our open keysets; you can control this via the Configure QuickReference Card command off the Option menu in the QuicKeys management window (see Figure 3-16).

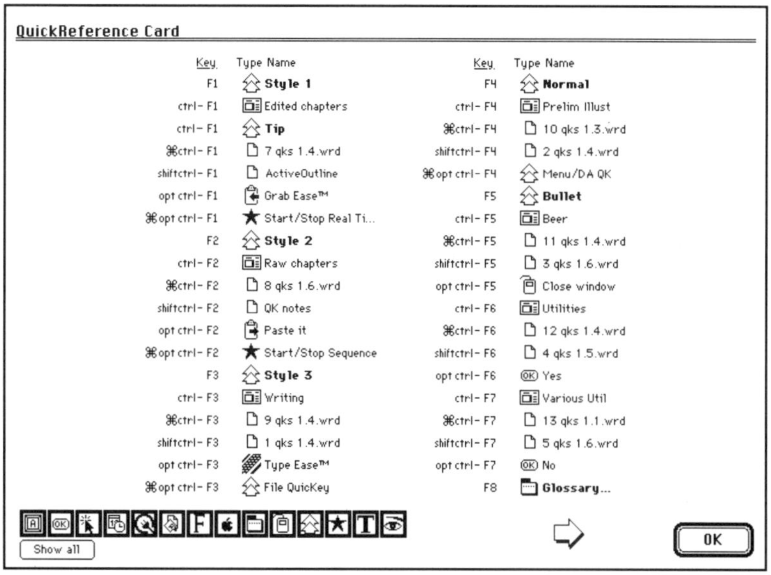

Figure 3-15
The QuickReference Card

The QuickReference Card is actually more than a reference. If a QuicKey has a message, the message icon lets you know. Press on the QuicKey, hold down the mouse button, and the message is displayed (see Figure 3-17).

Even better, you can invoke QuicKeys from The QuickReference Card by simply clicking on them. This is a great way to invoke QuicKeys whose keystrokes you can't remember. For more on the QuickReference Card, see Chapter 11, *QuicKeys Control*.

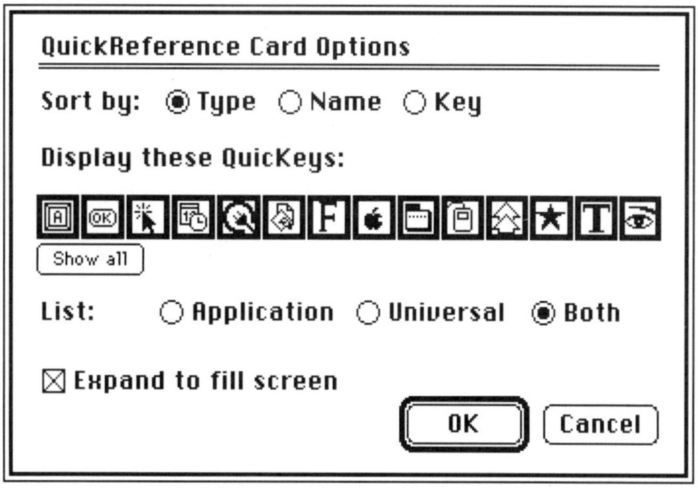

Figure 3-16
The Quick-Reference Card Options dialog box

Figure 3-17
Message displayed
in the QuickRef-
erence Card

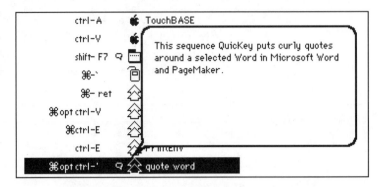

The Generic QuicKey Edit Dialog Box

We told you this chapter is about fundamentals. One QUICKEYS fundamental is a display you'll see frequently when you build a QuicKey: a QuicKey edit dialog box. Although every QuicKey type has a different edit dialog box to satisfy its own requirements, almost all edit dialog boxes have six features in common.

Common Edit Dialog Box Features

Take a look at the features of our generic edit dialog box (see Figure 3-18).

QuicKey Type. The QuicKey type is listed here. However, there are two exceptions to this. Each of the two QuicKey categories, Specials and Mousies, has its own special edit dialog box. With these QuicKeys, the category is listed in the upper-left corner, and the type is chosen through a pop-up menu.

Name. All QuicKeys can have a name. In most cases, you can name a QuicKey whatever you want, but some QuicKeys have a built-in naming process; the name is dependent on the function of the QuicKey. For example, choosing a menu item with the Menu/DA QuicKey automatically names it with that menu item; a File QuicKey is named identically to the name of its target file.

Keystroke. A regular key and any combination of modifier keys comprises the keystroke. The activating keystroke combination can be as simple as one key on your keyboard, or it can include one regular key and any combination of modifier keys (Shift, Option, Command, and Control). Below are

Figure 3-18
The generic QuicKey
edit dialog box

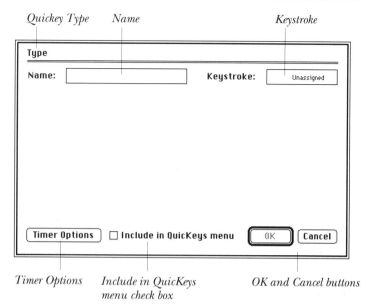

Quickey Type   *Name*   *Keystroke*

Timer Options   *Include in QuicKeys*   *OK and Cancel buttons*
                    menu check box

a few "dead" keys that should not be used to activate a QuicKey (because they're used to put foreign-language accents on characters).

- ~ (Shift-`)
- Option-E
- Option-I
- Option-N
- Option-O
- Option-U

Timer Options. Clicking the Timer Options button invokes the Timer options dialog box (see Figure 3-19). There are three (well, two and a half) options.

- **Mac or application start.** This option invokes a QuicKey a set time after the Finder (Finder or Universal Keyset) or application (specific application keyset) loads.

- **Preset value.** You can trigger the QuicKey at any time you want by filling in the time here. QUICKEYS automatically fills in the present time.

- **Repeat option.** If you have checked the previous option, you can repeat the invocation at a set interval. For example, you could have a QuicKey beep at you every day at 5 P.M.

Figure 3-19
The generic Timer
options dialog box

*Timing based on Mac or
application start*

Timing based on preset value

Repeat option

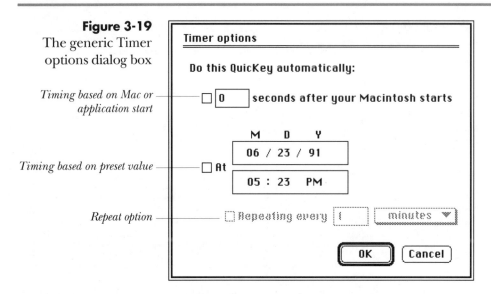

Include in QuicKeys menu check box. We used this option in
our sample QuicKey at the beginning of the chapter. It puts
your QuicKey on the QuicKeys submenu off the Apple menu.

OK and Cancel buttons. You figure. Yup, you're right.

High-level Control

There are a few configuration indicators and controls that
you'll access rarely. One of these is the memory indicator in
the QUICKEYS management window, and the others are hidden away in the QuicKeys control panel (choose Control
Panel from the Apple menu, and then select "QuicKeys"
from the scrolling list on the left side of the Control Panel).

Memory Indicator

If you click on the little thermometer icon in the upper-left
corner of the management window, you'll get a display of
memory statistics (see Figure 3-20).

The bottom part of the display shows the memory that
each of your open keysets occupies; the top displays their total and the percentage of allocated memory occupied.

Sometimes QUICKEYS starts acting a little befuddled when
the memory used becomes a large percentage of that allocated
in the buffer. There is no magic percentage at which increas-

ing your memory buffer is necessary, but it must be pretty high. You can reset your buffer size through the controls in the QUICKEYS section of your Control Panel, discussed next.

Figure 3-20
The Statistics dialog box showing QUICKEYS' memory usage

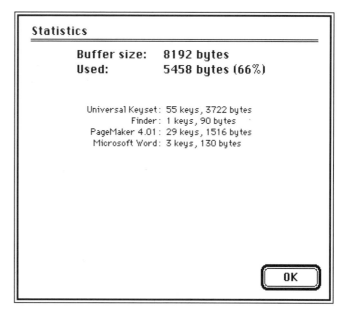

Statistics

Buffer size: 8192 bytes
Used: 5458 bytes (66%)

Universal Keyset : 55 keys , 3722 bytes
Finder : 1 keys , 90 bytes
PageMaker 4.01 : 29 keys , 1516 bytes
Microsoft Word : 3 keys , 130 bytes

OK

QUICKEYS in the Control Panel

There are a few controls for QUICKEYS in the Control Panel (see Figure 3-21), all but one of which are straightforward. Click on the Configure button and you will be rewarded by the QUICKEYS Options window (see Figure 3-22). You can use this window to control three things. The second and third options are only extant on newer versions.

Figure 3-21
THE QUICKEYS control panel

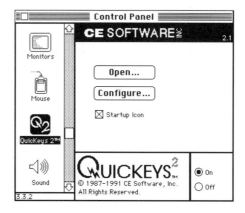

Figure 3-22
QUICKEYS Options
window

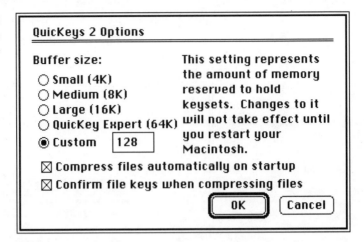

```
QuicKeys 2 Options

Buffer size:                This setting represents
                            the amount of memory
   ○ Small (4K)             reserved to hold
   ○ Medium (8K)            keysets. Changes to it
   ○ Large (16K)            will not take effect until
   ○ QuicKey Expert (64K)   you restart your
   ● Custom    [  128  ]    Macintosh.

   ☒ Compress files automatically on startup
   ☒ Confirm file keys when compressing files

                    [  OK  ]   [ Cancel ]
```

Buffer size. This tells QUICKEYS how much room to allocate in memory for your QuicKeys. Question: How many QuicKeys does it take to fill up a 4K space? Somewhere between one and a whole lot. QuicKeys come in different sizes. Alias keys can be very small, and long sequence QuicKeys can be large—or relatively large; our largest is 19K, and that's a Real Time QuicKey. They can get big. So how big does your QUICKEYS buffer have to be? It's best to set it at bigger than big enough. You can tell how much memory QUICKEYS is using by clicking on the Memory indicator in the QUICKEYS management window.

Compress files automatically. This feature compresses any new Sequence or Real Time QuicKeys you've created every time you start your Mac. It saves disk space. We leave it off because it's a time-consuming procedure, and using a lot of beta software, we restart somewhat more than we would like. We also use lots of INITs and cdevs, so startup is long enough as it is. We prefer to compress files occasionally, using the command on the Options menu in the QUICKEYS management window (see "Options" earlier in this chapter).

Confirm file keys when compressing. This feature checks your File QuicKeys (the ones that will open files for you) to verify the location of the files they call. By selecting "Confirm file keys," you ensure that QUICKEYS won't attempt to call a nonexistent file—which would happen if you make a File

QuicKey and then move, rename, or delete the target file.

However, this indemnification is not without cost; it includes a small bug that CE is working on as of the writing of this book. If you create a File QuicKey in the Universal Keyset (a QuicKey to open your Microsoft Word file named "Things To Do," for instance) and then you trash the "Things To Do" file and you have "Confirm file keys" checked, when QUICKEYS starts up it looks all over (and we mean *all* over—it checks all of your drives) for this file. When it can't find it, it gives you a dialog box that has the most logical response ("Remove") disabled! So after waiting for all of this to occur, you have to click Cancel then open QUICKEYS and remove the offensive, offending file. This problem does not show up in any keyset except Universal and it's not the end of the world; CE will probably have it fixed by the time you read this.

Beyond the Basics

That's it for the basics. The next series of chapters investigates QuicKey types in detail so you'll know their particular personalities and quirks. Then subsequent chapters introduce you to the rarefied universe of keyboard strategies and virtuoso-like control.

Thinking About QuicKeys

Before you wander farther along the path to QuicKeys nirvana, it might be best to sit back and reflect for a moment. Subsequent chapters explore the QuicKey types—the basic tools that will supercharge your work on the Mac. But once this power is in your hands, will you wield it wisely? Will you be the sorcerer or the apprentice? Luckily, being the sorcerer is easy, so this chapter will be short. In it, we review the evolution of QuicKeys with an eye to introducing two important macro concepts—using the right tool, and exploiting existing shortcuts. And we present our own functional categorization of the QuicKey types.

The Ugly Macro

Dave Reed, the technical support guru at CE Software, told us about a call he once received. The caller, Bob Faineant, had made a QuicKey for opening a particular file. Bob understood that macro programs are supposed to automate what he does when operating his boss's Mac. Bob wanted to open a Microsoft Word file that was buried in a bunch of folders. He wasn't exactly sure of the best way to accomplish this, but he knew that QuicKeys had a special feature that could help him, the Record Sequence function.

So to open his file, Bob started Record Sequence and then clicked on his folder labelled "Bob's folder." That folder opened to display a lot of other folders. He then clicked on the "Miscellaneous" folder, and then on the file labeled "Do Immediately!" he had stored there.

QuicKeys recorded and interpreted Bob's actions. When Bob tried to open the file by invoking the QuicKey, it worked—until his boss told him that the "Do Immediately" file should be moved to another folder. Bob moved his file, but when he tried to open it with his old QuicKey, another file opened instead! Bob called Dave Reed for help. If you tap out your own resources, CE Software Support likes to be called early in the morning—9-11 A.M., Central Time—that is when their lines are the least busy, and their minds the least boggled.

QuicKandDirty

Dave Reed realized that Bob's QuicKey looked something like Figure 4-1.

Figure 4-1
Bob's QuicKey

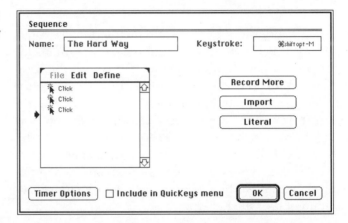

The Record Sequence feature had interpreted Bob's actions of opening his file as three double-clicks in different areas of the screen, and had dutifully recorded them. Now that Bob's target file was moved, there was no way to simply edit his QuicKey to return its functionality.

This is why managers often find support personnel in fixed positions, staring at their Macs, drooling and mumbling about Truk, Samoa, and their lost youth. Bob didn't understand the basic rules of writing a macro.

The Elegant Macro

Bob's QuicKey worked, but it was the wrong QuicKey type for his job. A QuicKey needs to be tailored to the specifics of its task, and it also needs to be adaptable to normal changing conditions within the Mac environment. You can fulfill both of these requirements by using the right tool.

The Right Tool

The key to choosing the right tool for your job is to first consider how the Mac goes about doing the job you want it to do. Hang on. You don't have to know the specifics of how the ROM talks to the ADB in the entire Mac family; you just need to have a sense of some of the Mac's broad functions. Learning more about how your computer works is fundamental to becoming more efficient with it. Luckily, you have aid.

Don Brown, the author of QUICKEYS, regards his program as something besides an automator of your actions with the Mac. He believes that using QUICKEYS can *educate* you about how the Mac works. Doing the job right with QUICKEYS means you know a bit more about the thinking of your Mac. Sounds great, right? It is, in most cases, but unfortunately, the user interface of QUICKEYS was not designed to always enhance this happy effect.

The Soul of a Macro Machine

QUICKEYS evolved from a small idea into a big one. Originally it was just to comprise some added functions for the utility program DiskTop. But Don Brown kept coming up with new ideas (with many suggestions from his function-hungry friends in the Mac community). CE Software's president, Richard Skeie, realized that QUICKEYS could be a stand-alone program. So QUICKEYS was born.

But that wasn't the end. QUICKEYS kept growing, helped by outside programmers; menus sprouted submenus, and categories became blurred within the program. This luxuriant growth attests to the program's basic value, but it also causes some confusion in the program's user interface. In QUICKEYS it is *not* always evident which QuicKey type to use, because the categories that QuicKey types are arranged in are not arranged by user function.

But they can be.

Order and Reorder

In this book, we present QuicKeys in categories arranged according to function—what you want to achieve. This organization is different from the program's classification scheme, which developed with the program. Our organization by function should make it easy to find the tools you need for your specific task.

QuicKeys Classic Classification

All different QuicKey types can be found under the Define menu and its submenus (see Figure 4-2). However, the menu is a bit of a hodgepodge.

Figure 4-2
Classic QuicKey Categories

Basic	Alias	
	Buttons	
	Click	
	Date/Time	
	File	
	FKEYS	
	Menu/DA	
	Text	
	Real Time	
Mousies	Line up	
	Line down	
	Page up	
	Page down	
	Home	
	End	
	Column left	
	Column right	
	Page left	
	Page right	
	Close window	
	Zoom window	
Specials	QuicKeys 2	
	Transfer	
	Shut Down	
	Restart	
	Select rear window	
	Select second window	
	QuickQuotes	
	Double QuickQuotes	
	QuickReference Card	
	Toggle QuicKeys on/off	
	Start/Stop Sequence	
	Start/Stop Real Time	
	Pause	
Extensions	Choosy	
	CursorWait	
	DisMounty	

Display
Grab Ease
Location
MenuDecision
MenuWait
Message
Mounty
Panels
Paste Ease
Repeat
Screen Ease
Sound
Speaker Changer
Stuff
Type Ease
UnStuff
Wait
WindowDecision
WindowWait

Finder Events   Show Clipboard
Sleep
Get Info
Show
Open
Print

System 7 Specials Balloon Help On
Balloon Help Off
Toggle Balloon Help
Next Application
Last Appliation
Start FileSharing
Stop FileSharing

- Some of the items under the main menu are QuicKey types, and some are QuicKey categories.
- Some of the categories contain types grouped by user function (Mousies), some are grouped by method of creation (Extensions), and some are grouped in ways that we find inexplicable (Specials).
- All submenus contain QuicKey types except for Date/ Time, which actually gives you format choices. The

items in the FKEYs submenu aren't officially QuicKey types, either.

QuicKeys Classification Reclassified

Figure 4-3 shows our functional QuicKey classification system. You can refer to it when creating a QuicKey. We've grouped all the QuicKey types into categories by function. We've even made functional subgroups within the new and improved QuicKey categories.

Figure 4-3
New and improved
QuicKey categories

Launching and Opening	File
	Menu / DA
	Location
	Transfer
	Stuff
	Unstuff
Window Control	Line up
	Line down
	Page up
	Page down
	Home
	End
	Column left
	Column right
	Page left
	Page right
	Close window
	Zoom window
	Select rear window
	Select second window
	Menu/DA
	Buttons
Keyboard and Mouse	Alias
	Click
System Control	Shutdown
	Restart
	Choosy
	Mounty
	DisMounty
	Panels
	Screen Ease
	Speaker Changer
	FKEYS

System 7 Stuff	Apple Events
	Show Clipboard
	Sleep
	Get Info
	Show
	Open
	Print
	Balloon Help On
	Balloon Help Off
	Toggle Balloon Help
	Next Application
	Last Appliation
	Start FileSharing
	Stop FileSharing
Text Manipulation	Text
	QuickQuotes
	Double QuickQuotes
	Date/Time
	Grab Ease
	Paste Ease
	Type Ease
	Display
QuicKeys Control	QuicKeys 2
	Toggle QuicKeys on/off
	QuickReference Card
	Start/Stop Sequence
	Start/Stop Real Time
Sequence Control	Pause
	Wait
	MenuWait
	WindowWait
	CursorWait
	MenuDecision
	WindowDecision
	Repeat
	Message
	Sound

These categories are not cast in a stealthy carbon-glass-epoxy composite. Occasionally, a type within a certain category is used in a manner that falls under another functional category. But most of the time, these functional categories hold true. One QuicKey type, Menu/DA, is put into two categories because it functions in two distinct ways.

We discuss each QuicKey type extensively in subsequent chapters—construction, examples, pitfalls, and anomalies are included for each QuicKey type. Each discussion includes a Tactics section, whose first paragraph succinctly states each QuicKey type's use.

The subsequent list directs you to the discussion of each QuicKey type.

Launching and Opening

Launch QuicKeys help in opening applications, documents, and (in the case of System 6) desk accessories.

File. You'll use File QuicKeys most of the time. They open files and applications.
- File, Chapter 5, page 61

DA. You can use the DA form of Menu/DA QuicKeys to open items on the Apple menu.
- DA, Chapter 5, page 64

Transfer. The Transfer type (on the Specials menu) launches an application or document you choose when you invoke the QuicKey.
- Transfer, Chapter 5, page 66

Location. The Location QuicKey (an Extension) takes you to a particular folder when an Open File dialog box is active.
- Location, Chapter 5, page 67

StuffIt Stuff. The Stuff and UnStuff QuicKeys (Extensions) compress and uncompress files in conjunction with the archive application StuffIt Deluxe.
- Stuff, Chapter 5, page 71
- UnStuff, Chapter 5, page 72

Window Control

Here's where you manipulate the standard Mac window. Window Control has four subgroups.

Document Windows. The first and largest set of Window Control QuicKeys affect document windows. They are all

Mousies (Line up, Line down, Page up, Page down, Home, End, Column left, Column right, Page left, Page right, Close window, Zoom window).
- Mousies, Chapter 6, page 77

Application Windows. The application window controls, both from the Specials menu, let you choose which window of a particular application is "on top" and active.
- Select rear, Chapter 6, page 81
- Select second, Chapter 6, page 81

Menu. The Menu form of Menu/DA QuicKeys select menu items (but only from top-of-screen menus, not from menus within windows).
- Menu, Chapter 6, page 82

Buttons. Button QuicKeys click buttons and check boxes.
- Buttons, Chapter 6, page 87

Keyboard and Mouse

Here's your chance to fool the Mac about the input from your keyboard and mouse.

Keyboard. An Alias QuicKey can make the Mac think that one keystroke (plus modifiers) is any other keystroke (plus modifiers).
- Alias, Chapter 7, page 91

Mouse. A Click QuicKey can mimic any mouse movement and clicks (plus modifiers).
- Click, Chapter 7, page 92

System Control

The System Control QuicKeys manipulate some basic functions of your Mac.

Switches. The Switch QuicKeys (they're Specials) turn the machine off, and back on.
- Shutdown, Chapter 8, page 101
- Restart, Chapter 8, page 101

Choosy. Choosy (an Extension) selects any of your available printers.

- Choosy, Chapter 8, page 102

Mounty and DisMounty. Mounty and DisMounty are two Extensions that mount and dismount AppleShare volumes.
- Mounty, Chapter 8, page 104
- DisMounty, Chapter 8, page 104

Control Panels. The Control Panels QuicKeys (all Extensions) access the Control Panel and the Chooser.
- Panels, Chapter 8, page 107
- Screen Ease, Chapter 8, page 109
- Speaker Changer, Chapter 8, page 111

FKEYs. FKEY QuicKeys are not to be confused with function keys on an extended keyboard. FKEYs are special utilities made available on early Macs that have hung around and are still used by some folks. This QuicKey type accesses any FKEYs you may have on your machine.
- FKEYs, Chapter 8, page 112

System 7 Stuff

These are the new Extensions for System 7 users only. Some of them perform tasks that are similar to other QuicKey types, but most take advantage of the new bells and whistles in System 7.

System 7 Specials. The System 7 Specials access some of the functions that are new with System 7. System 7 Specials switch balloon help and file sharing on and off, and toggle between open applications.
- Balloon help on, Chapter 9, page 117
- Balloon help off, Chapter 9, page 117
- Toggle balloon help, Chapter 9, page 117
- Next Application, Chapter 9, page 117
- Last Application, Chapter 9, page 117
- Start FileSharing, Chapter 9, page 118
- Stop FileSharing, Chapter 9, page 118

Apple Events. Apple Events are System 7 protocols for passing instructions and information from one application to another. The Apple Events Extension creates Apple Events for transmission on CEIAC.

- Apple Events, Chapter 9, page 119

Finder Events. These QuicKeys send Apple Events to the Finder—so they need CEIAC in order to function. Most of them are powerful tools to invoke certain Finder commands, even when you are in the middle of another application.
- Sleep, Chapter 9, page 125
- Get Info, Chapter 9, page 125
- Show, Chapter 9, page 126
- Show Clipboard, Chapter 9, page 126
- Print, Chapter 9, page 126
- Open, Chapter 9, page 126

Manipulating Text and Graphics

If you want to do anything with text or graphics, use one of these QuicKeys.

Text. This is the progenitor of the category. Text QuicKeys type the text you want into documents, dialog boxes, and windows.
- Text, Chapter 10, page 127

Copiers. These Copier QuicKeys (all Extensions) copy and paste text blocks. Paste Ease and Type Ease are nearly identical, except that Type Ease works in dialog boxes and applications that don't support paste functions.
- Grab Ease, Chapter 10, page 129
- Paste Ease, Chapter 10, page 130
- Type Ease, Chapter 10, page 130

Date/Time. Date/Time QuicKeys, not surprisingly, type the current date or time in a variety of formats.
- Date/Time, Chapter 10, page 132

Quotes. Quotes QuicKeys (they're Specials) type curved or "sexed" quotation marks and apostrophes.
- QuickQuotes, Chapter 10, page 133
- Double QuickQuotes, Chapter 10, page 133

Display. Hold onto your hat. The Display QuicKey (an Extension) allows you to display a text file in its own little text editor window.

- Display, Chapter 10, page 135

QuicKeys Control

The QuicKeys Control QuicKeys are the knobs and valves that allow you to control aspects of QuicKeys itself.

QuicKeys 2. QuicKeys 2 (a Special) invokes the management window.
- QuicKeys 2, Chapter 11, page 138

Toggle QuicKeys on/off. This powerful QuicKey type (a Special) makes the QuicKeys program go to sleep until you wake it up again.
- Toggle QuicKeys on/off, Chapter 11, page 138

QuickReference Card. The QuickReference Card (a Special) shows you a listing of the QuicKeys in your two active keysets. Your QuicKeys can be activated directly from the QuickReference Card.
- QuickReference Card, Chapter 11, page 139

Sequence Switches. These two types (Specials) start and stop the two different categories of QuicKey Sequences.
- Start/Stop Real Time, Chapter 11, page 143
- Start/Stop Sequence, Chapter 11, page 145

Sequence Control QuicKeys

Most of these types are only useful within Sequences.

Loafers. These delay Sequences until certain conditions are met.
- Pause (a Special), Chapter 13, page 160
- Wait (an Extension), Chapter 13, page 163
- WindowWait (an Extension), Chapter 13, page 165
- MenuWait (an Extension), Chapter 13, page 170
- CursorWait (an Extension), Chapter 13, page 172

Branchers. The branchers (all of these Extensions) allow a Sequence to proceed in one of two directions, dependent upon circumstances.
- WindowDecision, Chapter 13, page 173
- MenuDecision, Chapter 13, page 177

Looper. The Extension Repeat replays part of a Sequence or a QuicKey type a predetermined number of times.
- Repeat, Chapter 13, page 178

Message. Message (an Extension) displays a message, and can wait for input before proceeding.
- Message, Chapter 13, page 182

Sound. Sound (an Extension) plays a sound.
- Sound, Chapter 13, page 183

The Bottom Line

There are two main ways to make QuicKeys work for you: use the right tool, and take advantage of available shortcuts in applications and the operating system.

Do You Have the Tool?

When you make a QuicKey, ask yourself which category your tool is in.
- Am I launching something? Use Launching and Opening.
- Am I manipulating a window, button, or menu item? Use Window Control.
- Am I intervening in the keyboard output, or using the mouse? Use Keyboard and Mouse.
- Am I controlling the Mac system? Use System Control.
- Am I doing something special in System 7? Use System 7 Stuff.
- Am I working with text? Use Manipulating Text and Graphics.
- Am I controlling the QUICKEYS program? Use QUICKEYS Control.
- Do I need a Sequence? Use any of the appropriate QuicKeys above, and one or more of the Sequence QuicKeys.

Tips for Power-keying

After you have the right tool, use it well. Use *existing* keyboard shortcuts wherever possible.
- Command-Up arrow in Open and Save dialog boxes backs you up a folder level.
- Enter is the same as OK or the outlined default button, in most situations.

- Command-. (period) is often the same as Cancel, especially in Open and Save dialog boxes.
- Tab is the same as the Drive button in Open and Save dialog boxes (in System 6).
- Use predefined command-key equivalents (use literals to access these Sequences).
- Use Enter instead of the OK (or default) buttons.
- Use literals instead of text QuicKeys in Sequences, where feasible.
- Use DialogKeys in Sequences with literals.

The Great Beyond   You've finished the basic course. The subsequent chapters discuss each QuicKey type in detail. Then we go on to discuss sophisticated QuicKey strategies.

Launching and Opening

The process of opening applications and documents is automated neatly in QUICKEYS. The only trouble might be the abundance of launching QuicKey types—File, Menu/DA, Transfer, Location, and the StuffIt Extensions. You'll most often find yourself using File as the launching QuicKey type of choice. Menu/DA, Transfer, and Location give you finer control over launching or opening in specialized situations. If you use System 7, The Open QuicKey of Finder Events can be used instead of File, and has the added ability to open multiple documents (see "Finder Events," in Chapter 9, *System 7 Stuff*). The two Extensions, Stuff and UnStuff, enhance the popular compression utility, StuffIt Deluxe (see Appendix, *Resources*) to squeeze and unsqueeze your files.

The File QuicKey opens an application or document. Don has 33 File QuicKeys in his Universal Keyset alone. While working on this chapter, he generally used a File QuicKey to open it. Choosing "File" from the QUICKEYS Define menu invokes a standard Open dialog box from which you can choose an application or document (see Figure 5-1).

After you make your choice, QUICKEYS displays the File edit dialog box with the document or application title you've chosen displayed (see Figure 5-2). Type the keystroke you want (Don uses his function keys for often-utilized files), and when you invoke your File QuicKey, its target opens. You usually put your File QuicKeys in the Universal Keyset so you can access them at any time.

File

Figure 5-1
Open dialog box

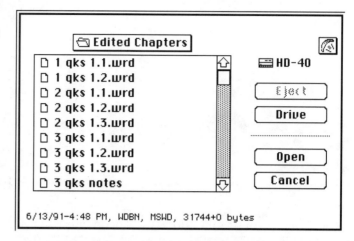

Figure 5-2
File edit dialog box

*File name with pop-up
path available*

File type/creator

Change button

Pressing the Change button displays an Open dialog box that you can use to change your target application or document.

File Considerations

The innards of the File type were enhanced in QUICKEYS 2.1. File QuicKeys now execute faster, and QUICKEYS keeps track of moved files better (see "Options" in Chapter 3, *QUICKEYS Doctrine*). However, any File QuicKeys you created in previous versions will not be automatically updated—they might still work, but in a slower, less stable manner. You can update a File QuicKey by taking your extant version through the standard editing process—pressing the Change button and selecting your target file.

The File QuicKey has just a few potential bugaboos.

Files with no application. When you choose "File" from the Define menu, the Open dialog box gives you a choice of *every* file that exists within a volume or folder, even files which have no application that opens them. If you target one of these hidden files, you'll get an error message when you try to invoke it (see Figure 5-3).

Figure 5-3
Unopenable file error message

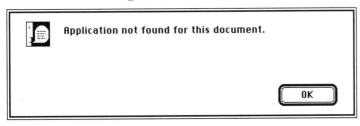

Application not found for this document.

OK

Moved and renamed files in System 6. When operating in System 6, the File QuicKey can sometimes stumble when you move or rename files or applications. The Compress files item in the Options menu fixes some problems. A File QuicKey will still find its target if you move a target into a deeper folder from where it was originally, or rename its folder. If you move a target into a shallower folder from its original location, or rename its hard drive, a File QuicKey will still finds its target after you choose "Compress Files" from the Options menu. But if you rename the file, your File QuicKey won't be able to find it.

In System 7, the System's Alias manager keeps track of QuicKey target files, so they aren't as easily "misplaced."

File Tactics *Use a File QuicKey as your first choice to launch an application or open a document.*

Here's an example of a typical File QuicKey. Don keeps a permanent Microsoft Word file titled "To Do." He modifies it during his workday (and sometimes worknight) as he completes tasks and takes on new ones. He has a Universal Keyset File QuicKey on a timer—so it opens his To Do file after his computer boots up.

File QuicKeys generally break down into two classifications: permanent and short-term.

Permanent. You can access your applications with a keystroke by making a File QuicKey for each one. Most QUICKEYS mavens use a keystroke strategy consisting of a modifier keystroke (like Control or Control-Option) and a letter key that corresponds to the first letter (or an easily remembered alternative letter) of the application's name (see Chapter 15, *Keystroke Strategies*). For example, Control-W opens Microsoft Word, Control-P opens PageMaker.

Short-term. Documents that you work with intensively but briefly can be accessed with a File QuicKey. Keystroke strategists often use function keys to invoke these files (see Chapter 15, *Keystroke Strategies*). If you're working on a longer document, for instance, you could assign the first eight chapters to the first eight function keys.

DA

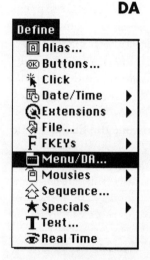

When we talk about DA QuicKeys, we're really talking about Menu/DA QuicKeys. But since "Menu" and "DA" are conceptually different functions, we deal with them in separate chapters (see "Menu" in Chapter 6, *Window Control*).

In System 6, the DA QuicKey launches only desk accessories—the miniprograms that show up on the Apple menu. In System 7, the DA QuicKey will launch anything on the Apple menu—you can put any application, document, folder or volume on the Apple menu by placing it (or its Alias) in the Apple Menu folder. DA QuicKeys can also launch applications from the Application menu in System 7.

The DA type, as we discuss it here, is best used for launching desk accessories in System 6. Here's how to create a DA QuicKey that opens the Chooser.

1. Select Menu/DA from the Define menu; your cursor turns into a menu and a dialog box appears (Figure 5-4).

Figure 5-4
Menu/DA dialog box

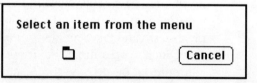

2. You can select "Chooser" from the Apple menu, which invokes the Menu/DA edit dialog box (see Figure 5-5). This box is slightly different depending on whether you have chosen a DA or a menu item, but the box always has the name "Menu" at the top left.

Figure 5-5
Menu/DA edit
dialog box for a DA

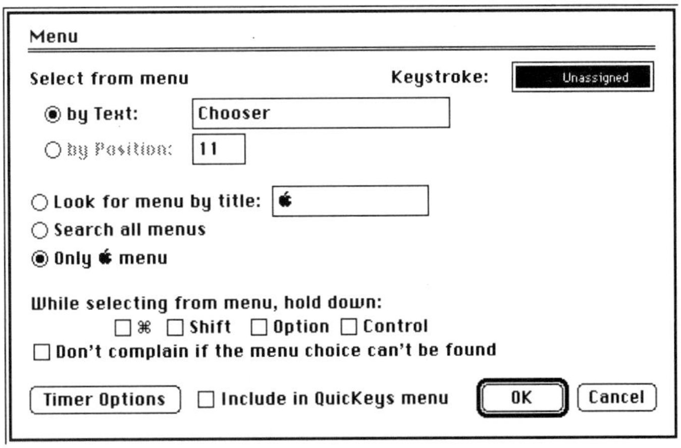

```
Menu

Select from menu                          Keystroke:    [ Unassigned ]
  ◉ by Text:       [ Chooser            ]
  ○ by Position:   [ 11 ]

  ○ Look for menu by title:  [ ⌘            ]
  ○ Search all menus
  ◉ Only ⌘ menu

While selecting from menu, hold down:
      □ ⌘  □ Shift  □ Option  □ Control
  □ Don't complain if the menu choice can't be found

[ Timer Options ]   □ Include in QuicKeys menu    ( OK )  ( Cancel )
```

3. For this QuicKey, it is best to leave QUICKEYS' "Select from menu" and button choices (Figure 5-6) as they are. Generally, whenever you construct a DA QuicKey, the QUICKEYS-entered options are best. We discuss these options in "Menu" in Chapter 6, *Window Control.*

Figure 5-6
Menu/DA
options

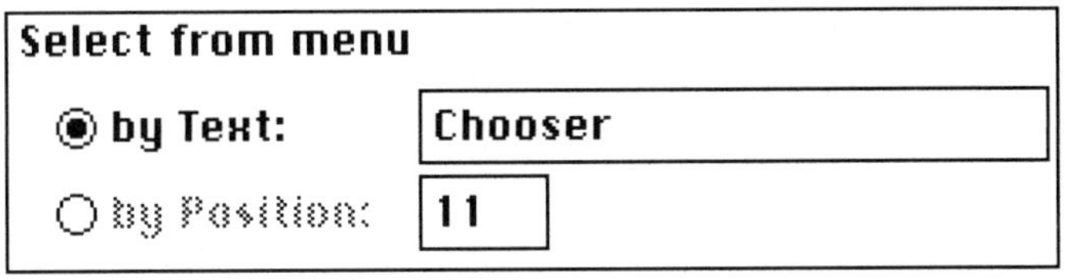

```
Select from menu

  ◉ by Text:       [ Chooser            ]
  ○ by Position:   [ 11 ]
```

Select from menu area

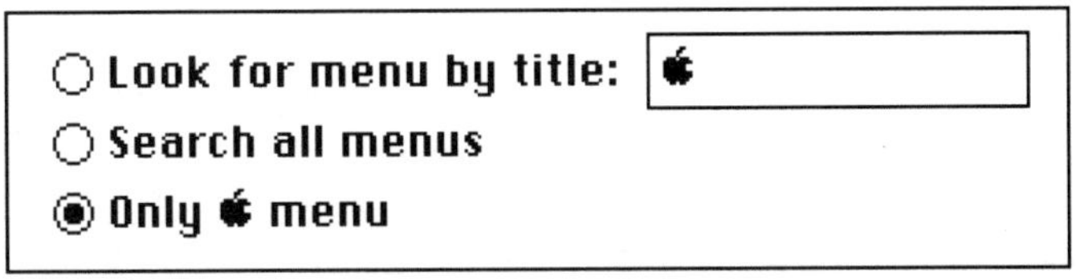

```
  ○ Look for menu by title:  [ ⌘            ]
  ○ Search all menus
  ◉ Only ⌘ menu
```

Additional menu control area

4. You can then enter your activating keystroke, and click OK or press Return.

DA QuicKeys are shown in the QuicKeys window preceded by little apple icons. Menu QuicKeys are shown preceded by little menu icons. The filter bar allows you to exclusively view either subtype (see Figure 5-7). Sorry, System 7 fans, Application menu items don't have their own icon.

Figure 5-7
Menu/DA QuicKeys in
the QuicKeys window

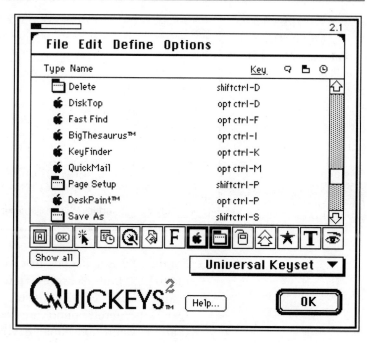

DA Tactics   *Use DA QuicKeys to open desk accessories in System 6.*

You usually want to be able to open desk accessories from any application at any time. So these QuicKeys are almost always stored in the Universal Keyset and accessed with a keystroke that can be applied permanently. In System 7, the Apple menu potentially contains many different types of choices—applications, former System 6 desk accessories, and folders—but generally it is better practice (and faster) to access these items directly with a File type QuicKey.

Transfer   Transfer QuicKeys open applications or files that you choose with an Open dialog box that appears when the QuicKey is invoked. When operating under Finder, Transfer quits the application you are in if you open a different one (it will ask you if you want to save any unsaved files). Under MultiFinder or System 7, it leaves the present application open.

The Transfer QuicKey is a Special that essentially functions like half of a File QuicKey: it opens files, but Transfer doesn't have a built-in target; you must choose the target file

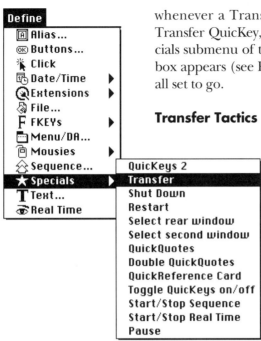

Define
- Ⓐ Alias...
- ⓄⓀ Buttons...
- ✳ Click
- 🔢 Date/Time ▶
- Ⓠ Extensions ▶
- 📄 File...
- F FKEYs ▶
- 🖥 Menu/DA... ▶
- 📋 Mousies ▶
- 🏠 Sequence...
- ★ Specials ▶
- T Text...
- 👁 Real Time

QuicKeys 2
Transfer
Shut Down
Restart
Select rear window
Select second window
QuickQuotes
Double QuickQuotes
QuickReference Card
Toggle QuicKeys on/off
Start/Stop Sequence
Start/Stop Real Time
Pause

whenever a Transfer QuicKey is invoked. To construct a Transfer QuicKey, you can choose "Transfer" from the Specials submenu of the Define menu; the Transfer edit dialog box appears (see Figure 5-8). Assign a keystroke, and you're all set to go.

Transfer Tactics

Use the Transfer QuicKey to open applications or documents that don't have their own dedicated opening QuicKeys.

Transfer tactics are simple, because you only need one Transfer QuicKey. You can keep your it in your Universal Keyset, ready to open files that have not been assigned to specific File QuicKeys. It is easier to open these untargeted files by using Transfer than by going through the alternatives (switching to the Finder or choosing from the Application menu in System 7). Command-Option-O (for "opens anything," a hierarchical level above Command-O for "open") is a possible keystroke for your Transfer QuicKey. Don finds his Transfer QuicKey so useful, he has assigned his function key, F14, to it.

Figure 5-8
The Transfer edit
dialog box

Special
Name: `Transfer`   Keystroke: `Unassigned`
Special choices: `Transfer ▼`
`Timer Options` ☐ Include in QuicKeys menu `OK` `Cancel`

Location A Location QuicKey jumps to a preselected folder. You usually use a Location QuicKey when you are working in an ap-

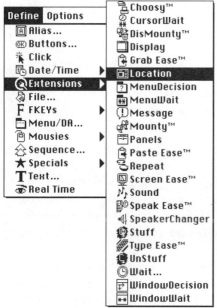

plication and ask it to open a document. An Open dialog box is displayed with a folder—seldom the folder you want—already selected. Invoking a Location QuicKey changes the selected folder in the Open dialog box to a folder you've preselected.

What's cool about this QuicKey is that the Open dialog box doesn't have to be open for it to work—you can invoke your Location QuicKey, then ask your application to open a document, and the dialog box will appear with your target folder selected.

To construct a Location QuicKey, you can select Location from the Extension submenu on the Define menu—the Location edit dialog box appears (see Figure 5-9). The box contains two radio button choices.

Set Standard File Location. This makes the Location QuicKey jump to the folder you have preselected using the Select Location button. You'll choose this option, which assigns a specific folder to the Location QuicKey, almost exclusively.

Figure 5-9
Location edit
dialog box

Restore Standard File Location. This makes the Location QuicKey return to the file location that was present when you invoked your last Location QuicKey. Since this QuicKey has no set target, you only need to make one of these. Many people have no use for a Location QuicKey like this—they just want to jump to preselected folders, not back to where they were. Restore Location QuicKey will remember the last-used Location QuicKey until you restart. After you restart, invoking this key just selects the startup disk .

To create a targeted Location QuicKey, choose "Set Standard File Location" and then press the Select Location button (Figure 5-10), a Select location dialog box like that in Figure 5-11 appears. It gives you access to all the folder choices available.

Figure 5-10
File location choices

When you work with the Select location dialog box, you might think that highlighting a folder and then pressing "Select" will give you that folder as your target. It won't. Pressing "Select" chooses the folder that is displayed at the top of the Select location dialog box, even if you have a folder highlighted. You must *open* your desired target folder (not just highlight it) to select it as your target.

Figure 5-11
Select location
dialog box

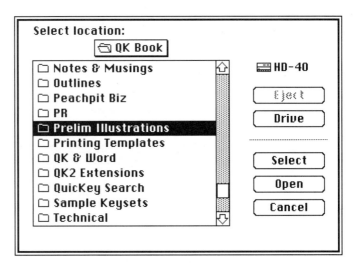

Location Considerations

Those of you with Boomerang probably realize that Location merely mimics a capability you already enjoy. But you can use it to augment Boomerang's keystroke folder selection, since

Boomerang's folder selection only uses the Command key as its modifier, and can't use many of the extended keyboard keys. QUICKEYS gives you a much bigger choice of invoking keystrokes.

Location Tactics   *Use Location QuicKeys to select your most often-used folders.*

It is easy to let the surgical-strike power of File QuicKeys make you overlook the broad strengths of Location. Location is a great asset if your work is set up so that you often access only a few different folders for a multitude of files. Location is the perfect QuicKey for desktop publishers, those tiny-file and many-folder freaks. When we wrote this book, we took a bunch of screen shots. We didn't want QuicKeys that opened each one separately (we'd have run out of keystroke combinations), but a QuicKey that instantly took us to their folder; and we used that one QuicKey repeatedly.

StuffIt Stuff   Stuff and UnStuff are two Extensions that integrate QUICKEYS with the third-party compression utility, StuffIt Deluxe, to compact and expand your files.

You can use the Stuff and UnStuff QuicKeys to process preselected target files, or you can create generic StuffIt QuicKeys which will ask you which files you want to process. Some people just stuff files to be transmitted over a telecommunications network. Others, especially those short on disk space, use StuffIt Deluxe as an integral part of their file storage and retrieval process.

Don (the curmudgeon) didn't want to discuss these Extensions in this book, because a third-party program is necessary to make them function. Steve said that everyone should know about StuffIt (ubiquitous in the world of file transfer), and those poor souls who didn't could just skip this section. Guess who won.

In a nutshell, StuffIt Deluxe works like this: to stuff a file, you must first choose the file to be stuffed. After the file is stuffed, it becomes an archive which you name. It is traditional and good practice (but not necessary) to designate a Stuffed file with a suffix of .sit (for example: 5.1.1.sit or Pix.sit). Unstuffing an archive is even easier than stuffing a file: you only have to choose the archive to unstuff. The unstuffed file automatically names itself with its previous name.

Stuff   When you select Stuff from the Extensions submenu of the Define menu, you are rewarded with an edit dialog box (see Figure 5-12). The non-generic controls are ordered a bit illogically (for us) so we'll discuss them in an order that we prefer.

Figure 5-12
Stuff edit
dialog box

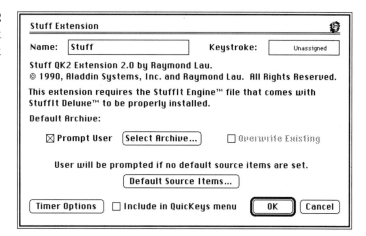

Default Source Items button. Near the bottom of the edit dialog box is the Default Source Items button, with which you can select the file (or files) to be archived. If you don't press this button, you will be asked what you want to archive when you activate this Stuff QuicKey. So don't press this if you want to make a generic "Stuff anything" QuicKey.

Prompt User check box. This check box deals with the name the archive will have—a check mark here means that when you activate the QuicKey, you will get an Open dialog box prompting you for the archive name. If you want to create a generic "Stuff anything" QuicKey which will also ask you for the name that the archive is saved under, then check this box.

Select Archive button. Click this if you want the Stuff QuicKey to save your compressed file to a preselected archive. Clicking this button will display an Open dialog box from which you can choose the archive you want. Note that although this control is an alternative to the Prompt User check box, it remains active when that box is checked. However, as soon as you select an archive here, the Prompt User check box automatically unchecks itself.

Overwrite Existing check box. This Overwrite Existing check box on the Stuff edit dialog box remains dimmed until you select an archive with the Select Archive button. Then it becomes potentially active, so if you check this, the Stuff QuicKey recreates (rewrites) its target archive every time the QuicKey is activated. If you leave this box unchecked, then any stuff command you direct to an already extant archive will elicit a dialog box asking if you want to replace the archive with the new, compressed file. In other words, this feature avoids the annoyance of going through the warning dialog box, if you know you want to replace the old archive with the new one.

You cannot use a Stuff QuicKey to *add* a file to an archive (a feature accessible through StuffIt Deluxe itself).

UnStuff UnStuff is a bit simpler than Stuff. Choosing UnStuff from the Extensions submenu of the Define menu conjures up the UnStuff edit dialog box (see Figure 5-13). This dialog box has only three unfamiliar controls.

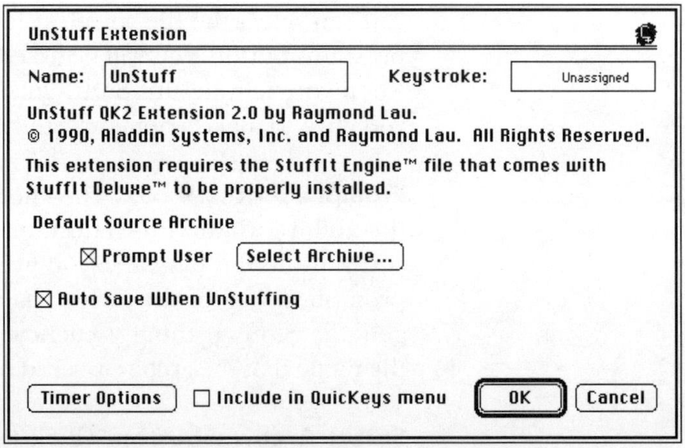

Figure 5-13
UnStuff Extension
edit dialog box

The Prompt User check box. If the Prompt User check box is checked, you are asked to name the archive you want to uncompress when the UnStuff QuicKey is activated. If the archive contains multiple files, you can then designate which you want to unstuff. Check the Prompt User check box if you want to make a generic "unstuff anything" UnStuff QuicKey.

The Select Archive button. Pressing the Select Archive button elicits an Open dialog box in which you can choose a target archive from which this QuicKey will unstuff.

Auto Save When UnStuffing check box. Checking the Auto Save When UnStuffing check box takes out some of the options when your UnStuff QuicKey is invoked. With this option checked, once you choose the archive (either by preselecting it, or if the Prompt User check box is checked, selecting it at the prompt), it is immediately and completely uncompressed into its own folder. When you check this option, you are *not* prompted to enter the file names of multiple-file archives you wish to uncompress—they just uncompress. It's quick....

Stuff Files Dialog Box

Sometimes when you use the Stuff QuicKey, you'll confront the Stuff files dialog box, from which you choose the file (or files) you want to compress. It's pretty spiffy (see Figure 5-14). It consists of two scrolling lists: the files available to stuff are on the left, and the files you want to stuff are on the right. You select a file from the list on the left, and add it to the list on the right. At the top of the box on the right is an information line which tells you how many files you are allowed to stuff, and how many are on the to-be-stuffed list. You can choose a file from the list on the left and then press the Add button, which adds the file name to the list on the right. There is no way to select multiple files from one list and add them all at once to the other list.

At the bottom of the list on the left is the Compression pop-up menu. You can use it to select the degree of sophistication of your compression. As sophistication increases, speed decreases, which accounts for the apples-and-oranges nature of the items listed. You can choose "None" if you wish to archive some files without compressing them. Even the most sophisticated compression level, "Better" (shouldn't it be "Best"?), is pretty darn quick.

Figure 5-14
Stuff Files
dialog box

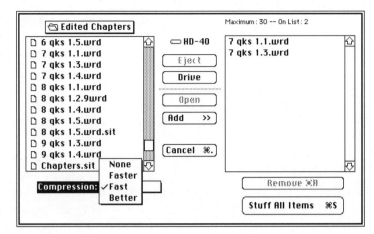

You can remove any item from the list on the right by choosing it and pressing the Remove button. When you are ready to activate the stuffing mechanism, press the Stuff All Items button.

Stuff and UnStuff Considerations

The Stuff and UnStuff Extensions were written by Raymond Lau, who knew more about computers when he was 12 years old then we will ever know. These QuicKeys are pretty sublime, but they are a compromise. Their major asset is that they are quick—you don't have to open your StuffIt Deluxe application to get some of its benefits. But the accompanying drawback is that you don't get all the bells and whistles available through the mother application. Here are a couple of limitations.

No way to append an archive. StuffIt Deluxe lets you add files to an archive; you can't do that with the Stuff Extension.

No way to automatically delete a file that is archived. StuffIt Deluxe gives you the option of erasing the source files that you have archived. You can't do that here.

Another consideration is that stuffing an open file may not work. We couldn't get Microsoft Word files to stuff while they were open. So if you want to stuff active files you must test the files of a particular application to see if they will stuff when they are active.

If for some reason your StuffIt QuicKeys don't work, it could be that you are missing something from the StuffIt Deluxe program. One critical item is the StuffIt Engine, which lives in the Extensions folder of your system folder.

Stuff and
UnStuff Tactics

Use Stuff to quickly compress files through StuffIt Deluxe.
Use UnStuff to quickly uncompress StuffIt Deluxe archives.

We have a generic QuicKey for each of these Extensions, as part of our Universal Keyset. But in special circumstances we could see having QuicKeys that targeted specific files and archives. If we were constantly dealing with one large file and we were short of disk space, we might dedicate a Stuff QuicKey and an UnStuff QuicKey to it. But one note of warning in this situation: if you do have a StuffIt QuicKey that targets a specific archive, it will always wipe out what that archive had on it before. You might be given warning (depending on how you set your options), but it will be replaced. So you will usually only target the archive to save to in situations where you are repeatedly saving one constantly-updated file to one target archive.

Window Control

Window Control covers a long list of QuicKey types that control four objects: document windows, application windows, menus, and buttons. QuicKeys that control document windows constitute the lion's share of window-control QuicKeys, but they're all functionally similar, so they're easy to remember and use. We employ almost all of the types in this chapter on a day-to-day basis.

Document Windows (the Mousies)

Document-window QuicKeys adjust windows. All of these QuicKey types are found in the Mousies submenu, which makes good sense as most of them directly mimic mouse clicking in different control areas of a document's window frame. And a couple of them give you control options not found on most applications' windows. Because all of these types are functionally similar, we'll treat them as group, but discuss their individual peculiarities.

The edit dialog box is the same for all the Mousies (see Figure 6-1). Although the dialog box displays the Mousie type you chose from the submenu, you can press on the Mousie choices pop-up menu and select any of the others (see Figure 6-2).

```
┌──────────────────────────────────────────────────────────────┐
│  Mousie                                                        │
│  ──────────────────────────────────────────────────────────   │
│  Name:  │ Line up              │    Keystroke:  │ Unassigned │  │
│                                                                │
│                                                                │
│  Mousie choices:    │ Line up            ▼ │                   │
│                                                                │
│                                                                │
│                                                                │
│                                                                │
│                                                                │
│                                                                │
│                                                                │
│  ( Timer Options )   ☐ Include in QuicKeys menu  (( OK )) ( Cancel )  │
└──────────────────────────────────────────────────────────────┘
```

Document Window Considerations

Most of the Mousies are stand-ins for clicking in a standard Mac document window (see Figure 6-3). Two additional Mousies, Home and End, move the vertical scroll bar to the top and bottom, respectively. Here are a few Mousie considerations.

```
┌────────────────┐
│ ✓Line up       │
│  Line down     │
│  Page up       │
│  Page down     │
│  Home          │
│  End           │
│  Column left   │
│  Column right  │
│  Page left     │
│  Page right    │
│  Close window  │
│  Zoom window   │
└────────────────┘
```

The type you choose from the Mousies submenu is checked.

Figure 6-2
Mousie choices
pop-up menu

No box, no click. The window you are attempting to adjust with a Mousie must have the feature to be clicked present, or the Mousie won't work. For example, the Close window Mousie won't function if there is no close box on the active window. However, if the feature *is* included, the Mousie might be able to make it function even if you can't. For example, if you have a very large word-processing document, it is often impossible to click between the scroll box and the scroll arrow when the window is near the document's beginning or end. The Page up or Page down Mousie can.

Mutant windows. Mutant document windows (those that don't follow the Mac guidelines) can sometimes fool the Mousie to click where it shouldn't, or there won't be any click at all. Some programs have double sets of arrows, some have weird scroll bars (see Figure 6-4), and some are just bizarre.

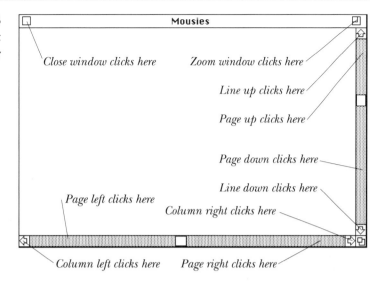

Figure 6-3
Standard Mac
document window

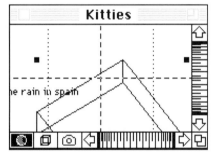

Figure 6-4
A different
document window

*Mousies don't work
with this creature.*

Sometimes Mousie QuicKeys scroll work windows instead of the main document window. Aldus PageMaker is a good example of this. If the Colors Palette or Styles Palette is open and its scroll bar is visible, then Mousies will adjust them. If these windows are closed, or they are enlarged so that their scroll bars go white (that is, their entire contents are showing), then control goes back to the main document window. We asked Ole Kvern (who probably knows more about the convolutions of PageMaker than anyone) why. He said, "That's just the way it is."

Insertion-point movement in word-processing programs.
Many word-processing programs, especially Microsoft Word, have a quiver full of keyboard shortcuts that can make you really fly. Many of them use the keys on the extended key-

board such as Home, End, Page up, and Page down that are designed for these tasks. Just because these keys have names identical to certain Mousies doesn't mean that the application-dedicated functions they invoke are also identical. Sometimes it's close, but not the same; where the insertion point ends up often accounts for the difference. The Mousies don't move the insertion point, just the window. Many applications move the window and the insertion point together. Neither way is superior, they're just different, and you can take advantage of that.

Figure 6-5
PageMaker windows

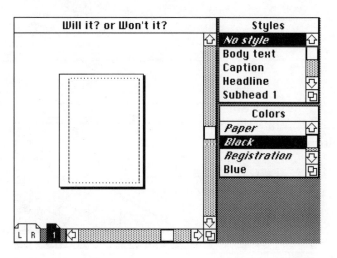

The Styles Palette is controlled preferentially over the main document.

The Colors Palette is controlled preferentially over the Styles Palette.

Document Windows Tactics

Use Document-window QuicKeys (Mousies) to manipulate an individual document's window.

Mousies are generalists, so you don't need more than one copy of each. Because there are so many Mousies and because some of them aren't too useful in our day-to-day work, we have standardized only six Mousies Mac-wide by putting them into our Universal Keyset. Page up, Page down, Home, and End are dedicated to the keys of the same names on our extended keyboards. Because this preempts the built-in function of these keys in Microsoft Word, Don redesignated those functions (Command-Home, Command-End, and so on) using Word's Commands dialog box. This procedure borrows keystrokes from a couple of other of

Word's shortcuts, but their functions are so obscure that Don didn't mind losing them.

The only other Mousies we use regularly are Zoom window and Close window. The keystrokes you use for them and for any additional Mousies you find valuable depend on your layout strategy (see Chapter 15, *Keystroke Strategies*)

Application Windows

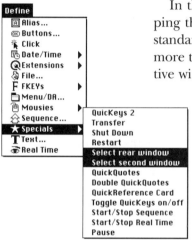

The two Application-window QuicKey types move between open windows within an application.

In the Specials submenu are two QuicKey types for flipping through windows, Select rear and Select second. The standard procedure for applications which allow you to have more than one document open is to push the previously active window behind the newly opened one. So if you first open Document A, and then B and then C and then D, their respective windows are layered as in Figure 6-6.

Select rear will pull the window off the bottom and bring it to the top. Repeatedly invoking Select rear will loop through all the open windows in an application. Select second brings the previously active window to the top. Repeatedly invoking Select second will toggle between the two previously active windows.

Application Window Considerations

To activate a window, it is usually quicker to invoke an Application-window QuicKey than to use the mouse to choose from a menu list of the open documents within an application (which is how most applications are engineered). Sure, a menu item is more precise, but you can use QUICKEYS to toggle through windows as fast as an IRS auditor can find an anomaly in your tax records (we're talking pretty quick).

Figure 6-6
Layers of document windows

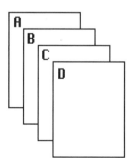

One trick to speed the process is to make your windows as small as possible. The Mac waits until one window is drawn on the screen before it draws the next one, and smaller windows are faster for the Mac to draw. You can facilitate this with the Zoom Mousie described in the previous section ("Document Windows"), but unless you are punching your way through a zillion open windows, the speed gain is not worth the trouble of shrinking each one.

Application Window Tactics

Use Application-window QuicKeys to move to different open windows within an application.

Select rear and Select second are powerful QuicKeys. They're generalists, so we include one of each in our Universal Keysets. Don invokes Select rear with Command-Option-Right arrow on his extended keyboard. He thinks of it as his application window's "Show Me" key because most of the time he has no idea on what layer different document windows exist (often he has little idea which docs he has open). He just jams through the windows until he finds the one he's looking for. Don uses the Select second QuicKey to toggle back and forth between two windows—for example, when he is doing a lot of cutting and pasting between two documents.

Menu

Menu QuicKeys select commands (or items) from a standard menu bar. Menu is the other and generally more powerful guise of the Menu/DA QuicKey (see Chapter 5, *Launching and Opening*). It allows you to choose an item (usually thought of as a "command") from a standard Mac application menu. This type is powerful because it is precise, and QUICKEYS gives you various controls to fine-tune the tool to your particular application and needs.

The first step in building a Menu QuicKey is to ensure you are in the application whose menu you intend to target. Also, it helps if the specific menu item is listed (many applications have menu items which change, depending on conditions).

A good, overall Menu QuicKey is one that chooses "Save As" from the File menu. Because this command is available but without a keystroke shortcut in most applications, it is useful to make one for the Universal Keyset that will invoke "Save As" from wherever you are. In this case, you can be in any application that has a Save As menu item.

Choosing Menu/DA, on the Define menu, makes your cursor turn into a tiny Menu icon as a little instruction dialog box appears (see Figure 6-7). You can select "Save As" from the File menu (contrary to the manual, even if it is dimmed) with the cursor, and a Menu edit dialog box appears (see Figure 6-8) with many of the choices preselected by QUICKEYS.

Figure 6-7
Menu instruction
dialog box

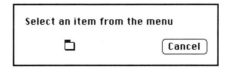

Menu Edit Dialog Box

The Menu edit dialog box has a number of controls that require a little explanation. These controls give you the power to work around *most* of the following menu anomalies.

- Some menu items change their names depending on recent events ("Undo" in Microsoft Word sometimes appears as "Undo Typing," "Redo Paste," and so forth).

Figure 6-8
Menu edit
dialog box

- Some menu items change their names depending on whether there is a modifier key pressed ("Open" in Word 4.0 changes to "Open Any File" if Shift is pressed).
- Some menu items toggle back and forth between two names (Show Ruler, Hide Ruler).
- Some menu items have similar but not identical names in different applications ("Word Count" in Microsoft Word is the same as "Statistics" in Vantage).
- Some identical menu items fall under different menus in different applications ("Bold" is on the Format menu in Word, but on the Type style submenu of the Type menu in PageMaker).

These menu-anomaly controls are grouped into three areas: Item selection control, Menu selection control, and Modifier key control (see Figure 6-9).

Figure 6-9
Menu-anomaly
control areas

Item-selection control

Menu-selection control

Modifier-key control

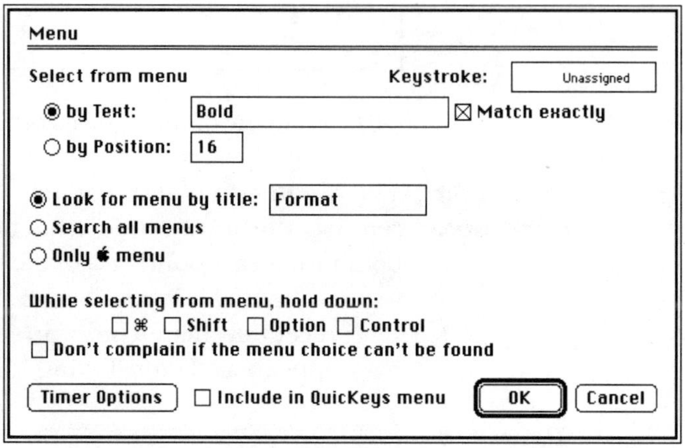

```
┌──────────────────────────────────────────────────────┐
│ Menu                                                   │
│ ══════════════════════════════════════════════════════│
│ Select from menu              Keystroke: [ Unassigned ]│
│  ◉ by Text:      [Bold        ]   ⊠ Match exactly      │
│  ○ by Position:  [16]                                  │
│                                                        │
│  ◉ Look for menu by title: [Format    ]                │
│  ○ Search all menus                                    │
│  ○ Only  menu                                          │
│                                                        │
│  While selecting from menu, hold down:                 │
│      □ ⌘  □ Shift  □ Option  □ Control                  │
│  □ Don't complain if the menu choice can't be found    │
│                                                        │
│ [Timer Options]  □ Include in QuicKeys menu [ OK ][Cancel]│
└──────────────────────────────────────────────────────┘
```

How these fine-tuning controls are adjusted often depends on whether you are making a Universal QuicKey (one that selects an identical or similar menu item in a variety of applications) or an application-specific QuicKey. It also often depends on the extent to which the menu item changes.

Item-selection control (Select from menu). By default, the By Text option is checked and the Menu item you chose is listed by name.
- **By Text.** Use when you are targeting a menu item whose name does not change much or at all. One situation to check this is in an application-specific QuicKey where there is another menu item with a similar name. "By Text" can also be chosen in a Universal Keyset QuicKey.
- **Match Exactly.** "Match Exactly" means nearly what it says. It's not case sensitive, but it sure can tell the difference between three periods in a row and an ellipsis.
- **By Position.** Use this option when the item name changes significantly (for example, "Undo Typing" becomes "Redo Paste"). By Position is almost always application-specific, because identical menu items are often in different positions in different applications.

Menu-selection control. This control area determines how QuicKeys looks for the menu in which your target item is located. Menu-selection control defaults to "Look for menu by title" and QuicKeys fills in the title of the menu you chose.

- **By Title.** Use this default for most application-specific situations, and in Universal Keyset QuicKeys when you are sure that the target menus all have identical names in every possible application.
- **Search all menus.** Use this option when a Universal Keyset QuicKey invokes a command located on menus that carry different names in different applications. It's also useful when QuicKeys, for some reason or another, can't seem to find the menu item.
- **Only Apple menu.** This is a interloper from the DA form of the Menu/DA QuicKey type, and so does not concern us here.

Modifier-key control. Some menu items change their form if a modifier key is pressed while the menu item is selected. These modifier-key control options tell QuicKeys which modifiers you want held down so the target menu item will appear.

When you construct a Menu QuicKey that needs a modifier, you can hold down the correct modifier key when you pick the menu item with the little menu cursor. For example, holding down Shift when you press on the File menu in Microsoft Word changes the Open item to "Open Any File." To build a menu QuicKey which accesses this Open Any File item, you can press the appropriate modifier (in this case Shift) while making the menu selection. This causes QuicKeys to fill in the correct name of the target menu item and to check the appropriate modifier key box in this control area.

Menu Considerations

You're usually best off using the automatic entries that QuicKeys makes in the Menu edit dialog box. But sometimes you will have to change them, especially in situations where you want to select a menu item that has a name with an ending that varies somewhat from application to application (or within an application). If you enter a truncated version of the menu item name and *uncheck* "Match exactly," QuicKeys searches through the menu items top to bottom and left to right and selects the first one that matches. For example, entering "Undo" in the text edit box and unchecking "Match exactly" allows the QuicKey to select "Undo Typing" or "Undo Paste" and so forth.

Checking "Match exactly" sometimes leads to problems when you type the menu item name into the text edit box yourself. This is because the true menu item name is often slightly different from your entered version of it. Check to see if spaces and special symbols are correct (don't worry about an initial space; QUICKEYS ignores it). And the three dots you see in menu items which bring up a dialog box are almost always the ellipsis character (Option-;).

Certain applications employ menu designs that deviate from the Mac interface standards. Sometimes what appears to be a menu isn't generated by the program in a standard manner. Sometimes an application can think a menu has a different name than it displays. The QUICKEYS automatic entries in a Menu edit dialog box are occasionally frighteningly perspicacious in determining a workable suggestion. For example, Figure 6-10 shows a hierarchical menu item chosen in PageMaker. The menu title is Type and the submenu is Type style, but the automatic entry that QUICKEYS made in the Menu edit dialog box has the submenu name as Format. And, of course, it finds the menu item perfectly when it thinks it is looking in the Format menu (wherever *that* is—it's not on the Menu bar). However, if you try a similar procedure in QuarkXPress, QUICKEYS doesn't deign to suggest what the menu title might be. The fix here, and a good one for similar problems, is to check "Search all menus." The menu item is selected, tickety-poo.

If your Mac beeps when you make the menu choice while constructing a Menu QuicKey, it's an indication that this is a non-standard menu and there probably is not a way to use QuicKeys to access it. And Pop-up menus within dialog boxes are not accessible with QUICKEYS—maybe someday.

Figure 6-10
PageMaker's Type style submenu

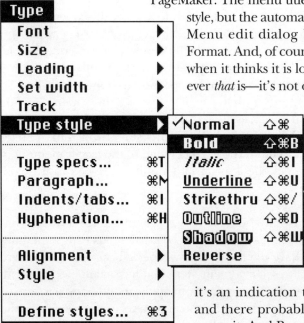

Menu Tactics   *Use Menu QuicKeys to select a menu item.*

The most common use of Menu QuicKeys is to give an application's menu command a keystroke equivalent (for example, assigning keystrokes to the Clear and Define menu items in FileMaker). This type of job can also be done (sometimes easily) with ResEdit, but some people don't want to mess with a utility program that is so powerful (and unforgiving).

The More Universal Keys keyset that comes with your QUICKEYS package suggests four universal Menu QuicKeys (see Figure 6-11). These standardize the basic Edit menu commands and assign them to the function keys with the appropriate labels on the Mac extended keyboard. This approach works for some folks, but we wonder why you should waste perfectly good function keys when these menu items already have standard keystroke activation in most applications. So we standardize them the old-fashioned way (see Figure 6-12).

Figure 6-11
More Universal Keyset

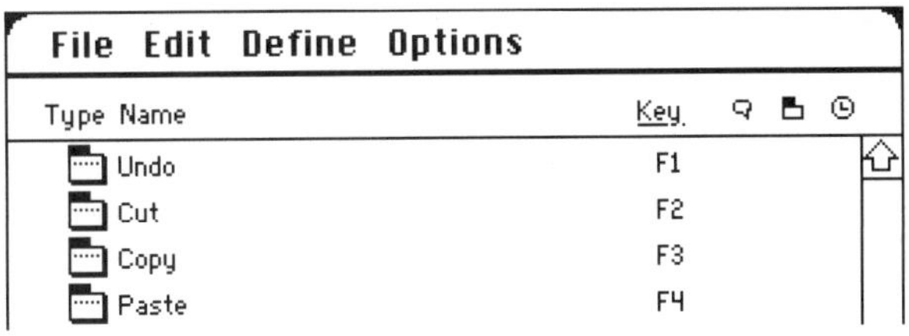

QUICKEYS-suggested keystrokes

Figure 6-12
Our Universal Keyset

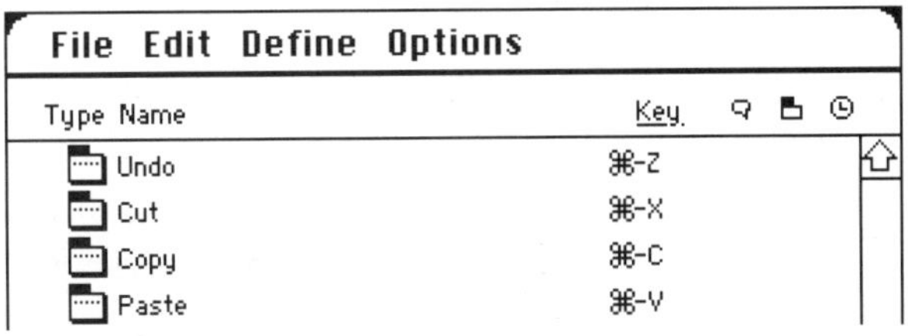

With the old-fashioned keystrokes

Buttons   Button QuicKeys click a button or check box in a dialog box. There's no mystery here; the Button type has an obvious task and simple controls. Just choose Button from the Define menu, and the Button edit dialog box appears.

Button Edit Dialog Box

The Button edit dialog box is designed so that you enter into the Name text box the name of the button you want to press.

QUICKEYS can choose the correct button even if you only type the first letter or few letters, as long as there are no other buttons in that dialog box which start the same way (see Figure 6-13).

The options area of the Button edit dialog box was created to give you specialized control of check boxes—but it can affect the clicking of buttons so always choose the top option (Always click button) for buttons.

Figure 6-13
QUICKEYS button title discrimination

Button named "A" picks Arabic numeral.

Button named "L" picks Lower Roman (not Lower alphabetic).

Button named "Lower a" picks Lower alphabetic.

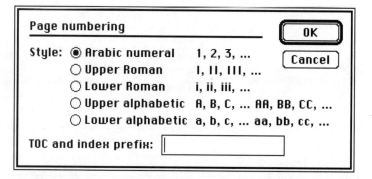

Unlike buttons, a check box toggles between two modes when it is clicked. Generally, you won't want to worry about whether the check box is already checked; you just want to change it to either the checked or unchecked mode. That's what options two and three are for. If you choose the first option, Always click button, for a check box, the QuicKey will reverse the mode of the check box.

A Button QuicKey will not display a notice if its target button is not available.

Button Tactics   *Use Button QuicKeys to click a button or a check box.*

You'll probably use Button QuicKeys in application-specific areas. Often, Sequences contain at least one Button QuicKey.

Many times, applications have keystroke shortcuts to press buttons in dialog boxes. But you might find yourself in a situation where you must repeatedly press buttons that don't have these shortcuts built in. Application-specific button QuicKeys fill this role nicely.

If you find yourself in this situation only occasionally, you might just want to use the DialogKeys application which came in your QUICKEYS package. This allows you to tab through the buttons in a dialog box and press the one you want without using the mouse.

Don has a few Button QuicKeys in his Universal Keyset, just because he doesn't use DialogKeys often (see Figure 6-14). Steve uses DialogKeys.

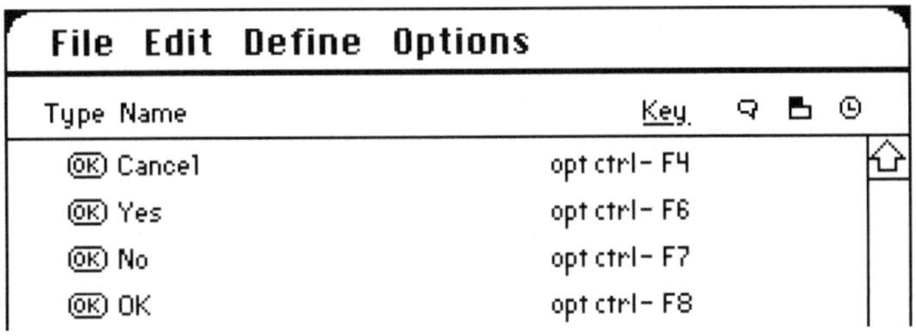

Figure 6-14
Don's Universal
Button QuicKeys

File Edit Define Options			
Type Name	Key		
(OK) Cancel	opt ctrl– F4		
(OK) Yes	opt ctrl– F6		
(OK) No	opt ctrl– F7		
(OK) OK	opt ctrl– F8		

Keyboard and Mouse

CHAPTER

7

This chapter discusses two similar QuicKey types, Alias and Click. Both act as stand-ins for different parts of the Apple Desktop Bus (the keyboard and mouse), and both perform simple tasks. Although creating an Alias QuicKey is easy, making Click function properly sometimes might seem like you're battling the controls of a crippled 747.

Alias

Alias QuicKeys remap one keyboard key (and any modifiers) to another keyboard key (and any modifiers).

A good example of this type is an Alias Quickey that Steve created to overcome a hardware/human interface glitch. The extended Apple keyboard has its Help key just about half an inch to the right of the Delete key. Sometimes, when Steve is burning up the keyboard trying to meet a deadline, his killer Delete index finger overshoots its intended touch-down on Delete and instead bounces off Help and back to Delete. This causes the Help feature of Microsoft Word to seize control of his machine, ponder a bit, and finally deliver a Help screen on deleting text and graphics. Steve fixed this using Alias (see Figure 7-1).

Steve's fix fools the Help key into thinking it is Delete. The Delete key still invokes the Delete function, but now Help does the same. In order to retain the Help function, Steve created a second Alias QuicKey to invoke it using Command-Help. This problem occurs in enough applications (word processors, desktop publishers, art programs, and so forth) that Steve put these Alias QuicKeys in his Universal Keyset.

Define

- Ⓐ **Alias...**
- ⓞⓚ **Buttons...**
- ⁂ **Click**
- **Date/Time** ▶
- **Extensions** ▶
- **File...**
- F **FKEYs** ▶
- **Menu/DA...**
- **Mousies** ▶
- **Sequence...**
- ★ **Specials** ▶
- T **Text...**
- **Real Time**

Figure 7-1
Steve's fix

File	Edit	Define	Options

Type Name | Key ♥ 🖿 🕐
🅰 del | help | ⬆
🅰 help | ⌘-help |

Alias Considerations

The Alias QuicKey is almost foolproof. The only hazard to worry about is inadvertently mapping over a function that you want to retain. Don't.

Alias Tactics

Use Alias QuicKeys to make a keystroke combination invoke a different keystroke combination.

Except for situations like Steve's, where you want one key on the keyboard to do what another does, you probably won't find yourself using a lot of Alias QuicKeys as single units. However, Sequences (see Chapter 12, *The Sequence*), often employ an Alias QuicKey as one of their steps.

Click

The Click QuicKey mimics mouse clicking and movement.

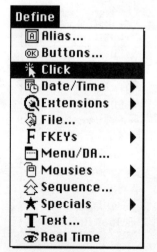

Define
🅰 Alias...
🆗 Buttons...
🔆 Click
🔒 Date/Time ▶
🔍 Extensions ▶
🗒 File...
𝖥 FKEYs ▶
🗔 Menu/DA...
🗐 Mousies ▶
🔼 Sequence...
★ Specials ▶
𝗧 Text...
👁 Real Time

The first steps in creating a Click QuicKey are simple, and if QUICKEYS fills in selections for the Click edit dialog boxes that fit your situation (and it usually does), then Click will give you no problem. However, if you have to tweak or edit your Click QuicKey, you may find the multiple edit dialog boxes fairly daunting, but we'll show you what you have to worry about and what you don't.

Creating a Click Quickey involves a QUICKEYS-aided process of recording. Some of the sights that you see during the process are very similar to those you see when you record a sequence (see Chapter 12, *The Sequence*).

A useful example of this QuicKey type is a QuicKey that will shrink a document window down to its smallest size. It's easiest to begin the process with a document that's open to a fairly normal size. Then you can select Click from the QUICKEYS Define menu. This causes a little microphone-icon cursor to appear (if you have Display "Record" cursor item chosen on the Options menu of the management window) as the QUICKEYS management window disappears. Use this cursor to click and drag the bottom-right corner of the box all the way to the top left of the screen (the box will stop shrinking at some point but you can continue your drag all the way to the screen's top-left corner).

After you release the mouse key, a Click edit dialog box appears (see Figure 7-2). The center part of this dialog box contains three buttons (Click, Window, and Control area). To the right of each button is a report on its settings. Under the buttons are two additional settings. If you want multiple clicks on something, you need to fill in the appropriate number in the Click times box. If you want modifier keys held down as you click, you can enter them in the Hold down area.

Pressing on the Click button invokes the Click Location edit dialog box.

Figure 7-2
Click edit dialog box

Click

| Name: | Click | Keystroke: | Unassigned |

Click: From:(560,424) from top-left corner
To:(-560,-464) from current location

Window: Window #1 from front

Control area: None

Click [1] time(s)

Hold down: ☐ ⌘ ☐ Shift ☐ Option ☐ Control

[Timer Options] ☐ Include in QuicKeys menu [OK] [Cancel]

The Click Location Edit Dialog Box

The Click Location edit dialog box has a right and a left section (see Figure 7-3). Each section corresponds to a different location that the Click QuicKey records when you create a Click QuicKey.

Figure 7-3
Click Location edit dialog box

The click control area—where you pressed down on the mouse button

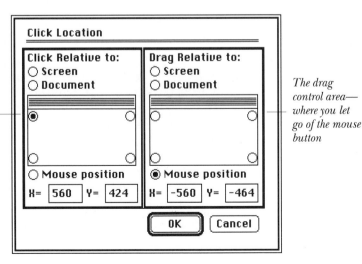

The drag control area—where you let go of the mouse button

The two sections. QUICKEYS remembers two things:

- It records where you pressed down on the mouse button (click-down). This location is displayed on the left side of the dialog box.
- It records where you let go of the mouse button (click-up). This location is displayed on the right side of the dialog box.

These positions are displayed in the bottom "x=" and "y=" boxes in the dialog box.

The units of measurement. The numbers in the bottom "x=" and "y=" boxes are in measured in *pixels*, which are the little dots that make up the image on your Mac monitor. A pixel equals about 1/72 inch on most monitors, but it has no exact size; a pixel array can contract or expand depending on what monitor you're using. However, each standard class of monitor displays a set number of pixels (see Table 7-1).

Table 7-1 Monitor Pixel Arrays

Mac 11-inch black-and-white monitor	640 x 480
Mac 13-inch color monitor	640 x 480
Mac Classic monitor	576 x 378

Original sin. Although each section of the Click Location edit dialog box only contains one location (specified by an x and a y coordinate), each possesses various other controls. These are the options for locating where the x and y coordinates are measured from (which, as you might remember from your first geometry class, is called the *origin*). QUICKEYS automatically selects one of these options and fills in the x and y coordinates where you click. If you choose a different option, QUICKEYS automatically recalculates the coordinates. You will only need to fill in the coordinates yourself if you are tweaking the automatic entry.

There are three different options areas (see Figure 7-3) on each side of the Click Location edit dialog box that you can select.

- **Screen.** If this option is chosen, the coordinates are measured from the top-left corner of the entire screen.

So the top-left corner pixel of Don's 13-inch monitor has the coordinates of (0,0) and the bottom-right corner pixel has the coordinates (639, 479). Use this option when you want to pick out something relative to the whole screen, like the Trash Can.

- **Document.** This gives you the option of measuring from any corner of a document window. The graphic within the Document section might be a little misleading. There are five buttons: Document, and one for each of the four corners. The Document button is redundant with the top-left corner button in the window beneath it. The corner buttons measure from the extreme corners of the document window (outside the scroll bars, for instance), not from within the window as it appears in the graphic. Use this option when you want to click on something relative to the window, like the "grow region" in the lower-right corner of most document windows.

- **Mouse position.** This is a little different depending on which section it is in. In the left-hand section of the Click Location edit dialog box, this coordinate represents a point measured from where the mouse cursor was when you pressed the button down. So when this option is chosen the coordinates displayed are always initially (0,0), since you always clicked where the mouse was when you recorded the QuicKey. The option can then be used to tweak the click position by changing the coordinate entries.

  In the right-hand section, the Mouse position option represents the coordinate of where the cursor was when you let go of the mouse button (a click and drag) relative to where the button was pushed down. If you just make a click QuicKey (no drag) then the Mouse position option is automatically checked in the right-hand section and the coordinates (0,0) are filled in, to show that there was no movement between where the mouse was pressed down and where it was released.

You may notice that x-coordinates *increase going toward the right* of the screen and y-coordinates *increase going toward the bottom* of the screen. This is different from the standard Cartesian coordinate system (increases right and up) but makes perfect sense in this context.

The Click Window Edit Dialog Box

The Window button on the main Click edit dialog box invokes the Click Window edit dialog box (see Figure 7-4). This dialog box selects the window in which the Click QuicKey does its click. There are three options.

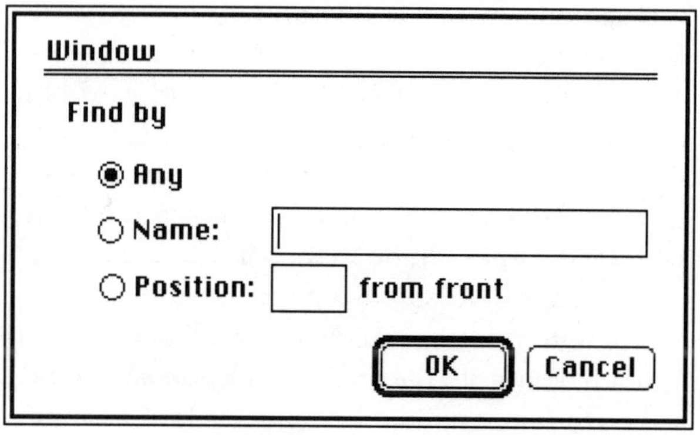

Window

Find by

◉ Any
○ Name: [   ]
○ Position: [   ] from front

[OK] [Cancel]

Figure 7-4
Click Window edit dialog box

• **Any.** Any is the automatic choice if the click is not within an application window. The click is made regardless of what is showing on the screen.

• **Name.** This button and its text edit box choose the document to be clicked on by its name. If you choose this option it means that the click will only happen if the active window has the same name as you enter in the text edit box. The text box of this option is automatically filled in with the name of the application document when you click on it. But if you want this option you need to select it yourself.

• **Position.** If you click on an application window, the document's position is entered in the text edit field and the Position button is selected. If you choose this option the click will occur in the window that is as many layers back from the front as you enter in the text edit box. This is particularly useful in applications like PageMaker where the "main" window is rarely the top window.

The Control Area Edit Dialog Box

Pressing the Control area button on the main Click edit dialog box invokes the Control Area edit dialog box (see Figure 7-5). This dialog box controls how the Click QuicKey finds its target if the click occurs on a button or a scroll bar.

If your Click QuicKey was recorded by clicking in a scroll bar, check box, or a button, then the name of that control area appears in the text edit box after the Name radio button. Also, the Position radio button will be on, with the position of the control area automatically filled in. You probably don't want to mess with the Click Control Area edit dialog box. If you want to click on a button, try using a Button QuicKey, instead. Use this option in the very unusual circumstance that the control area (Button) doesn't have an apparent name.

```
┌─────────────────────────────────────────────┐
│  Control Area: Includes Buttons and Scroll bars │
│                                               │
│  Find by                                      │
│    ◉ None                                     │
│    ○ Name:    [                    ]          │
│    ○ Position: [    ]  from front             │
│    ◉ Always click button                      │
│    ○ Only click if button is on               │
│    ○ Only click if button is off              │
│                          ( OK )  ( Cancel )   │
└─────────────────────────────────────────────┘
```

Figure 7-5
Click Control Area
edit dialog box

• **None.** "None" will be on if you haven't clicked in a Control Area.

• **Name.** If you want the Click QuicKey to target a control area by name, then click this radio button and fill in the name of the control area. (QUICKEYS probably already filled it in for you).

• **Position.** Different control areas occupy different transparent layers that can be used to identify the particular area you want. QuicKeys often fills in the correct position for you.

• **Button click options.** There are three options that can be used to ensure the button is clicked correctly.

Click Considerations

The biggest tip regarding the Click QuicKey is to only use it when no other QuicKey will do. In certain situations, Button, Mousies, File, or Menu/DA might be a better choice than Click. Use Click as a last resort, because it is sometimes tricky to modify and isn't as adaptable to most changes in conditions as a QuicKey that's more specialized for a particular job.

Click coordinate manipulation. Occasionally, you might want to change the coordinates that QUICKEYS automatically enters in the "x=" and "Y=" fields. This might happen if you set up the Click QuicKey on some icon and then you move the icon.

The thing to remember here are that x-coordinates increase to the right and Y-coordinates increase going down. These coordinates are approximately 72 to the inch, so use that as your benchmark. For example, replacing x=400 and Y=200 with x=418 and Y=182 moves the click point a quarter inch to the right and a quarter inch up. When you find your Click is missing the point you want it to hit, you can actually measure the screen with a ruler—from the transitory arrow that appears when you invoke the Click QuicKey to the object you wish to target. Then work out the arithmetic and change the settings in the Click Location window appropriately.

Click in sequences. Sequences are important enough to have two chapters devoted to them (Chapter 12, *The Sequence* and Chapter 13, *Sequence QuicKeys*), but the Click QuicKey presents a special situation within the Sequence and so we want to mention it here. When you are constructing a Sequence the Click QuicKey is not made available to you from the Define menu. Instead, you must either use the Record More or Import buttons on the Sequence edit dialog box to create a Click QuicKey or import an already-extant QuicKey into your sequence. For more, see "Import," in Chapter 12, *The Sequence.*

Click Tactics   *Use Click to click or drag something when other QuicKeys can't be used.*

We often find ourselves using a Click QuicKey when we tried to use another QuicKey, but it just didn't work. This sometimes occurs with programs that don't comply with the Apple guidelines for control areas. So when we try to use a Button QuicKey to press what appears to be a button and it doesn't work, we resort to a Click.

Our few Click QuicKeys tend to be in application-specific keysets or within Sequence QuicKeys. Don has two Click QuicKeys he uses enough to keep in his permanent collection.

Trash It. This Click lives in the Finder Keyset in System 6, the Universal Keyset in System 7. It drags whatever icon the cursor is on to the trash. Figure 7-6 shows the appropriate settings.

Figure 7-6
Trash It
Click QuicKey

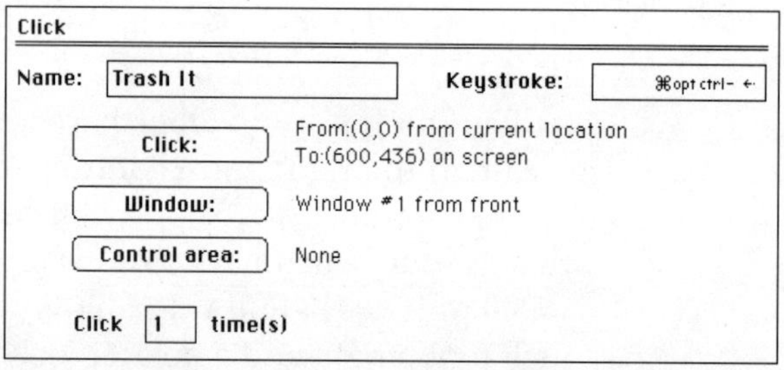

Close Zoom. This Click QuicKey drags the image size box in the lower-right corner of the top application window up and to the left so that it shrinks to its smallest size. Don keeps this QuicKey in his Universal Keyset and its activating key is right next to his Zoom Mousie QuicKey (which essentially performs the opposite function). Figure 7-7 shows the settings for Close Zoom. Some applications (such as PageMaker) do not work with this QuicKey, as their main window is never on the top layer.

Figure 7-7
Close Zoom
Click QuicKey

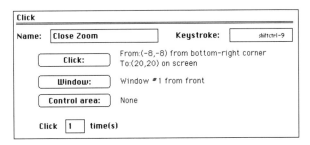

System Control

System Control QuicKeys make high-level adjustments to your Mac; they automate the switches, knobs, bells, and whistles of your Mac's interface. Some automate processes found on certain menus; others instantly change the settings on control panels. Many of the QuicKeys in this chapter perform one job—they don't have multiple targets—so you usually need just one of each in your QUICKEYS environment.

Switches

Restart and Shut Down are the two "switches" for your Mac that are normally activated from the Special menu (in the Finder). You can make QUICKEYS restart or shut down your Mac by using a Menu QuicKey to choose each option directly from this Special menu, but only when you're in the Finder. The Restart and Shut Down Specials offer a more direct route to these switches, no matter what program is running.

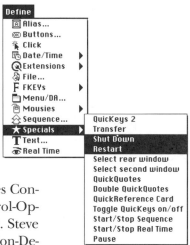

Choosing either Restart or Shut Down from the Specials submenu of the Define menu gives you the Special edit dialog box (see Figure 8-1); its operation is completely self-evident.

We both have Shut Down and Restart QuicKeys as part of our permanent Universal Keysets. Don uses Control-Option-Delete to activate Shut Down and Control-Option-= (the key adjacent to Delete) to invoke Restart. Steve uses Control-Delete for Shut Down, and Control-Option-Delete for Restart, because they're far apart and hard to press by accident. Whatever keystroke strategy you use, you don't want to be able to invoke either of these QuicKeys inadvertently, so multiple modifiers accompanied by a long stretch of the fingers help to create a fail-safe guard.

Figure 8-1
Special edit
dialog box

Special

Name: | Shut Down | Keystroke: | Unassigned |

Special choices: | Shut Down ▼ |

[Timer Options]   ☐ Include in QuicKeys menu   [OK]   [Cancel]

Switches Tactics   *Use Shut Down and Restart QuicKeys instead of accessing these switch functions from the Finder's Special menu.*

Choosy   Choosy QuicKeys let you use a keystroke or menu selection to choose from among different printers in the Chooser (which you normally access from the Apple menu).

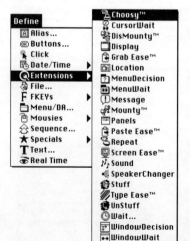

Selecting "Choosy" from the Extensions submenu of the Define menu invokes the Choosy Extension edit dialog box (see Figure 8-2). You can press on the Types of printers available pop-up menu to reveal the printer drivers on your System. After you make your selection, the dialog box changes to give you text edit boxes for the specific printer and zone. You can press the Choose Printer button to select a printer; a dialog box is displayed which shows the zones and printers available (see Figure 8-3).

If you only have one network available, QUICKEYS enters an asterisk in the Zone name text edit box, which means "current zone" in AppleTalk-ese. Networks in big companies can get pretty huge, and therefore contain a bunch of zones. One local company has a network so extensive that an employee can choose to print out a document on any of the printers in any of their offices—national or international. So one could create a Choosy QuicKey that would select the LaserWriter IINTX in the Tokyo office. Pretty cool stuff.

Figure 8-2
Choosy edit
dialog box

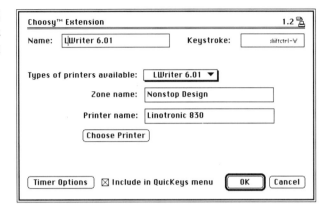

Figure 8-3
Selecting a zone and a
printer for a Choosy
QuicKey

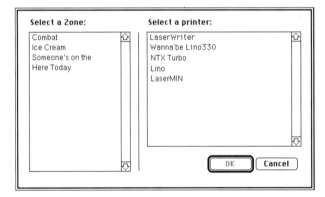

Choosy Tactics and Considerations

Use Choosy to switch printers.

If you have trouble with the Choosy Extension, it may be that your printer name is not entered *exactly* as it is listed in the Chooser; choose a printer using the Choose Printer button so you're sure you've got it right. Also, Choosy versions up to and including the current one (1.2) have bugs in two areas.

- You can't make a Choosy QuicKey for a non-AppleTalk printer driver—one dedicated to a printer that is connected directly to your Mac (like an HP DeskWriter or non-AppleTalk ImageWriter).

- You can't make a Choosy QuicKey for a non-printer device like Preview, because it doesn't have a zone.

CE says they'll have these bugs fixed in version 1.2.1, so you might want to check out your version number (it's listed in the upper-right corner of the edit dialog box) to see if you need an upgrade.

One Choosy problem (or feature, depending on your point of view) is that it doesn't let you know which printer you are choosing; it makes the selection in the background. This is great for many folks because it is fast, but some people like to be notified that something actually happened. It's easy to do: make your Choosy QuicKeys into two-step sequences with a Message QuicKey that tells you what printer you've changed to as the second step (see Chapter 12, *The Sequence*, and Chapter 13, *Sequence QuicKeys*).

Steve likes to put his Choosy QuicKeys on the QuicKeys 2 submenu, because there are so many of them and it's tough to assign a mnemonic keystroke to each one.

Mounty and DisMounty

Mounty and DisMounty are similar to Choosy—they deal with networks and zones—but they only work if you are connected to an AppleShare file server. Mounty and Dis-Mounty quickly select (mount) and deselect (dis-mount) a volume on an Apple-Share network. If you don't use AppleShare, you will have no use for these Extensions. If you do use AppleShare, you'll find them a great help in speeding your access to (and egress from) AppleShare volumes.

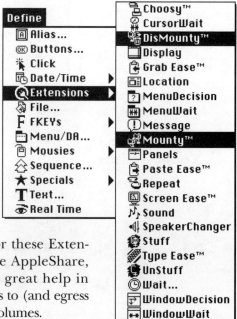

Mounty   You can choose "Mounty" from the Extensions submenu of the Define menu in the QuicKeys management window. The Mounty edit dialog box appears (see Figure 8-4). If you use AppleShare, then you are no doubt familiar with its terminology, so the different controls and text edit boxes are fairly straightforward. You can either fill in the names of the zone and the server manually (be sure to enter their names exactly; AppleShare is case-sensitive), or you can press the Choose Server button and the Choose Server dialog box appears (see Figure 8-5). You can select the zone and server in the Choose Server dialog box and press OK—they will be entered into the Mounty edit dialog box automatically.

Figure 8-4
Mounty edit
dialog box

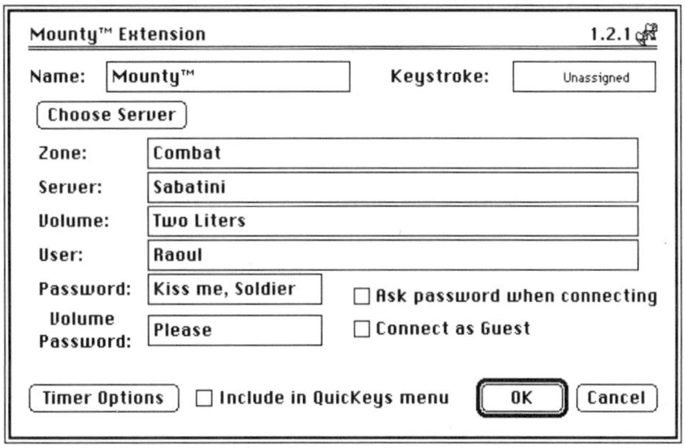

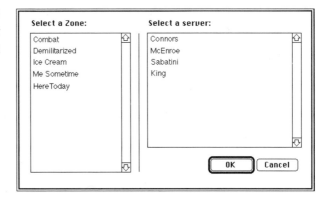

Figure 8-5
Choose Server
dialog box

You can either enter your password in the Mounty edit dialog box, or, if you prefer not to keep it in such an accessible place, you can check the Ask password when connecting check box; but then you will have to enter it whenever you invoke the QuicKey.

DisMounty

The DisMounty Extension is very simple in operation and setup—it dismounts the AppleShare volume that you name in its edit dialog box. To create a DisMounty QuicKey, choose "DisMounty" from the Extensions submenu of the Define menu in the QuicKeys management window. The DisMounty edit dialog box is displayed (see Figure 8-6). Enter the name of the volume you wish to dismount (it must be a precise duplication), assign a keystroke, and you are ready to go.

Figure 8-6
DisMounty edit
dialog box

DisMounty™ Extension		1.0
Name: DisMounty™	Keystroke:	Unassigned

© 1991 CE Software, Inc. Written by Jon Thelin.

QuicKeys 2 Extension to DisMount AppleShare® Volumes:

Volume Name: Two Liters

Timer Options   ☐ Include in QuicKeys menu   OK   Cancel

Mounty and DisMounty Considerations

Like Choosy, Mounty and DisMounty do not inform you that they have actually done anything when you invoke them. Even if you choose the Ask password when connecting option, the dialog box that asks you for your password doesn't tell you which server you are mounting. This can be annoying if you access many servers utilizing many passwords. As with Choosy, one solution is to make either of these AppleShare QuicKeys the start of a two-part sequence, followed by a Message Extension which will display a dialog box that informs you what server you are dealing with.

Mounty and DisMounty Tactics

Use Mounty to mount an AppleShare volume.
Use DisMounty to dismount an AppleShare volume.

Mounty and DisMounty can substantially accelerate the

process of mounting and dismounting AppleShare volumes. Mounty and DisMounty are targeted QuicKeys; they don't have a generic capability, so you will have to create two QuicKeys for each volume you want to be able to mount and dismount. For keystrokes, we like to use our function keys with a fairly obscure modifier combination (like Shift-Control-Command) with the mount and dismount functions tagged in pairs (for example, F1 mounts Connors, F2 dismounts Connors). We need to use a visual reminder (see Chapter 16, *Mechanical Memory Assist*) to remember which keys go with which servers—but it's easy to remember that the odd-numbered keys mount, and the even-numbered keys dismount.

As with Choosy QuicKeys, Steve likes to put Mounty and DisMounty QuicKeys on the menu so he doesn't have to remember the keystrokes.

Control Panels

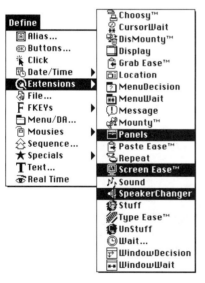

Control Panels is the category of QuicKeys that access the various control panels you have installed in your system. System 6 and System 7 vary in their treatment of control panels. In System 6, under the Apple menu, there's a desk accessory named "Control Panel" which, when activated, gives you scroll-bar access to various cdevs (control panel devices—located in your system folder) and their adjustments. In System 7, your cdevs are stored inside the Control Panels folder within your system folder, and they're accessible either from the Control Panels item on the Apple menu or from an individual icon within the Control Panels folder (or by using an Alias).

The Panels Extension enables you to invoke a specific control panel (without going through the DA in System 6 or the Finder in System 7). The Screen Ease and SpeakerChanger Extensions only adjust their two respective control panels.

Here's a rundown on these three useful QuicKeys.

Panels Choosing "Panels" from the Extensions submenu of the Define menu invokes the Panels edit dialog box. Initially, its Control Panels pop-up menu appears blank, but when it is pressed a listing of all your control panels appears (see Figure 8-7). This listing includes all the cdevs in your system folder, not just the ones that are loaded.

Figure 8-7
Panels edit
dialog box

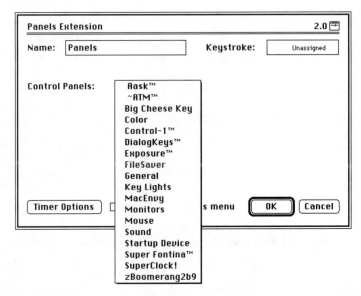

You can choose any control panel and assign it an invoking keystroke combination. Then, when you invoke that Panels QuicKey, your target control panel appears so you can make whatever adjustments you want to it.

Panels
Considerations
When using the Panels Extension, keep in mind that you may have control panels that were included in your system software that have no target in your configuration (for example, the color control panel when you have a black-and-white monitor). Don't invoke these control panels with QUICKEYS or, as CE Software states in the Read Me file, "unpredictable results may occur."

A more likely problem might occur if you are using System 7 (see below).

Panels problems in System 7. Control panels can be different sizes in System 7. In the case of a few control panels, this creates interference with the Panels Extension. However, there is an alternative path to open a control panel (or any file or folder) through the Finder Events Extension.

This procedure requires that you operate in System 7 and you have CEIAC (CE Software's interapplication communications program) installed. You can select "Finder Events" from the Extensions submenu of the Define menu. The Finder Events edit dialog box appears. Pressing on the Finder Events pop-up menu displays a list of all the Finder Events available; you can choose "Open," which invokes a standard Open file dialog box. Choose your target control panel, and assign an invoking keystroke combination (see "Finder Events," in Chapter 9, *System 7 Stuff*).

Panels Tactics   *Use Panels to access a control panel.*

We adjust a few of our control panels frequently enough to warrant our dedicating QuicKeys to them. However, many important control panel adjustments are available through specific Control Panel Extensions (see next section).

Screen Ease   The Screen Ease Extension adjusts various controls located on the Monitors control panel: with it, you can choose how you display different colors and shades of gray. Additionally, Screen Ease can make the changes permanent (until you change them again) or temporary (until you reboot). Screen Ease is designed to maximize the ways you can control your screen's characteristics. You can make QuicKeys which will select specific settings, or you can choose options which will vary settings in a particular direction.

You can make a Screen Ease QuicKey by choosing it from the Extensions submenu of the Define menu. The Screen Ease edit dialog box appears (see Figure 8-8). The left side of this dialog box gives you options for selecting the target monitor in multiple-monitor setups. The right side contains the adjustment options, including the Depth pop-up menu (see Figure 8-9). By pressing on the pop-up menu, you can choose a level of color or gray-scale display. Those available on your Mac are outlined. At the bottom of the menu are two cool option areas: Decrease/Increase and Minimum/Maximum. Decrease or Increase adjusts the depth level in steps; Minimum or Maximum takes you to the simplest or the most complex depth level available to you.

Figure 8-8
Screen Ease
edit dialog box

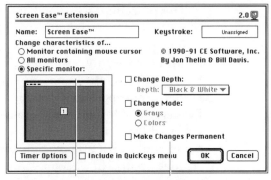

Monitor selection options   Display options

Figure 8-9
Depth pop-up menu

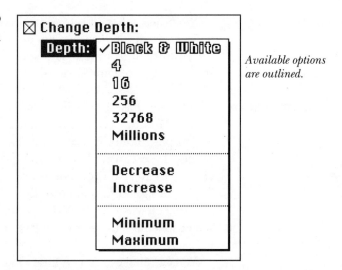

*Available options
are outlined.*

**Screen Ease Tactics
and Considerations**

Use Screen Ease QuicKeys to adjust your monitor settings.

How often and in what manner you use Screen Ease depends on your particular situation. If you need a Screen Ease QuicKey, you probably will want to make more than one of them; you'll want one for your standard monitor settings, and any others for special situations.

There are two basic tactics for Screen Ease QuicKeys.

- **Targeted.** Make one Screen Ease QuicKey for your standard setting, and any others for specialized applications. You can embed a Screen Ease QuicKey into a Sequence which opens a sophisticated graphics application (like Photoshop) to make the screen change to a higher rendition level automatically.

- **Toggled.** Make two Screen Ease QuicKeys—either Decrease and Increase, or Minimum and Maximum. Don uses a Decrease and an Increase combination within his Universal Keyset.

What if you don't know the level your monitor is rendering at the moment? There is a third-party Extension that can tell you—Bit Depth, written by Ed Ludwig of Vectre Systems. Bit Depth is a single-use Extension QuicKey that pops up a box containing the number of levels your monitor currently displays. See the Appendix, *Resources*.

SpeakerChanger

The SpeakerChanger Extension sets the volume of your speaker. When it is chosen from the Extensions submenu, the SpeakerChanger edit dialog box appears (see Figure 8-10). Any volume adjustments you make with the SpeakerChanger Extension will disappear when you reboot; your volume level will revert to the Speaker Volume setting in your Control Panel.

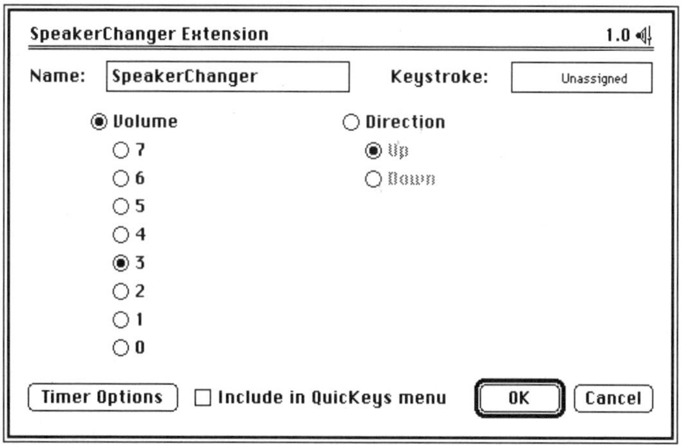

Figure 8-10
SpeakerChanger
edit dialog box

SpeakerChanger Tactics and Considerations

Use SpeakerChanger to adjust the volume of your Mac's speaker.

We have two SpeakerChanger QuicKeys: one to increase the volume, and one to decrease it. Every time we invoke one of them, we get a beep signifying the new volume level. Two beeps indicates we have hit the maximum setting; the menu bar flashing without any beeps indicates we have reduced the setting to zero.

FKEYs

FKEY QuicKeys give you the power to invoke FKEYs with your own keystroke combination. You must have the FKEY resident in your System for it to function.

Many folks who aren't too familiar with the Mac get confused about FKEYs. They *aren't* the function keys (F1, F2, F3, and so forth) on an extended keyboard. They *are* little utility programs that come inside your System that you can invoke from your keyboard. You can also get third-party FKEYs and install them using a program like Suitcase or Master-Juggler.

The FKEY QuicKey is available straight from the main Define menu, which is perhaps too prominent a position for such a seldom-used commodity. When you press on the FKEY menu item, a submenu of all your available FKEYs appears. However, we have some FKEYs in our system (like Command-Shift-1, which ejects the floppy in the internal drive) that don't show up on this list, because the System handles them in a nonstandard manner. You can use an Alias QuicKey to access these.

Choosing one of your FKEYs from the submenu invokes the FKEY edit dialog box (see Figure 8-11). All the FKEYs that QuicKeys can access are listed in the FKEY choices pop-up menu. Choose the FKEY you want, enter your keystroke combination, and you're ready to go.

Define
- 🅰 Alias...
- 🆗 Buttons...
- ✳ Click
- 🕰 Date/Time ▶
- ⌚ Extensions ▶
- 📄 File...
- F FKEYs ▶
- 📁 Menu/DA...
- 📱 Mousies ▶
- 🔼 Sequence...
- ★ Specials ▶
- T Text...
- 👁 Real Time

3-Screen to paint
4-Screen to printer

FKEYs Considerations and Tactics

Use FKEY QuicKeys to access FKEYs with your own keystrokes.

Many folks believe that FKEYs belong on that great big pile of unrecyclable paraphernalia (you know that pile—the one that's full of vinyl records, reasonable prices, entertaining

Figure 8-11
FKEY edit dialog box

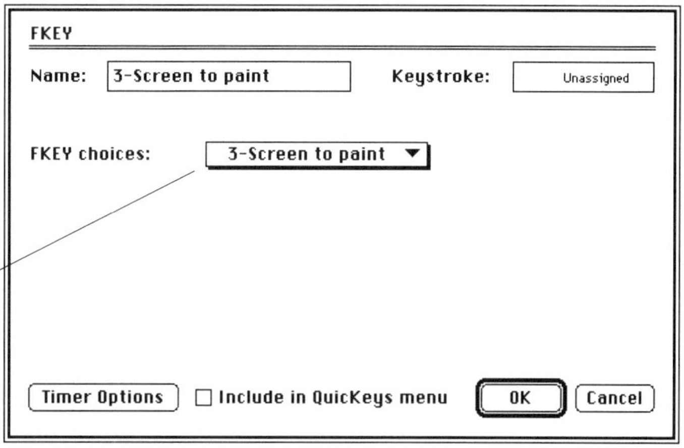

```
FKEY
────────────────────────────────────────────────────────────
Name:    [ 3-Screen to paint ]        Keystroke:   [ Unassigned ]


FKEY choices:        [ 3-Screen to paint  ▼ ]
```

FKEY choices pop-up menu

```
[ Timer Options ]   □ Include in QuicKeys menu    (( OK ))  [ Cancel ]
```

television shows, and honorable political advertising). It is true that most FKEY functions can also be performed by INITs and cdevs. But there are a number of spiffy third-party FKEYs available from online services like CompuServe (see Appendix, *Resources*). Some of these are free, and some are shareware. Here's a sampling.

- FKEY Icon Maker by Kevin Collier. This FKEY grabs graphic images and saves them as ICN# resources.
- Applause FKEY by Tony Karp, TLC Systems. Press the FKEY combination (Command-Shift-5) and you'll get a heartwarming round of applause.
- Mickey 1.0 FKEY by Tony Karp, TLC Systems. Mickey 1.0 is an FKEY that lets you change mouse tracking (sensitivity) without going through the Control Panel.
- Large cursor FKEY by Andy Hertzfeld. This program installs an FKEY 8 resource, which implements a large (32-by-32-pixel) cursor, into your system file.
- Toggle Key 1.51 by Lofty Becker. Toggle Key 1.51 changes the < and > on the keyboard to , and . and back again. Convenient for touch typists.
- Screen Dump FKEY. The Screen Dump FKEY provides color and black-and-white dumps of the screen or top window, and saves the result to a PICT file with a name of your choosing.

System 7 Stuff

Here's where we consider the brave new Mac world. In this chapter, we discuss the recent QuicKeys created to enhance and capitalize on System 7.

- System 7 Specials
- Apple Events
- Finder Events

The introduction of System 7 has modified and generally enhanced the workings of the Mac. While not a complete reformation, it is more than a slight reinterpretation of the tried-and-true system dogma. Perhaps the most important aspect of System 7 (as of this writing, at least) is not what it is, but what it promises to be. The introduction of Apple Events and IAC (interapplication communication) sets the stage for a whole new evolution in the Mac interface. This promise won't be fully realized until the applications you use are rewritten to be System 7-savvy, but CE, with its introduction of CEIAC (which facilitates the transmission of Apple Events), has made a significant step towards this promising future.

This chapter discusses the QuicKeys that can only be used in System 7: Apple Events, Finder Events and System 7 Specials. They are all Extensions, and they allow you to profit from the new potential of System 7 (although some of their capabilities merely mimic the functions of other QuicKeys). Most of the QuicKeys listed in this chapter need both System 7 and CEIAC to function. A handful (the balloon help and application-switching QuicKeys of the System 7 Specials) require System 7, but don't need CEIAC.

Apple Events and CEIAC

In order to provide a foundation for IAC in System 7, Apple Computer developed Apple Events, a message format specialized to process and pass instructions and information from one application to another. CE Software developed CEIAC as a method of transferring Apple Events between applications and INITs or System extensions.

CEIAC was designed as an application that's launched by an INIT, so it starts automatically whenever you boot up your Mac; you can't launch it yourself by double-clicking. This design was due to some of the vagaries of System 7, but it can be a problem. In its present configuration, if you quit CEIAC, the only way you can restore it is to reboot. Why would you want to quit it? One of System 7's new features is its ability to add things to the System file, like fonts, without rebooting. However, you must close all applications to do so. Get the picture? But this flaw aside, CEIAC is a powerful device to beam you right down to the surface of interapplication communication.

All of the System 7 QuicKeys give you quick access to either Apple Events or some of the new interface design elements of System 7. Two of them (Finder Events and System 7 Specials) contain pop-up menus from which you can select their different QuicKey tools.

System 7 Specials

The System 7 Specials are QuicKeys that allow you to control some of the new features of System 7. You can open the System 7 Specials edit dialog box by choosing System 7 Specials from the Extensions submenu of the Define menu. The System 7 Specials edit dialog box contains a pop-up menu selection of seven QuicKeys tools (see Figure 9-1). These seven tools control three areas: balloon help, application switching, and file sharing.

Balloon Help Never let it be said that CE doesn't give you options. There's a QuicKey to turn balloon help on, one to turn it off, and one to toggle it on and off. What abundance! Unfortunately, we don't use any of them, because we find balloon help more of a marketing gimmick than a real feature. We might turn it on someday when we are in a totally foreign program that is well supported with balloon help. But until then, we just remember that these tools exist.

Figure 9-1
The System 7 Specials
edit dialog box

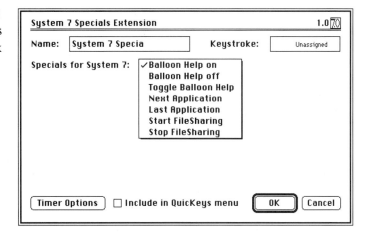

Application Switching We move from the ridiculous to the sublime. Here are a couple of QuicKeys that switch between open applications. They can be used in combination with a new feature of System 7 that's really hot—the ability to hide applications that aren't on the top (active) layer.

The two application-switching tools, Next Application and Last Application, allow you to march through all the applications you have open, in either direction. Applications are layered in the order in which they were opened, not in the order they appear on the Application menu (which is almost alphabetical, except that the Finder item is always last).

The ability to flip through your open applications in one direction is great; the ability to go in the other direction is sort of stupid. Maybe CE realizes that—their Extensions addendum to the manual states that the Last Application QuicKey "switches you to the last application you opened." Unfortunately, it doesn't—it merely switches in the opposite order. What would be really cool would be a QuicKey that would toggle back and forth between two applications—like the Select second window QuicKey.

We use a Sequence QuicKey that joins Next Application with a Menu QuicKey that chooses Hide Others from the Application menu (see Figure 9-2). Don uses Control-Option-Right arrow to invoke the Sequence. By repeating that keystroke, his open applications appear and disappear one after another.

Figure 9-2
Application menu

File Sharing

File sharing is a new feature of System 7 with a lot of potential. It's a lot like Tops, a networking package we've used for a long time. Although it does have more features than Tops, it is also more complicated and less intuitive to use. File sharing is for networked computers, so if you are working out in the woods with only your fax machine and the sound of a rushing brook to keep you company, you can ignore this. But if you are networked with other computers, System 7 has the ability to share files among them.

The two file-sharing QuicKeys control the master switch for your file sharing. One starts it, and the other stops it. We haven't found these QuicKeys too useful because we have file sharing activated constantly; we control access by exercising prudence when adjusting the settings when we select "Sharing" under the File menu. However, you might want to use these QuicKeys if you repeatedly turn file sharing on and off. However, note that the Stop FileSharing QuicKey acts a little differently from clicking Stop in the Sharing Setup control panel. Clicking Stop invokes a dialog box in which you enter a delay before file sharing actually ceases (see Figure 9-3). This

Figure 9-3
Delay end file sharing
edit dialog box

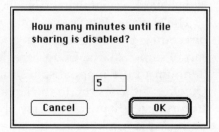

gives people who are sharing your files a chance to save what they are working on. The Stop FileSharing QuicKey shuts down file sharing immediately.

System 7 Specials Tactics and Considerations

Use System 7 Specials to enhance your use of ballon help, application switching, and file sharing.

You probably will want to access these new features of System 7 from any application, so System 7 Specials belong in your Universal Keyset. A good keystroke for the balloon help QuicKeys would be various modifiers with the Help key. Switching applications seems natural to Don using Option-Control-Right arrow, but many people like to use modifiers with the Tab key. File sharing control keystrokes depend on your own setup (see Chapter 15, *Keystroke Strategies*). But because of the immediate effect of Stop FileSharing, you might want its keystroke to be difficult to enter as a fail-safe device.

Neither set of QuicKeys—balloon help or the application switchers—needs CEIAC.

Apple Events

One of the most-hyped features of System 7 is Apple Events, the interapplication communication protocol that Apple says will help applications work together in universal peace and harmony. We doubt if this utopia will be realized for some time. Here's why.

QuicKeys 2.1 allows you to send Apple Events to other applications, and allows other applications to trigger QuicKeys through Apple Events. Unfortunately, many of the programs so far that support Apple Events either aren't documenting their Apple Events properly, or have defined Apple Events that, for the most part, duplicate functions that QUICKEYS already has.

**What is an
Apple Event?**

An Apple Event is a message sent by one application to another application. It works like this: the sender sends a message to the System. The System figures out which application the message needs to go to, and sends it along. The receiving application looks up the message to see if it knows it. If it does, it performs some action, like inserting a page or recalculating a spreadsheet. If it doesn't, it either returns an error message (the most appropriate response), or it sits placidly as though nothing had happened (the all-too-frequent response).

The Apple Event message consists of an address (generally the creator type of the receiving application), a class (the type of message; four letters), an ID (the actual message; also four letters) and possibly a lot of additional data. QuicKeys usually handles the address for you (you select the application, and it figures out the rest). The class, ID, and any extra data need to be known in advance, before you can send an Apple Event.

There are four core Apple Events that you may already have heard of: Open Application, Open Documents, Print Documents, and Quit. Their class name is "core" (three points for originality). Their message IDs are, respectively, "oapp," "odoc," "pdoc," and "quit." Open Application and Quit require no other parameters. Open Documents and Print Documents require a list of documents in a special Apple Event format.

"Great," you say, "but what about more…well…*useful* Apple Events?" The short answer is that there aren't any (yet). All applications are supposed to support these core events, if possible. Any other Apple Events are up to individual program developers. Apple is maintaining a registry of new events as they are defined, but so far the pickings are slim. As more applications (in their own inimitable fashions) support Apple Events, more companies will borrow classes and IDs from the existing list, and the core will grow. For right now, you are virtually guaranteed that applications from different companies will support completely different Apple Events, even if the applications do similar things.

Each company is free to define its own set of Apple Events. For example, HyperCard 2.1 defines a bunch of useful Apple Events for running scripts, evaluating mathematical expressions, and so on (we'll show you how to define one later).

Aldus has announced that they intend to define Apple Events which will allow complete control over all PageMaker's features from other applications. Microsoft and other manufacturers have pledged that they will soon support full-fledged suites of Apple Events.

Sending an Apple Event through QuicKeys

Sending an Apple Event from QuicKeys requires that you have installed the Apple Events Extension and the CEIAC application, and that you have both CEIAC and another Apple Event-aware application running. The CEIAC application is necessary because QuicKeys, not being an application, can't send Apple Events directly. QuicKeys sends the Apple Event to CEIAC via CE's own communication system, and CEIAC converts it to Apple's format and sends it.

The following example uses HyperCard's math processor to figure the result of a mathematical equation. To follow along, launch HyperCard 2.1.

Open the QuicKeys management window. Select "Apple Events" from the Extensions submenu off the Define Menu. You should see a dialog box like Figure 9-4.

Figure 9-4
Apple Events edit dialog box

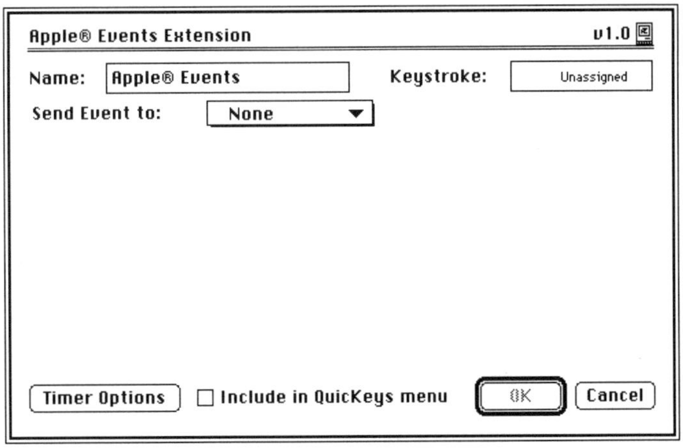

Next, select an application to which you want to send an Apple Event message. The pop-up menu shows all Apple Event-aware applications that are currently running on your machine. To send an Apple Event to an application on another machine on your network, select "Remote Applications." (In order to send an Apple Event to a remote machine, the remote machine must have Program Linking turned on in the File Sharing Control Panel. Otherwise, it works just like sending one to your own machine.) You shouldn't ever need to select "Other," unless you are creating an Apple Event for a program that isn't running. For the moment, select "HyperCard."

Once you have selected the application, you need to select the Apple Event. QuicKeys has predefined the four core events for you. (QUICKEYS calls the Open Application Apple Event "New Document," because for all intents and purposes, that's all Open Application does—make a new document.) There is a selection called "Lookup From Target" that looks in the application for an "aete" resource (an optional resource that describes the application's Apple Events, so you don't have to go rummaging through cryptic manuals). We haven't seen any applications that have an "aete" resource, except for CEIAC. You can go ahead and select it, but don't expect much. Most of your events will need to be custom-built, so roll up your sleeves and select "Custom" (see Figure 9-5).

Now you have a whole lot of choices before you. Let's take them one at a time. The Include in Event Menu check box allows you to add frequently used Apple Events to the Event Menu just to the left, much as the Include in QuicKeys Menu check box adds frequently used QuicKeys to the QuicKeys menu. Don't bother. The two edit items in the lower-right corner allow you to type the class and ID of your Apple Event. You'll need to get those from the application manual. For this

Figure 9-5
Event pop-up menu

particular example, type in "misc" for the class, and "eval" for the ID. This is HyperCard's "evaluate mathematical expression" Apple Event. The box in the center of the

Event:

New Document
Open Documents
Print Documents
Quit Application
....
Lookup from Target...
Custom Event

screen lists the parameters of the Apple Event. Again, your documentation should have these. (If it doesn't, and some don't, feel free to call tech support for that company and give them a tactful suggestion to update their manuals. Also see if they can give you the Apple Events parameters.) To add a parameter, click the New button.

At this point, you'll want to type a description for the parameter. It can be anything, so type "expression." The next field is labeled "Keyword." This tells the receiving application what this parameter represents. It's only used for Apple Events that have optional parameters. Most of the time, the keyword is "----" which means, in effect, "The receiving application already knows what this parameter is." Type "----" in this field. Now you can select a type of data. This should be in the documentation (sorry to sound like a broken record). In this case, select "Text" from the pop-up menu. The type will be entered for you. If the type you want isn't on the list, your documentation will have the four-character identifier (with luck), and you can type it into the box. Now you can type some data into the box, or tell QUICKEYS to get it, at the time it is run, from the Clipboard. Select "Clipboard." Click OK.

Last, but not least, you need to tell QUICKEYS what to do with the response it gets back. "Ignore" means, "Send the event and don't wait for a response." "Wait" means, "Send the event and wait until it's complete, but throw away the response." "Type" mean, "Type the text in the current window" (which is a text window, we hope). "Display" means, "Put up a dialog box with the response shown, if possible." (This only works for text and numbers.) "Clipboard" means, "Put the response on the Clipboard." Select "Type."

You have created a full-fledged Apple Event QuicKey (see Figure 9-6). Give it a name and a keystroke; "Evaluate" and Control-Option-Command-E would be good. Click OK.

Leave the QUICKEYS management window by clicking OK. Leave HyperCard running, and launch a text editor. Note Pad works best. Type an expression like "94/2." Select it, then copy it to the clipboard. Type Control-Option-Command-E (or whatever you set to invoke your QuicKey), and you should almost immediately see the response "47."

You can use this method to define Apple Events QuicKeys for your favorite applications, assuming that they support interesting Apple Events and that they document them somewhere in their manuals. Happy hunting.

Figure 9-6
Nearly complete Apple
Event edit dialog box

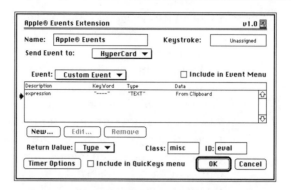

**Playing a QuicKey
with an Apple
Event**

If you have another application that can send Apple Events,
like Frontier, or if you would like to be able to trigger a
QuicKey over a network, then you can use the CEIAC set of
Apple Events to trigger a QuicKey. Here's how.

Select "CEIAC" in the Apple Events edit dialog box, then
select "Look up from application" in the Event pop-up menu.
You should see a list of event "suites," and a list of events.

Select the QuicKeys suite, as the core suite doesn't mean
much to CEIAC. You'll see three Apple Events in the right-
hand list. Select "Play QuicKey by Name." Click OK, and
you'll see that all the class, ID, and parameter information
has been filled in for you. All you need to do is fill in the parameter data. Double-click on the parameter, or click on it,
then click "Edit." Type the name of the QuicKey you want to
run, and click OK. Select the "Ignore" or "Wait" return type,
since QuicKeys doesn't return anything anyway. Presto! You
can now run a QuicKey, simply by typing a…QuicKey. This
may seem a wee bit strange, but keep in mind that you can
use this to run a QuicKey on a remote computer. Just select
"CEIAC" on that computer, and the rest is easy.

**Apple Events Tactics
and Considerations**

Use Apple Events QuicKeys to play practical jokes.

At this stage, the best thing we can say about Apple Events is
that the possibilities for practical jokes are endless. Define a
Sound Extension QuicKey on your friend's computer. Use the
digitized sound of their phone ringing. Turn on Program
Linking in their File Sharing Control Panel. Now, at your lei-
sure, you can link to their CEIAC, and define a QuicKey to
play the one on their computer. Whenever you invoke your

QuicKey, it sounds like their phone is ringing. It's best to stop the ringing just before they pick up the phone.

With a little thought, you can probably think of practical reasons for remote Apple Event QuicKeys, too!

Finder Events

Finder Events is an uneven Extension. It contains some tools that are powerful and useful, but it also contains tools that we don't use, and never will. Because Finder Events accesses specific menu commands in the Finder, you end up in the Finder even though you might have invoked the Finder Event QuicKey from another application.

The Finder Events pop-up menu lists six tools (see Figure 9-7). Two of the tools (Sleep and Show Clipboard) perform unalterable tasks. The other four allow you to choose multiple target files, so they have Change buttons on their text edit boxes. Choosing any of these four targeted Finder Events from the pop-up menu invokes a File Selection dialog box. You choose the files you want to target in this box, and then press "Done."

Let's look at the Finder Events tools in order of increasing utility.

Sleep. Sleep puts your Macintosh portable to sleep. Haven't got a Mac portable? Don't use it.

Get Info. Get Info switches to the Finder and then gives you

Figure 9-7
Finder Events
pop-up menu

✓**Show Clipboard**
Sleep
Get Info
Show
Open
Print

the Info Box on any number of preselected files. We cannot figure out why you would want to do this.

Show. Show switches to the Finder and then opens the folders of preselected files. We don't know why you would want to do this either, but you might know.

Show Clipboard. Show Clipboard switches to the Finder and displays the contents of the Clipboard. You might find this useful enough to devote a QuicKey to it; we don't.

Print. Here's something you might use. Print switches to the Finder and then prints out your preselected list of documents (by first launching the document's application). However, if the application of the target is already open, Print won't work unless the application is Apple Event-aware.

Open. Open is by far the most useful of the Finder Event tools. It can open applications, documents, and folders. It is able to open preselected files (the manual says only six at a time, but we've opened more). The files can be applications or documents, of various types. If you are in the Finder, Open can open preselected folders. Unlike Print, Open is not confounded by having the target application already open.

**Finder Events
Tactics and
Considerations**

Use Finder Event QuicKeys to access many of the features of the System 7 Finder.

The best thing to say about Finder Events is not to forget about them because sooner or later you'll have that occasion when you need one. We often use Open. It comes in handy when we want to simultaneously launch multiple files, often the case on big jobs. Usually, these "bundles" are pretty short lived, so we invoke them with a function key plus modifiers.

You'll want to keep Finder Event QuicKeys in your Universal Keyset so you can invoke them at any time.

Manipulating Text and Graphics

This chapter discusses QuicKeys for working with text and graphics. There are five QuicKey types in this category, most of which manipulate text.

Text. These QuicKeys simply type text.

Copiers. Grab Ease, Paste Ease, and Type Ease QuicKeys let you create multiple clipboards to store text and graphics, and copy and paste in places where normal cut, copy, and paste functions don't work.

Date/Time. If you want to insert the date or time in a text stream, use a Date/Time QuicKey.

Quotes. Use QuickQuotes and Double QuickQuotes to type curly quotation marks and apostrophes.

Display. The Display QuicKey is actually a mini word processor for working with text files.

The following sections explore each of these QuicKey types in more detail.

Text

Text QuicKeys are simple. When you invoke them, they type text. To create a text QuicKey, select "Text" from the Define menu in the QUICKEYS management window. The Text edit dialog box appears (see Figure 10-1). You can assign a name and invoking keystroke, and enter up to 255 characters in the Text to type box. You can cut, copy, and paste text in this

box, using the standard Macintosh Command-X, Command-C, and Command-V keyboard shortcuts.

The characters you type in the Text to type box can include carriage returns (what you get when you press the Return key), tab characters (they appear as little diamonds), and all the special characters you get when you press Option and Shift together with various keys. The text is probably displayed in Geneva (the Macintosh default font), so the special characters you type may not be the ones you get when you've applied a different font in your application.

Text

Name: FutureMedia   Keystroke: ⌘opt ctrl-F

Text to type:

FutureMedia△The Company
1222 Past Venue Avenue
Present Tense, CA, 14777|

Timer Options   ☐ Include in QuicKeys menu   OK   Cancel

Figure 10-1
The Text edit
dialog box

Text Tactics   *Use Text QuicKeys to type text into applications such as word processors, databases, spreadsheets, and page-makeup programs.*

The primary use for Text QuicKeys is to store boilerplate text for use in various applications. They're great for dropping your online signature at the end of all your electronic mail messages, or for putting your closing and full name at the end of letters, bracketing your signature. If you have a standard disclaimer or series of formulas, you can store each of these in a Text QuicKey.

You can also use Text QuicKeys within Sequences. A string of letters in a Text QuicKey plays out more slowly than a string of Alias QuicKey steps, so it often works (the application can keep up with it) where the Alias steps don't.

Text QuicKey Considerations

The main point to consider when you're planning to use a Text QuicKey is how long your text is, and whether it includes any formatting. If your text contains more than 255 characters, you'll either have to use multiple Text QuicKeys, or use a Type Ease or Paste Ease QuicKey instead.

You can't paste text copied from Microsoft Word into the Text to type box. The solution is to use the Grab Ease, Paste Ease, and Type Ease QuicKeys discussed later in this chapter to grab the text and paste or type it into the dialog box. Alternately, first paste and copy the text into and out of another program, like the Scrapbook or McSink text-editing DA.

Copiers

The Grab Ease, Paste Ease, and Type Ease Extension QuicKeys—we call them Copiers—work together to provide multiple, named clipboards in which you can store text, graphics, and in some cases, a combination of the two. The basis of the set is Grab Ease, the one that creates the clipboards and places in-formation in them. Paste Ease and Type Ease get the information back out. None of these has anything to do with similarly named Screen Ease, aside from the fact that they're all QuicKeys Extensions.

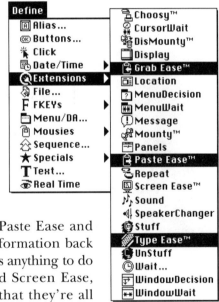

Grab Ease

To begin with, create a Grab Ease QuicKey by selecting "Grab Ease" from the Extensions submenu off the Define menu. The Grab Ease edit dialog box appears (See Figure 10-2). There's not much to do in this dialog box except to choose an invoking keystroke.

Figure 10-2
The Grab Ease edit
dialog box

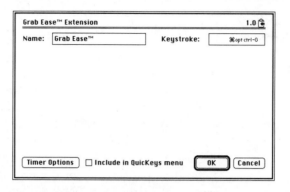

Next, select some text or a graphic in your favorite application, and invoke the Grab Ease QuicKey. You'll see the dialog box in Figure 10-3. Type into it the name of the clipboard file in which you want to save the information. Grab Ease saves the item in a file of its own, stored in the Clipboards folder (System:Preferences:QuicKeys Folder:Clipboards).

Figure 10-3
Grab Ease
dialog box

Now that you have some information stored in a Grab Ease clipboard, you can insert it somewhere using either Paste Ease or Type Ease. To create a Paste Ease QuicKey, select "Paste Ease" from the Extensions submenu off the Define menu. You'll see the Paste Ease dialog box shown in Figure 10-4.

**Paste Ease and
Type Ease**

Your Paste Ease QuicKey can either paste the information from one of the named clipboards (you press the key, it pastes from the clipboard), or it can ask you which clipboard to paste from when you invoke it. If you use the Ask when pasting option, you'll see the dialog box in Figure 10-5 when you use the QuicKey.

Type Ease QuicKeys work in exactly the same way, except that they act as if they're typing the information, rather than pasting it, so you can use them in certain dialog boxes and other places where pasting doesn't work. Type Ease only works with text. You can't type graphics with it.

Figure 10-4
The Paste Ease
dialog box

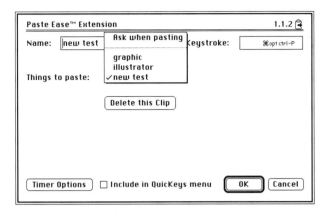

Figure 10-5
The Ask when pasting
dialog box

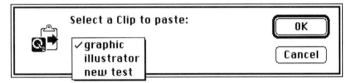

Copier Tactics *Use Grab Ease, Paste Ease, and Type Ease to build your own library of text and graphic elements for placing anywhere.*

To use these keys, you first need a Grab Ease QuicKey. We use Command-Option-Control-G. Then you need keys for generic Paste Ease and Type Ease QuicKeys—the ones that ask you which clipboard to use each time you invoke them. Steve uses Command-Option-Control-P and Command-Option-Control-T for these.

Then there are the specialized Paste Ease and Type Ease QuicKeys—the ones that are preloaded with things like your address or name. You'll need to choose keystrokes for these based on how frequently you use them.

Copier Considerations Copiers work with either text or graphics, or both. The primary exception is Microsoft Word. You can grab text, or you can grab graphics, but if your selection includes both text and graphics, the graphics disappear in their journey through Ease-y land. Word's version 5 purportedly doesn't suffer from this deficiency.

131

Date/Time Date/Time QuicKeys do exactly what you'd expect: they type in the current date or time, in your choice of format. When you choose one of the Date/Time formats from the Date/Time submenu off the Define menu, you see the Date/Time edit dialog box (Figure 10-6).

No matter which format you chose, you can change your mind here and switch to another format. Then apply an activating keystroke, and you're done.

```
Define
 🔲 Alias...
 ⊙ⓚ Buttons...
 ✱ Click
 🗐 Date/Time        ▶    7/17/91
 ⊛ Extensions       ▶    Wednesday, July 17, 1991
 🗐 File...               Wed, Jul 17, 1991
 F FKEYs            ▶    July 17, 1991
 🗐 Menu/DA...            Jul 17, 1991
 🗐 Mousies          ▶    17 July 1991
 △ Sequence...           17 Jul 1991
 ★ Specials         ▶    91/07/17
 T Text...               11:21 AM
 👁 Real Time             11:21:33 AM
                         11.21
```

Figure 10-6
The Date/Time
edit dialog box

```
Date/Time
───────────────────────────────────────────────
Name:  [Wed, Jul 17, 1991    ]    Keystroke:   [ Unassigned ]

                      7/17/91
                      Wednesday, July 17, 1991
Date/Time choices:  ✓Wed, Jul 17, 1991
                      July 17, 1991
                      Jul 17, 1991
                      17 July 1991
                      17 Jul 1991
                      91/07/17

                      11:24 AM
                      11:24:15 AM
                      11.24

[ Timer Options ]  ☐ Include in QuicKeys menu    [ OK ]  [ Cancel ]
```

**Date/Time Tactics
and Considerations**

Use a Date/Time QuicKey to type the date or time.

The main characteristic to remember about Date/Time QuicKeys is that they insert the *current* time, and that inserted time doesn't change. If you want a date or time stamp that continuously updates, you'll have to use the one in your word processor, spreadsheet, or page-makeup program.

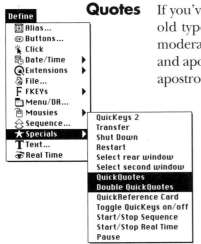

Quotes

If you've read *The Mac is not a typewriter,* you know that ugly old typewriter-style straight quotes are anathema to even moderately skilled Mac users. If you want to use curly quotes and apostrophes (', ', ", and ") instead of straight quotes and apostrophes (' and "), QuicKeys can help you.

To create a Quotes QuicKey, select either QuickQuotes or Double QuickQuotes from the Specials submenu off the Define menu. The Special edit dialog box appears, with the appropriate Quote options selected in the pop-up menu (Figure 10-7)

The normal technique for using the Quotes keys is to invoke QuickQuotes with the apostrophe ('), and Double QuickQuotes with Shift-Apostrophe (") key. That way every time you type ' you get ' or ', and when you type " you get " or ".

Figure 10-7
The Special
edit dialog box

But how does QUICKEYS know whether to give you an open or close quote? It's based (not terribly intelligently) on your last action before using the Quote QuicKey. As explained in the manual, if it's a {, (, [, <, ", ', Return, Space, Tab, or a mouse click, you get a left quote. In any other situation, you get a right quote.

Quotes Tactics

Use Quotes QuicKeys to type single and double curly quotes.

The Quotes QuicKeys aren't super smart, so you might want to take advantage of the smart-quotes capability in your application software, if it exists (Word's is excellent, as is QuarkXPress'; so is PageMaker's when you're importing text, though not while you're typing). If you're working in some other application, check out Quote Init (Figure 10-8), a wonderful shareware cdev that handles smart quotes on the fly as you type, in addition to ligatures, em dashes, and double spaces.

Figure 10-8
Quote Init

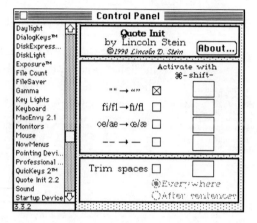

Quotes Considerations

No matter what method you use to generate smart quotes, be aware that in some cases—notably when you're sending electronic mail—you want straight quotes instead of curly ones. When you send a message with curly quotes, they tend to come out as little Qs and such.

There are a few ways to to turn off your Quotes QuicKeys, once you've set them up. Choose the one that's best for your circumstances.

- Turn off QUICKEYS. Steve uses Command-. (period) for that task, so if he wants to type a straight apostrophe, he presses Command-. (period) then the Apostrophe key, then Command-. (period) again. Both Microsoft Word and Quote Init give you keystrokes to toggle smart quotes on and off.

- Make an Alias QuicKey for your straight apostrophe. Since your unmodified apostrophe key is tied to QuickQuotes, just give yourself another keystroke that types a straight apostrophe—Command-'(apostrophe) might do.

- Make an Alias QuicKey for your application keyset that overrides the Quotes QuicKeys in your Universal Keyset. You would only do this if your setup would be enhanced by having Quotes active in most applications, but inactive in one.

Display

Who would have thought it? A QuicKey that's a word processor! Well, it's not a full-blown word processor, but a little editor that lets you view, edit, and even (minimally) format straight text files. That's the Display Extension.

To create a Display QuicKey, select "Display" from the Extensions submenu off the Define menu. You'll be rewarded with the Display edit dialog box (Figure 10-9).

Figure 10-9
The Display
edit dialog box

Assign an invoking keystroke to the QuicKey, and if you want to, click the Change button to select a text file for this Display QuicKey to open. If you don't select a file, when you use the QuicKey you'll get a standard Open dialog box asking which file you want to open. (We've had a lot of trouble getting this method to work consistently. Most of the time, after you select the file, nothing happens; you're back to where you were. Display QuicKeys that are dedicated to particular files seem much more reliable.)

In either case, Display comes up as a stand-alone word-processing window (see Figure 10-10) in which you can manipulate the text. You can edit text in the normal ways, change the font, size, type style, and color of any group of characters, search for a text string, and save the file. That's it.

**Display Tactics and
Considerations**

Use Display QuicKeys to view and edit text files.

There are better pop-up text editors in the world than Display (the shareware DA McSink comes to mind), but few that can bring up a designated file so quickly and easily. Display QuicKeys are great for maintaining text files like your to-do list, Rolodex file, or other commonly accessed text file. One keystroke and it's up and ready for you. Another keystroke and you're searching.

Figure 10-10
Display's word-processing window

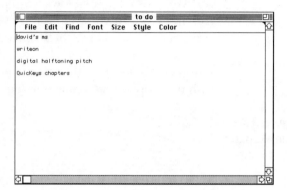

When you apply formatting to a text file with Display, it performs a little bit of magic. It formats the text, so the next time you open the file with Display, all your formatting will be there. But it doesn't change the nature of the straight text file by inserting formatting information. You can open the file with any other word processor or text editor, and it opens right up as an unformatted text file.

For those who care, Display manages this magic by adding a couple of new resources to the text file. The data stays the same, so other programs can read that, but Display also looks at the new resources for the formatting information.

QuicKeys Control

11

QUICKEYS controllers are the QuicKeys that give you power over various QUICKEYS functions. Some of the QUICKEYS controllers are trivial, some are indispensable, and some are redundant with items in the QuicKeys 2 submenu. QUICKEYS controllers break down into two groups: those that access parts of the QUICKEYS program, and those that start and stop macro recording. All the QUICKEYS controllers appear on the Specials submenu off the Define menu.

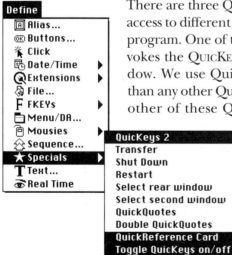

There are three QuicKeys that give you access to different parts of the QUICKEYS program. One of them, QuicKeys 2, invokes the QUICKEYS management window. We use QuicKeys 2 more often than any other QuicKey we possess. Another of these QUICKEYS controllers, Toggle QuicKeys on/off, is arguably the most powerful of all QuicKeys. Toggle QuicKeys on/off puts the QUICKEYS program to sleep; it deactivates all QuicKeys except one (itself)—so even though you

QUICKEYS Access QuicKeys

can turn QUICKEYS off, there is one QuicKey left active to turn the program back on again. QuickReference Card can display a list of QuicKeys in both the Universal Keyset and the current application's keyset. We seldom use QuickReference Card, but some folks activate it frequently—it does have some cool features.

Each of these QuicKeys has only one target or purpose, so you only need one of each in your Universal Keyset. When you create one, the only entry you need to make into the edit dialog box is your activating keystroke combination.

QuicKeys 2

This is the QuicKey we built as our first prototype, way back in Chapter 3, *QUICKEYS DOCTRINE*. What could be simpler? Invoke the QuicKeys 2 QuicKey, and the QUICKEYS management window appears. Of course, you can always get the management window by choosing "QuicKeys 2" from the Apple menu, but why go menu pulling when you have a utility program that does what you want with only a keystroke?

QuicKeys 2 Tactics and Considerations

Use the QuicKeys 2 QuicKey to bring up the QuicKeys management window.

We could not live without the QuicKeys 2 QuicKey, since we are constantly building new QuicKeys (or modifying old ones). Invoking the management window is the first step in this process (most of the time—see "Recording Switches," below). Don uses Control-Option-Q to invoke QuicKeys 2; Steve uses Control-Q.

Interesting to note is that the More Universal Keyset, which is included in your QUICKEYS package as a starter set of universal QuicKeys, does not have this—the most useful QuicKey—included in it. However, when you first install QUICKEYS, a Universal Keyset is automatically created for you that does contain this QuicKey (among others).

Toggle QuicKeys on/off

Power. Toggle QuicKeys on/off gives you the ultimate power over QUICKEYS. If for some reason you want QUICKEYS off—for example, if it's overriding a keystroke shortcut in a particular application—you can stun it with this keystroke, and it seems to go to sleep. However, invoking Toggle QuicKeys on/off a second time wakes QUICKEYS up again.

Power requires control, and there are a couple of silly situations you can get into with Toggle QuicKeys on/off that you have to watch out for. First, it is possible to create a Toggle QuicKeys on/off QuicKey without assigning it an invoking keystroke combination; for example, you could just check the Include in QuicKeys menu option in the edit dialog box. If you do so, and choose this QuicKey from the QuicKeys 2 submenu off the Apple menu, QUICKEYS deactivates itself— and the Toggle QuicKeys on/off menu item disappears. There is no apparent way to turn QUICKEYS back on again without rebooting! But there is a fail-safe On button lurking in the QUICKEYS control panel.

A similar situation can occur if you just create one Toggle QuicKeys on/off QuicKey, and make it part of a Sequence. When you invoke the Sequence, as soon as it gets to the Toggle QuicKeys on/off step, QUICKEYS goes dormant. You can't use the same Sequence to turn QUICKEYS back on, because the dormant QUICKEYS will only recognize *one* QuicKey—Toggle QuicKeys on/off. QUICKEYS will not recognize any Sequences, even those containing the Toggle QuicKeys on/off QuicKey.

Toggle QuicKeys on/off Tactics and Considerations

Use the Toggle QuicKeys on/off QuicKey to play God over QuicKeys.

The insurance is to *always* have a pure Toggle QuicKeys on/off QuicKey as part of your Universal Keyset. The More Universal Keyset has one, with the keystroke combination Command-Option-. (period). CE Software suggests that you don't change that keystroke (so everybody who uses the machine knows how to toggle QUICKEYS on and off), but Don doesn't like it much—it doesn't fit his keystroke strategy (see Chapter 15, *Keystroke Strategies*). Don uses Control-Option-Command-Q as his QUICKEYS toggler.

QuickReference Card

The QuickReference Card QuicKey gives you access to the QuickReference Card, a display of your active QuicKeys. It is usually set up to display the QuicKeys in two keysets, the Universal Keyset and the keyset of your active application

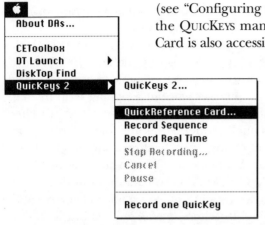

Figure 11-1
QuickReference Card
on the Apple menu

(see "Configuring the QuickReference Card," below). Like the QUICKEYS management window, the QuickReference Card is also accessible as a menu item under QuicKeys 2 on the Apple menu (see Figure 11-1).

The QuickReference Card looks and acts a lot like the QuicKeys window in the QUICKEYS management window but has some important and useful differences (see Figure 11-2). First, let's look at the similarities.

- **Display sorting.** You can change how the display is sorted (by Key, Type, or Name) by pressing on the entries in the Sort bar under the key display.

- **Display sieve.** You can reduce the number of QuicKeys displayed by pressing on the appropriate QuicKey icon in the Filter bar. Multiple selections can be made by holding down Shift when clicking on an icon.

Figure 11-2
The QuickReference
Card

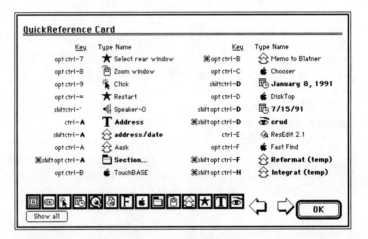

Here are some of the differences between the QuicKeys window and the QuickReference Card.

- **Two keysets.** Instead of displaying one keyset, the QuickReference Card can show two: the Universal Keyset and the keyset of your active application. Names of QuicKeys in the active application's keyset are displayed in bold type.

- **Pages vs. scrolling window.** Instead of a scrolling window, the QuickReference Card is displayed in a page format. Turning pages is accomplished with the left and right arrows next to the OK button; your keyboard arrows perform the same function.
- **Hot key.** Pressing anywhere on the display of a single QuicKey in the QuickReference Card returns you to the application you were in, and plays that QuicKey.
- **No edit or keystroke change.** You can't edit or change a QuicKey's activating keystroke from the QuickReference Card.
- **Comment.** In the QuickReference Card, you can press on a QuicKey listing and its comment (if it has one) will be displayed. In the QuicKeys window, you can view (and edit) a comment by clicking in the Comment column.

Configuring the QuickReference Card

On the Options menu of the QUICKEYS management window is a menu item called, "Configure QuickReference Card" (see Figure 11-3). Choosing this item displays the QuickReference Card Options dialog box (see Figure 11-4). The QuickReference Card Options dialog box should probably be named the Preferences dialog box, since that really is closer to its function—it sets your preferences for the QuickReference Card display. Two of the adjustments (Sort by and Display these QuicKeys) can also be changed within the QuickReference Card itself. The other two (List and Expand to fill screen) can only be set here. We generally want to list both keysets, and have the card expand to fill the screen.

Figure 11-3
Configure QuickReference Card on the Options menu

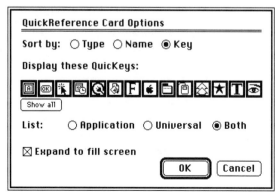

Figure 11-4
QuickReference Card Options dialog box

QuickReference Card Tactics and Considerations

Use the QuickReference Card QuicKey to invoke the QuickReference Card

We don't often find it helpful to invoke the QuickReference Card. Steve doesn't even have a QuicKey for it; he just chooses it from the Apple menu when he wants it. Nevertheless, for many people it's a valuable mnemonic aid to go along with keystrokes and placement of QuicKeys on the QuicKeys submenu off the Apple menu.

Recording Switches

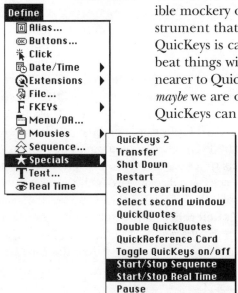

Like Superman and Bizarro Superman, these two QuicKeys sort of look the same, but one is a distorted and contemptible mockery of the other. Start/Stop Sequence is a fine instrument that unlocks all the power and finesse of which QuicKeys is capable. Start/Stop Real Time is a crowbar to beat things with, when all else fails. The former leads you nearer to QuicKeys nirvana, the latter to QuicKeys hell. Well, *maybe* we are overstating the case a bit, because both these QuicKeys can be useful in the appropriate situations. But don't confuse the two. They both start and stop the recording of actions, but one does it intelligently, the other like a clod.

Either a Real Time or a Sequence QuicKey recording can be initiated in one of three ways.

• Choose "Record Sequence" or "Record Real Time" from the QuicKeys 2 submenu off the Apple menu.

• Choose either the Sequence or the Real Time option from the Define menu of the QUICKEYS management window.

• Invoke either a Start/Stop Real Time QuicKey or a Start/Stop Sequence QuicKey.

A Real Time or Sequence QuicKey recording can be terminated in either of two ways.

• Choose "Stop Recording" from the QuicKeys 2 submenu off the Apple menu.

• Invoke either a Start/Stop Real Time QuicKey or a Start/Stop Sequence QuicKey.

Start/Stop Real Time

Start/Stop Real Time records the mouse movements, clicks, and keystrokes you make, and plays them back as quickly (or as slowly) as you made them. Real Time recordings are played back "blind": they don't know what applications they are in, or what menu items they are choosing. They can remember mouse movements by screen position only.

If you want to be able to initiate a Real Time recording with a keystroke, you need to include a Start/Stop Real Time QuicKey in one of your keysets (the Universal Keyset is the most logical). Just choose "Start/Stop Real Time" from the Specials submenu of the Define menu on the QuicKeys management window, enter a keystroke combination, and you are ready to make Real Time recordings. If you intend to record Real Time QuicKeys often, it is a good idea to make an easy-to-invoke one-handed keystroke for Start/Stop Real Time. This allows you to create the QuicKey as efficiently as possible.

Real Time Recordings

"Real Time" is a good name for this kind of recording. "Real Long Time" might be more descriptive, because you can't shorten a Real Time recording to its essential components; you can't edit it in any manner, except by adding to it. Real Time recordings have limited usefulness.

You might find a use for a Real Time recording as a demonstration device: you can record cursor movements, menu pull downs and such so that it looks like an invisible operator is in charge of your Mac (the potential for practical jokes has not escaped us). We don't have any use for invisible operators, but we create a Real Time recording every so often when an application has a nonstandard interface—for example, if the way the application builds menus is screwy enough that a Menu/DA QuicKey doesn't work with it. A Real Time QuicKey might just do the trick.

Making a Real Time recording starts with invoking your Start/Stop Real Time QuicKey (or using one of the other two methods listed above). Your cursor will turn into a little microphone (if you've previously chosen this option from the Options menu in the QuicKeys management window). Then you do your thing, and Real Time will record and record and record (you can make very lengthy recordings this way) until you tell it to stop. The easiest way to stop recording a Real Time QuicKey is by invoking Start/Stop Real Time again. A Real Time edit dialog box appears which is very simple; the only option unique to it is the Record More button which lets you do just that.

Real Time Tactics and Considerations

Use Real Time QuicKeys when nothing else will work.

The key to recording a Real Time QuicKey is speed. Set up everything in advance, so you can start creating the QuicKey as quickly as possible after you start recording. In some situations you may even want someone else to work in tandem with you, in order to make things as efficient as possible. This may sound like overkill, but a sluggish Real Time QuicKey will quickly drive you nuts.

Real Time Trouble

When you invoke a Real Time QuicKey, you are giving up control over your computer to QUICKEYS. There is just a slight chance that a Real Time recording can get you into trouble—really big trouble. Here's how.

Let's say that you're in QuarkXPress and you have a bunch of items for which that you want to change one of the Runaround Specifications. So you start recording a Real Time QuicKey, choose "Runaround" from the Item menu, and a Runaround Specifications dialog box appears. You double-click in a text edit box, type in 2 pt, and click OK. Then you stop the Real Time QuicKey, give it a keystroke combination, and try it out. It works. A bit slowly, but, hey, you've got a bunch of boxes to change and it's better than having to make all the entries for each one yourself.

But what happens if, in the middle of your work, you switch to the Finder and then inadvertently invoke this Real Time QuicKey? If you placed the QuicKey in the Universal Keyset, it goes up to the menu—a different menu now, but it doesn't realize that—and chooses the item in the same position as "Runaround." In the Finder, this is "Erase Disk." Then the QuicKey tries to double-click on the Left text edit box, but instead it clicks the right-hand button in the modal dialog box, which is "Initialize" (see Figure 11-5).

We almost gave David Blatner, the author of *The Quark-XPress Book*, heart failure with a demonstration of this perilous possibility. Surprisingly, computer programmers and baseball managers use the same phrase to describe situations like this, but we can't print it.

Figure 11-5
What can happen when a Real Time QuicKey goes wrong

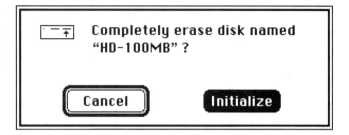

The key point to remember is this: clicking the mouse button stops a recording playback, and presents a dialog box that allows you to terminate the Sequence. This gives you some control over rogue Real Time recordings—if you are fast enough with your fingers.

Don Brown, the author of QuicKeys, thinks we are too hard on this QuicKey. Maybe that's true, and maybe you'll discover all sorts of spiffy uses for it. At any rate, we don't use Real Time recordings enough to warrant having a Start/Stop Real Time QuicKey as part of our permanent repertoire. If we want to create a Real Time QuicKey, we record it using the controls in the QuicKeys 2 submenu.

Start/Stop Sequence

Start/Stop Sequence initiates the recording of a QuicKeys Sequence. Sequences are analyzed exhaustively in the next two chapters (see Chapter 12, *The Sequence*, and Chapter 13, *Sequence QuicKeys*). Start/Stop Sequence is one of the switches to turn the recording of a Sequence QuicKey on and off.

Start/Stop Sequence Tactics and Considerations

Use the Start/Stop Sequence QuicKey to record Sequences.

Don keeps a Start/Stop Sequence QuicKey as part of his Universal Keyset. He made it by choosing "Start/Stop Sequence" from the Specials submenu of the Define menu on the the QuicKeys management window. He uses Control-Option-Command-F8 to invoke it; the F8 key is arbitrary, but the Control-Option-Command modifier combination denotes it as a powerful QuicKey, not to be invoked lightly.

The Sequence

This is the chapter that gives the ultimate answer. You've now arrived at the well where QuicKeys come to drink, the true source of QuicKeys power: the Sequence. Sequence QuicKeys give you the capability to incorporate individual QuicKey steps into series that function as distinct QuicKey units. The potential uses are only limited by your skill, imagination, and what you want to accomplish.

Making A Sequence

A Sequence QuicKey is a QuicKey that performs a series of steps. The makeup of a Sequence is such that these steps take the form of individual QuicKeys, so you can think of a Sequence as just a bunch of strung-together QuicKey functions. For example, if you want a QuicKey that will first choose a menu item, then type something in a text edit box, and then press a button, you can can create this composite QuicKey by making a Sequence with Menu/DA, Text, and Button QuicKeys as the steps. There are some QuicKeys that are designed to work *only* as steps in a Sequence; we discuss these in the Sequence Control QuicKeys section in the next chapter.

There are two ways to build a Sequence. First, you can record a Sequence (don't confuse this with Real Time recording; it's different); second, you can build a Sequence with the Sequence edit dialog box (a.k.a. the "Sequence editor"). Which way to go depends on what your Sequence is like.

Recording a Sequence

You record a Sequence by starting a Sequence recorder, performing the actions you want to record, and then stopping the Sequence recorder. Then QUICKEYS displays the Sequence editor, with a listing of the editor's *interpretation* of the different steps you made.

Here's an example. You find yourself constantly using the Word Count feature in Microsoft Word. "Word Count" is a menu item on the Utilities menu and has its own keystroke shortcut in Word (Option-F15). But once you choose "Word Count," you get a dialog box in which you always have to press the Count button to get the Word Count feature operating. So you decide to record a Sequence QuicKey to do both steps for you.

First, make sure you are in the correct application (with the correct document, if that matters). Then you can start recording a Sequence in any one of three ways.

- Invoke your Start/Stop Sequence QuicKey (see Chapter 11, *QUICKEYS Control*).
- Choose "Record Sequence" from the QuicKeys 2 submenu of the Apple menu.
- Select "Sequence" from the Define menu of the QUICKEYS management window, and click the Record More button.

Next, you can choose "Word Count" from the Utilities menu, and press on the Count button. Then stop the recording in either of two ways.

- Invoke your Start/Stop Sequence QuicKey again.
- Select "Stop Recording" from the QuicKeys 2 submenu of the Apple menu.

QUICKEYS then displays the Sequence editor, with its interpretation of your actions (see Figure 12-1).

Figure 12-1
The Sequence editor

Insert arrow

Sequence window

Editing control buttons

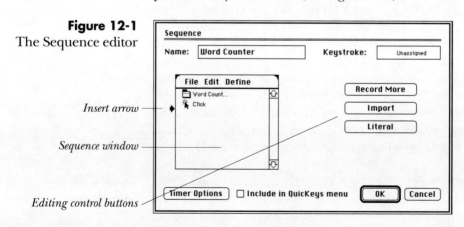

The Sequence window displays the recorder's interpretation of your Sequence's two steps of choosing an item from a menu and clicking on a button. If you now assign a keystroke combination to this Sequence and activate it, you find that it works satisfactorily. However, you may notice that not all is in perfect QUICKEYS harmony. The Sequence recorder interpreted your second action, clicking the Count button, as a Click QuicKey rather than a Button QuicKey. Yes, it works, but it isn't the best QuicKey for the job.

Sequence Recorder Strengths and Weaknesses

The Sequence recorder can only make the correct interpretation (determine the most appropriate QuicKey) for *some* of your actions. For example, if you type out some text, the Sequence recorder will correctly interpret that as a Text QuicKey; if you click on a Close box, the Sequence recorder will attribute that action to a Close window QuicKey (Mousie). Table 12-1 shows actions which are *correctly* interpreted by the Sequence recorder.

Table 12-1
Actions and Sequence recorder interpretations

Your action	Type of QuicKey recorded
Typing text	Text
Typing a modifier-keystroke shortcut in an application	Alias
Clicking in a window	Click
Clicking on a Close box	Close window (Mousie)
Clicking on a Zoom box	Zoom window (Mousie)
Clicking on a different application window	File
Choosing a Desk Accessory (System 6)	Menu/DA
Typing the invoking keystroke for one of your QuicKeys	Appropriate QuicKey except Sequence, Click, and Real Time

But the Sequence recorder interprets many (if not most) actions insufficiently. If you open the Control Panel and set the speaker level to three, the Sequence recorder interprets that as a Menu/DA QuicKey and a Click QuicKey, not as a SpeakerChanger QuicKey. If you type out the date, it will be interpreted as a Text QuicKey, not as a Date/Time QuicKey. Of course, creating a perfect Sequence editor would be nearly impossible. As it is, it's a good compromise between complexity and functionality.

One function the Sequence recorder does well is to put already extant QuicKeys into a Sequence, if you type their invoking keystroke combinations. For example, if you already have a QuicKey which sets the speaker level to three, invoking it while the Sequence recorder is running will place that SpeakerChanger QuicKey into your Sequence. However, this will *not* work with three types of QuicKeys.

- Sequence
- Real Time
- Click

If you try to invoke any of these QuicKeys types during a recording session, the Sequence recorder will stop functioning and peremptorily deliver you back to wherever you were before. A Real Time QuicKey step can never be included in a Sequence. However, there is a method of placing a Click or Sequence QuicKey into a Sequence with the Sequence editor (see "Import" below).

Don often uses the Sequence recorder when he builds a Sequence, but he always checks out the resulting Sequence critically, and often edits it substantially. The limitations of Sequence recorder demand that you test and review its created Sequence to determine if it is appropriate for your needs. If you only need a Sequence recorder-created QuicKey temporarily, and it functions well enough, you might want to use it as is, even though it may contain some inappropriate QuicKey steps. But if you want to make it part of a permanent keyset, we strongly suggest you edit it to make it as good as possible. For that, you use the Sequence editor.

Editing a Simple Sequence

Editing a Sequence is easy because the Sequence editor has some functions analogous to something you already know—the QuicKeys management window. In either one, you can invoke the edit dialog boxes to create and modify different QuicKeys. In the management window, they are individual

QuicKeys; in the Sequence editor, they are QuicKeys that are steps in a Sequence. The Sequence editor also contains Sequence-specific controls.

The Sequence window displays the different QuicKey steps in your Sequence. Within the Sequence editor, you can cut, copy, paste, and modify these individual QuicKey steps; and you can add more steps to the Sequence. Each QuicKey step shown in the window is "hot." Clicking once highlights it and allows you to copy or cut it; double-clicking invokes its edit dialog box.

The Sequence window contains three menus: File, Edit, and Define. They are based on the menus in the QuicKeys management window, but in many cases, items are dimmed because they have no function in this context.

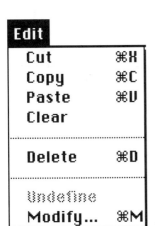

File. The Sequence window has most of its features dimmed. The only items active are Page Setup and Print. By choosing "Print" you can print a listing of the Sequence. This is a new feature with version 2.1 and has been long awaited; it's very useful for archiving and (especially) for debugging long Sequences.

Edit. When a QuicKey step is highlighted in the Sequence window, the Edit menu is almost completely active—only "Undefine" is dimmed because it has no purpose here. The other items are what you'd expect. "Clear" and "Delete" are functionally identical to each other, and "Modify" produces the same result as double-clicking the QuicKey step—it invokes its edit dialog box.

Define. The Define menu has an extra item here: "Pause" is added to the bottom of the list of QuicKey types. The Define menu functions as a source of QuicKey types that you can add to your Sequence. When you choose a QuicKey type from the Define menu, its edit dialog box appears (missing the keystroke box, because there is no need for it here). You can modify the QuicKey as necessary, and then click OK. The new QuicKey is inserted into your Sequence at the spot the Insert arrow points to.

Note that there are three QuicKey types dimmed on this Define menu. Click, Sequence, and Real Time QuicKeys cannot be added to a Sequence from this menu. However, Click and Sequence QuicKeys can be imported.

Editing Sequences

Let's edit the Sequence we made to count words in the Microsoft Word document. Double-clicking on the QuicKey in the QUICKEYS management window makes its Sequence edit dialog box appear.

We need to replace the Click QuicKey with a Button QuicKey. To obliterate the Click QuicKey, you can click on it in the Edit window, and then choose Cut, Clear, or Delete from the Edit menu (or press Command-X for Cut, or Command-D for Delete). The Click QuicKey disappears into the alternate universe.

To add a new step to the Sequence, you must first ensure that the Insert arrow is at the correct spot. When the Sequence editor opens, the Insert arrow always defaults to after the last QuicKey step, so if you want to add a step somewhere else you must move the arrow by dragging it, or by clicking above or below it (see Figure 12-2). You have to watch out for this when you are dealing with long Sequences.

In the case of our little Sequence, the Insert arrow should be below the only remaining step, the Menu QuicKey. You can now add the Button QuicKey by choosing "Button" from the Define

Figure 12-2
The Insert arrow in a long Sequence

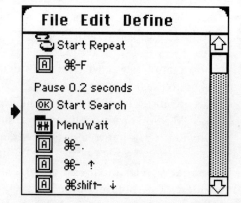

You can drag it up or down.

Click anywhere above or below to move the arrow to that point.

menu. The Button edit dialog box appears. You can enter the name of the Button ("Count") and ensure the correct click option is selected (the Always click option is correct) and then click OK. The QuicKey Button step appears in the Sequence window (see Figure 12-3).

Figure 12-3
Word count
Sequence

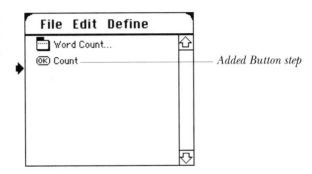

Added Button step

That's all there is to it. Clicking OK in the Sequence editor returns you to the management window. Clicking OK there returns you to your previous application, where you can try out your edited Sequence QuicKey to see how it works.

There is another school of thought concerning the make-up of this particular QuicKey. Instead of using a Menu QuicKey step to choose "Word Count" from the Microsoft Word Utilities menu, you could use an Alias QuicKey step to type Option-F15, the keystroke shortcut to invoke Word Count in Microsoft Word. There is a quick way of doing this, using one of the editing control buttons on the Sequence editor.

Editing-control Buttons

All three editing-control buttons are used to add QuicKey steps to a Sequence (see Figure 12-4).

Figure 12-4
Editing-control
buttons

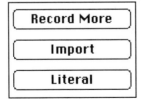

Record More. Clicking "Record More" pops you back into the Sequence recorder. Just perform whatever additions to the Sequence you wish to make. You can then turn off the recorder (see "Recording a Sequence," above) and you are returned to the Sequence editor, which displays the Sequence with the new steps added.

"Record More" is dimmed unless the Insert arrow points after the last step in your Sequence.

Import. The Import button, nestled between "Record More" and "Literal," seems innocuous enough, but it packs a lot of wallop and complexity. In its simplest sense, "Import" allows you to insert any existing QuicKey into a Sequence. It also gives you the only method of importing Click QuicKeys, or the steps of Sequence QuicKeys, into a Sequence.

You can click on the Import button and the Sequence editor undergoes a metamorphosis: its right side becomes a scrolling window that displays the QuicKeys contained in the keyset showing in the Keyset pop-up menu below it (see Figure 12-5).

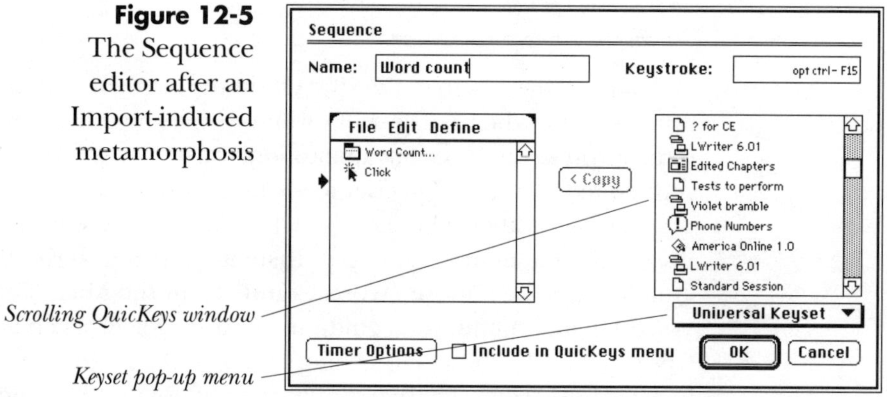

Figure 12-5
The Sequence
editor after an
Import-induced
metamorphosis

Scrolling QuicKeys window

Keyset pop-up menu

You can click on any QuicKey in the right-hand scrolling window, click on the Copy button, and it will be inserted into your Sequence in the position indicated by the Insert arrow (double-clicking on it achieves the same result). Pretty cool! But you ain't seen nothin' yet.

If you press on the Keyset pop-up menu, you see your open keysets listed (see Figure 12-6). Choosing any of them will result in their QuicKeys being displayed in the right-hand scrolling window, available for you to import into your Sequence. Note that Click QuicKeys are listed, and can be imported like any other type. Sequence and Real Time QuicKeys aren't listed. Real Time QuicKeys can never be steps in a Sequence, but Sequence QuicKeys can have their steps inserted by using the "Other" item in the pop-up menu.

Figure 12-6
The Sequence editor
Keyset pop-up menu

Choosing the Other menu item invokes an Open dialog box, displaying your KeySets folder. With it, you can choose any one of your keysets, which will display its QuicKeys in the Import window. But you can also use it to open your Sequences folder, where your Sequence

✓**Universal Keyset**
Finder
Microsoft Word
DA Handler
⋯⋯⋯⋯⋯⋯⋯⋯
Other...
None

QuicKeys are stored. The Sequences folder should be at the same level as your KeySets folder, so you can use the hierarchical pop-up menu to go up to the next folder and find it.

Choose your Sequences folder and all your Sequences are displayed in the scrolling window of the open dialog box. Choosing one Sequence (or double-clicking on it) returns you to the Sequence editor, with the steps of your chosen Sequence displayed in the Import window (see Figure 12-7).

You can now copy any step from the Import window to the Sequence window, or you can copy multiple steps by pressing Shift and clicking or dragging through a number of steps. By pressing Shift and dragging through the whole window (it automatically scrolls, if necessary), you can select and import all the steps in the Sequence.

Figure 12-7
Sequence steps in
the Import window

One of the strange things about Import is that it *seems* the only way to get out of the Import mode is by clicking OK, which returns you to the QuicKeys management window. You

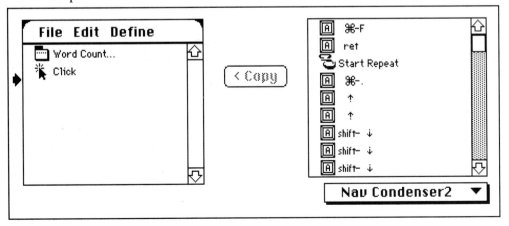

may *not* want to immediately return to the management window, especially if you wish to add some other steps after you do your importing. There is a way out, but it isn't obvious— it's by choosing "None" from the Keyset pop-up menu, which closes the Import window. "Close Import Window" or "End Import" might be more appropriate choices for the name of this menu item.

Another point to keep in mind is that importing a QuicKey into a Sequence is a copying procedure—there is no hot link between the original QuicKey and its imported version. For example, if you import into a Sequence a File QuicKey which opens QuarkXPress, and then later change the original File QuicKey to open Aldus PageMaker, the Sequence will still open QuarkXPress.

Literal. The Literal button is a useful shortcut to add an Alias step to your Sequence. In our Word Count Sequence, we can replace the Menu QuicKey (which chooses "Word Count") with an Alias QuicKey which enters Option-F15, the Microsoft Word shortcut that invokes the Word Count function. As before, the first step is to highlight the unnecessary step and cut it. Now, with the Insert arrow above the remaining Button step, you can click on the Literal button, and a prompt appears asking you to type a key. Type Option-F15, and you will return to the Sequence editor with an Alias key inserted and defined (see Figure 12-8). The same result can be obtained by choosing "Alias" from the Define menu, but that's more complicated. Think of the Literal button as an instant Alias maker.

Figure 12-8
The Sequence window after typing a Literal Option-F15

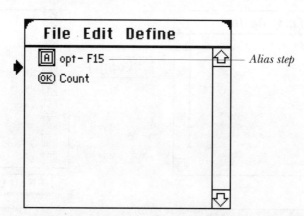

A note of caution on the Literal button. You cannot make an existing QuicKey a step in a Sequence by clicking the Literal button and then typing the invoking QuicKey keystroke. For example, let's say you have a Menu QuicKey with the keystroke Option-Command-S, that you want to include in a Sequence. You *cannot* click the Literal button and type Option-Command-S and have that step function correctly. You *can* import the QuicKey into the Sequence. You can also *record* the QuicKey into the Sequence *by typing the same invoking keystroke that didn't work with the Literal button.* In this case, the Sequence recorder realizes what's happening and puts the correct QuicKey step (in this example, a Menu QuicKey) into your Sequence.

Building Sequences

All the basic steps we used to edit Sequences can also be employed to build a Sequence from scratch. You can give yourself a *tabula rasa* Sequence window by choosing "Sequence" from the Define menu in the QUICKEYS management window. Then, you can start adding steps by choosing QuicKeys from the Sequence editor's Define menu, or by pressing the editing control buttons.

We build Sequences from scratch in situations that the Sequence recorder can't adequately handle. Sometimes we record the simple body of the Sequence with the Sequence recorder, and then add some Sequence control QuicKeys (see next chapter, *Sequence QuicKeys*) to the Sequence to enhance it.

Sophisticated Sequences

Sequences are often the solution to the knottier problems that QUICKEYS can handle. In the next chapter, *Sequence QuicKeys*, we introduce QuicKeys that are intended to work just within Sequences. And we illuminate some of the finer points of advanced Sequence technique.

Sequence QuicKeys

The bulk of this chapter introduces and discusses the Sequence QuicKeys—those QuicKeys that are designed mainly to work within Sequences. At the end of the chapter, we include a guide to troubleshooting a Sequence.

The Sequence QuicKeys break down into two functional categories.

- **Sequence control QuicKeys.** QuicKeys that can only work inside a Sequence (Pause, Wait, MenuWait, WindowWait, CursorWait, MenuDecision, WindowDecision, and Repeat).
- **Sequence helper QuicKeys.** QuicKeys that can function on their own, but are particularly useful in a Sequence (Message and Sound).

Sequence Control QuicKeys

You can use the extremely powerful Sequence control QuicKeys to vary how your Sequence plays. Pause, Wait, and Repeat are included in your QUICKEYS package. MenuWait, WindowWait, CursorWait, MenuDecision, and WindowDecision are Extensions written by a sharp programmer by the name of Simeon Leifer, and are available through online services such as CompuServe, or direct from Simeon (see Appendix, *Resources*).

A Sequence control QuicKey exerts one of three types of control in your Sequence.

- **Loafer.** A loafer QuicKey waits for a certain time or for something to happen, and then it allows the Sequence to continue. Pause, Wait, MenuWait, WindowWait, and CursorWait are loafers.

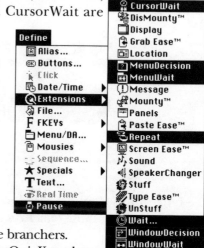

- **Brancher.** Brancher QuicKeys wait for a condition to occur, and then proceed in either of two directions; it continues the Sequence by jumping to either of two QuicKey options. MenuDecision and WindowDecision are branchers.
- **Looper.** The looper QuicKey plays part or all of your Sequence over and over again a selected number of times. Repeat is the only looper. Let's take a look at the Sequence control QuicKeys.

Pause

Pause is conceptually a very simple QuicKey. Placing Pause within a Sequence causes the Sequence to halt at that step and wait. You determine in which of the two ways that Pause can wait.

- **Time.** Pause will wait the length of time you choose.
- **User input.** Pause will flip into the QUICKEYS pause mode. To get it going again, you must choose "Pause" from the QuicKeys submenu (or invoke your special "Unpause" QuicKey—see below).

Figure 13-1
Pause options
dialog box

To put a Pause step into a Sequence, you choose "Pause" from the Define menu of the Sequence editor. The Pause options dialog box appears (see Figure 13-1). You can then choose how you want Pause to pause. If you choose the time option, you can enter the pause time in seconds (and tenths of seconds).

When a Sequence encounters a Pause step, QUICKEYS halts the Sequence QuicKey's actions and the cursor turns into the double line

Pause

- ⦿ Pause for [1.0] second(s)
- ○ Pause and wait for user

[OK] [Cancel]

Pause symbol. When the Pause step is countered (either by user input or by time), the Sequence starts up again.

Pause and Wait for User

The Pause and wait for user choice on the Pause options dialog box makes the Sequence pause and wait for you to tell it to continue. While QUICKEYS is in this Pause and wait for user mode, the cursor turns into the Pause icon, and you can use your Mac as if nothing unusual were happening. We can't say enough about the power of a Pause and wait for user step in a Sequence. We've found that it's helped us build some really terrific Sequence QuicKeys.

You can use a Wait for user Pause if you have a Sequence that needs user input in the middle of it. For example, you may have a Sequence which sets up a header for you in a word-processing document. It can enter the date and page number, but it requires you to enter the chapter title before it reformats. You place a Pause and wait for user step that allows you to type in the chapter name. Then you tell the Sequence to resume.

One way to trigger this resumption is by choosing "Pause" from the QuicKeys 2 submenu off the Apple menu. But there is an easier way: make your own Unpause QuicKey that you can trigger from your keyboard. Here's how.

Select "Pause" from the Specials submenu off the Define menu. Yup, this is another route to the Pause QuicKey that controls the QUICKEYS pause function. But unlike the Pause step available in the Sequence editor, you can give this Pause an invoking keystroke. We like to use our straight F15 key for Pause since it's already labeled that way. This QuicKey now becomes an easy way to "unpause" a Sequence that is in the Pause and wait for user mode.

It is worth noting that while you are in a Sequence, your Unpause QuicKey is just that: it only functions to make a Sequence resume. You can't use it to make a Sequence pause (to do that, click the mouse). However, you can use this QuicKey to pause and "unpause" the Sequence and Real Time recorders.

Pause Considerations

One of the things to watch out for in a Pause mode is that invoking another QuicKey during a pause can be as dangerous as walking through a child's room with the lights turned off—it's difficult to predict where you will stumble, but getting through without tripping is less than likely. What often happens is that at first nothing happens. You are still in the Pause mode. However, when you choose "Pause" from the QuicKeys 2 submenu (or use your Unpause QuicKey) to deactivate the Pause step, instead of finishing off the original Sequence, QUICKEYS flips to the QuicKey you most recently invoked, and plays that. Sometimes you sneak through.

However, in the worst case, invoking another QuicKey during a Pause can be hazardous to the health of your original Sequence. For example, we have a Sequence which has a "Pause and wait for user" step in it. If we invoke a Choosy QuicKey during the pause, nothing happens until we tell the Sequence to continue. Then the Chooser pops up. Okay, no big deal. But now if we open up the QUICKEYS management window, we discover that the original Sequence has no steps in it! They have been shipped (via Next Day Air?) into the alternate universe. It's not just Choosy that does this, so watch out for it!

Pause Tactics

Use Pause to suspend a Sequence when none of the other loafers (Wait, WindowWait, MenuWait, or CursorWait) will do.

A timed Pause is often put into a Sequence when the Sequence you've built doesn't work correctly, and you suspect that QUICKEYS is going too fast for the application it is working in. This is an endemic problem with QUICKEYS—it sometimes doesn't realize when an application is creeping along, so it goes right ahead and gives it more steps. Often the application just ignores the QUICKEYS messages until it gets its act together, so you find that QuicKeys steps occur in the wrong places—or do weird things. Placing timed Pauses in a Sequence is like telling QUICKEYS, "Hold on, wait for a while, maybe the application will catch up." If the application does catch up in time, then everything is okay; if not, you need a longer pause.

A timed Pause can be as simple as this: if you are making a Sequence in Microsoft Word that calls the spelling checker and then clicks the Start Check button, it won't work correctly without a Pause built into it because the button tries to execute before the checker is loaded. The spelling checker takes a few seconds while it loads the first time, so you want a Pause step that will wait just long enough (but not too long, that wastes time) for the button to become active. It often requires experimentation to determine the minimum safe time to pause.

Timed Pauses are often used to *debug* (analyze and correct) a Sequence. The sledge-hammer approach is to spread a bunch of timed Pauses throughout a nonworking Sequence. If the Sequence starts working, you know you have a problem with synchronization between QUICKEYS and the application. Start taking out the timed Pauses until the Sequence stops working. Then you know the last timed Pause you removed was a necessary one (there may be more than one timed Pause needed). Yes, it's convoluted and monstrous, but sometimes it's the best possible fix. For more on Pauses in debugging, see "Troubleshooting," later in this chapter.

In a perfect computing environment, there would be infrequent need for a timed Pause. If there is a reason to wait for an application to do something, it is much better to be able to put in a conditional step, not a timed step—"Wait until the cursor changes back to a pointer," or "Wait until the document window becomes active."

Wait   The Wait QuicKey pauses a Sequence until a particular condition (that you preselect from a pop-up list) occurs. The four available conditions all involve the status of the front (active) window.

- **Window changes.** The front window changes to anything else (for example, if you click on another open file within the same application, or if you invoke a command that brings up a dialog box).
- **Window is gone.** The window that was in front when Wait paused must *close* for the Sequence to resume. The window can be shoved into the background, but as long as it's open, the Sequence remains paused.
- **Dialog in front.** The Sequence waits until a dialog box is the front window. Usually it is obvious when something is a dialog box (a window which requests information or gives information), but sometimes you have to try this out to make sure it works.

- **Not dialog.** The Sequence waits until the window in front is not a dialog box.

You can add a Wait step to a Sequence by choosing "Wait" from the Extensions submenu of the Sequence editor. The Wait edit dialog box appears (see Figure 13-2). Two features are important in this dialog box—the Wait until pop-up menu (see Figure 13-3) and the Allow user actions while waiting check box.

Figure 13-2
Wait edit
dialog box

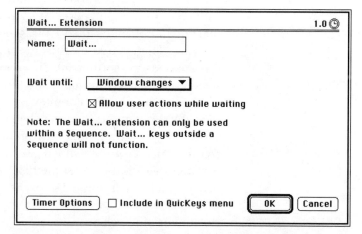

Wait Considerations

Wait is only aware of windows that exist within the application that's active when the Wait step occurs in the Sequence. If you manually flip to another application while Wait has paused your Sequence, it does not pick up the change in windows, or the change in any windows in that subsequent application.

When Wait pauses the Sequence, it does so by activating the QUICKEYS Pause function—so you can get the Sequence restarted (bypass the Wait conditional) by choosing Pause from the QuicKeys 2 submenu or invoking your Unpause QuicKey. But here's a warning: just like Pause (see section above), this mechanism can be confounded if you invoke a QuicKey while it has suspended a Sequence. Do so at your own risk.

Figure 13-3
Wait until
pop-up menu

Wait Tactics   *Use Wait to suspend a Sequence when you want the resumption to be triggered by a change in the active window. If Wait isn't flexible enough for the job, see WindowWait.*

Think of the Wait QuicKey as waiting for the *active* window. It can discriminate between dialog and non-dialog windows, and it can be triggered by a window moving from the top layer, or closing completely. Here's a good example. Steve works on long documents in PageMaker and he often re-indexes them, using the Create index feature (which displays a dialog box while it is working). Steve then flows the index into a page, using the loaded text gun that's displayed when the indexing is finished. In long documents the indexing can take a long time, so he tried to make a QuicKey that would choose "Create index" from the Options menu, click on OK, and then click in the space where he wanted the index to flow from (see Figure 13-4). However, it didn't work because the Click step occurred while the indexing was taking place.

Figure 13-4
Failed attempt at an indexing and flowing Sequence

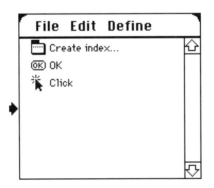

So he placed a Wait for window to change step into the Sequence (see Figure 13-5), and it worked perfectly. Wait until dialog is gone and Wait until window is gone also work for this step.

WindowWait   WindowWait is similar to Wait, but gives you finer control over the the window conditional that triggers the Sequence restart. Whereas Wait is only triggered by the top window activity, and whether or not it's a dialog window, WindowWait evaluates a window's *name* and/or *type*. WindowWait is third-party PWYTIW (pay what you think it's worth) ware.

Figure 13-5
Wait step to fix the
indexing and flowing
Sequence

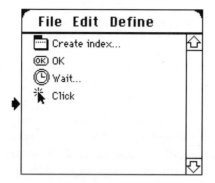

You can include a WindowWait step by choosing WindowWait from the Extensions submenu of the Sequence editor. The WindowWait edit dialog box appears (see Figure 13-6). The edit dialog box contains two pop-up menus (one for name and one for type), each with a check box below that activates it. There is also a text edit box to the right of the Window Name pop-up menu, in which you enter text that's considered by the criteria chosen.

Figure 13-6
WindowWait edit
dialog box

```
┌─────────────────────────────────────────────────────────────┐
│ WindowWait Extension                                   1.3 ** │
│                                                               │
│ Name:  │WindowWait                    │                       │
│         © 1991 Simeon Leifer          All Rights Reserved     │
│                                                               │
│ Window Name:  │ IS              ▼ │   ┌─────────────────────┐ │
│               ⊠ Check Window Name    └─────────────────────┘ │
│ Window Type:  │ DIALOG          ▼ │                           │
│               ☐ Check Window Type                            │
│                                                               │
│                                                               │
│                                     ( OK )  ( Cancel )        │
└─────────────────────────────────────────────────────────────┘
```

Window Name. The Window Name pop-up menu and the accompanying text edit box comprise the Window Name conditionals (see Figure 13-7). The four pop-up menu tests

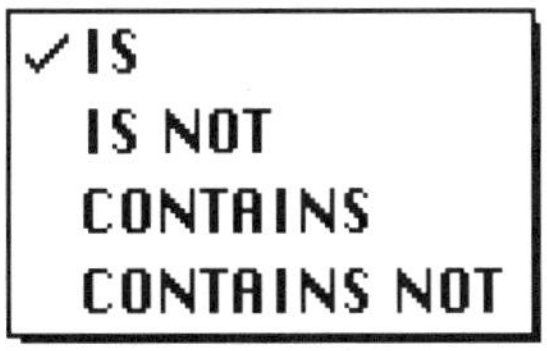

```
✓ IS
  IS NOT
  CONTAINS
  CONTAINS NOT
```

Figure 13-7
Window Name
conditionals
pop-up menu

are straightforward. Choose one, and enter the text upon which it acts in the text edit box.

Having four name-matching criteria gives this part of WindowWait a lot of dexterity in dealing with potential window names. Here's the lowdown.

- **Is.** Matches the name of the window exactly as you've entered it in the Window Name text edit box. Use this when you want to pause the Sequence until a specific window becomes active. For example, if you want the Sequence to wait for a window named "Spelling" to become active before proceeding, choose this option.

- **Is Not.** Waits until the active window is anything other than the window you have named exactly in the Window Name text edit box. For example, if you want to wait until the active window is not the Find window, this is the option to choose.

- **Contains.** Waits until the name of the active window contains text you enter into the Window Name text edit box. Use this when you want to wait until the active window has a generic quality—for example, if you wanted to wait until the window had a name containing the word "Untitled." "Untitled 1," "Untitled 2," and so on would all fulfill this condition.

- **Contains not.** This option waits until the name of the active window *doesn't* contain text you enter into the Window Name text edit box. An example similar to the one above might be what you're after: you want to wait until the window *doesn't have* a name containing the word "Untitled." "Untitled 1" or "Untitled 2" would make the Extension wait, with this option chosen. Any name that does not include the word "Untitled" allows it to proceed.

Under the Window Name pop-up menu is the Check Window Name check box. Check this if you want the Extension to wait, using the Window Name criteria.

Window Type. The WindowWait Extension also can wait for a certain window *type* before proceeding with the Sequence. Click in the Check Window Type check box if you want the Extension to wait for a certain type of window. Then press the Window Type pop-up menu to choose the condition you want to be met. There are three window types it can test for, and you can choose whether it waits for this type of window to become active (Is) or to become inactive (Is Not).

- **Dialog.** You've seen a zillion dialog windows (Figure 13-8) This category also includes alert boxes that the application displays.

Figure 13-8
Typical dialog windows

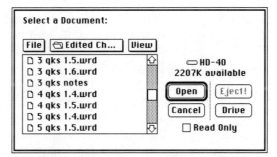

Open dialog box

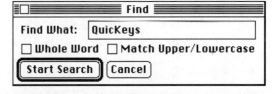

Find window in Microsoft Word

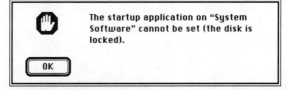

Alert box from the Finder

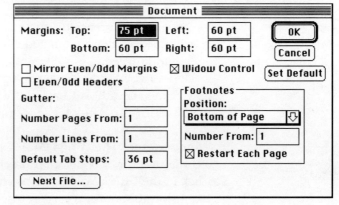

Document dialog box in Microsoft Word

- **System.** System windows (emanating from your System) show up rarely (see Figure 13-9).

Figure 13-9
Typical System window

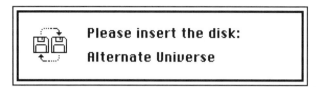

Disk swap alert box

- **User.** User windows comprise all windows that aren't dialog or System windows (see Figure 13-10).

Figure 13-10
Typical user windows

PageMaker user windows

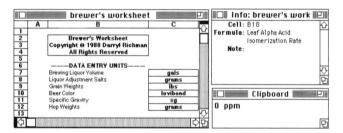

Excel user windows

WindowWait Considerations

You may have noticed that you can choose the Check Window Name option and the Check Window Type option simultaneously; they are not mutually exclusive criteria. If you do so, WindowWait waits until *both* conditions are met before proceeding. For example, if you ask it to wait until the window name is Find, and also that the window type is User, the Sequence will wait until a user window named "Find" is active; it *will not* proceed only on a dialog window named "Find."

Sometimes window types are not obvious. If your WindowWait step depends on a window type, you might want to test the type just to be sure you have it right. An easy way to do this is to create a two-step Sequence. The first step is your WindowWait Extension with the correct criteria chosen. The second step is a Message Extension or a Sound Extension that confirms that the WindowWait step preceded it. Invoke your test Sequence with the questionable window active. If you get your confirmation, you know that WindowWait's criteria were met.

WindowWait Tactics

Use WindowWait to pause a Sequence until a window with a preselected type and/or name becomes active.

In many instances, the Wait Extension can produce a result identical to WindowWait's. But there are situations where only WindowWait will do. Many of the jobs made for WindowWait test for the Window Name conditional. For example, you can use WindowWait to pause a Sequence that is copying paragraphs from a number of documents, and pasting them into just one. If you set up WindowWait to pause while the application is switching to the target document, you can ensure that your pasting is done correctly.

MenuWait

MenuWait is similar to WindowWait except it waits for a menu item's condition to be met before it proceeds..

It is easy to create a MenuWait step in a Sequence. Choose MenuWait from the Extensions submenu of the Define menu in the Sequence editor. The MenuWait edit dialog box appears (Figure 13-11). You can press the Select Menu button—your cursor turns into a little menu cursor—and you can use it to choose the menu item on which you want to base the MenuWait. After you have chosen a menu item, the Menu Name and Item Name fields are filled in.

Now you can choose from the conditionals options. Basically, there are two areas to test for: whether or not a menu item is checked, and/or whether the menu item is enabled (a disabled menu item is displayed in gray). If you don't want to test in any of these areas, then check the Don't Care option.

MenuWait Considerations

If you ask MenuWait to consider two conditionals (you haven't chosen the Don't Care option for either the Checked condition or the Enabled condition), then both conditions must be met before MenuWait will allow the Sequence to proceed.

Menu item conditionals ——

```
┌─────────────────────────────────────────────────────────────┐
│ MenuWait Extension                                    1.3 ▦   │
│                                                              │
│ Name:  ┌──────────────────────────┐                          │
│        │ MenuWait                 │                          │
│        └──────────────────────────┘                          │
│    © 1991 Simeon Leifer              All Rights Reserved      │
│                                                              │
│   ┌──────────────┐   Menu Name:                              │
│   │ Select Menu  │   Item Name:                              │
│   └──────────────┘                                           │
│    ○ Is Checked  ○ Is Not Checked  ◉ Don't Care              │
│    ○ Is Enabled  ○ Is Not Enabled  ◉ Don't Care              │
│                                                              │
│                                                              │
│  ┌───────────────┐  ☐ Include in QuicKeys menu  ┌──────┐ ┌────────┐ │
│  │ Timer Options │                              │  OK  │ │ Cancel │ │
│  └───────────────┘                              └──────┘ └────────┘ │
└─────────────────────────────────────────────────────────────┘
```

Some applications seem to have their own way of generating menus that may look like menus, act like menus, and smell like menus—but actually don't follow all the Apple guidelines for true menu-ness. So before incorporating MenuWait as an integral part of a long Sequence, check your particular application to see if MenuWait works the way it is supposed to.

MenuWait Tactics

Use MenuWait to pause a Sequence until preselected conditions for a menu item are met.

Whether a menu item is able to be checked depends on the application. Many applications do not have any (or many) menu items that can be checked. Most menu items can be disabled (dimmed) depending on certain conditions, so you will probably use the Enabled conditionals much more often than the Checked conditionals.

Generally, we don't use MenuWait very often, but we're glad it exists because we like to have as many tools available as possible, even those that we use infrequently. We sometimes include MenuWait in a Sequence, to ensure that a particular menu item is checked before proceeding. Sometimes a menu is enabled or disabled for a reason that's not connected with what you're trying to do, but that nevertheless signals that an event has occurred that *is* important to what you're doing. MenuWait can let you create workarounds that you couldn't create otherwise.

CursorWait

CursorWait is a dandy Extension that pauses a Sequence until the cursor (pointer) conforms or does not conform to a particular shape. You can put a CursorWait into a Sequence by choosing CursorWait from the Extensions submenu of the Define menu in the Sequence editor. The CursorWait edit dialog box appears (Figure 13-12). The CursorWait dialog box contains a cursor display box and two pop-up menus (Figure 13-13). If you choose "Other" from the Cursor pop-up menu, the Select cursor window appears, which gives you a passel of additional cursor choices (See Figure 13-14).

Figure 13-12
CursorWait edit dialog box

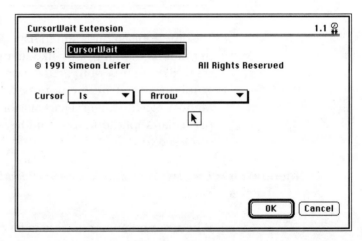

CursorWait Considerations

CursorWait Extension QuicKeys search for a specific type of cursor resource within the open file. If the application you are in does not treat cursors in this standard manner (using a "curs" resource), it may be impossible to get CursorWait to work.

Figure 13-13
Conditional and Cursor pop-up menus

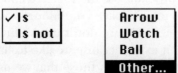

CursorWait Tactics

Use CursorWait QuicKeys to pause a Sequence until preselected conditions for the cursor are met.

Figure 13-14
Select cursor window

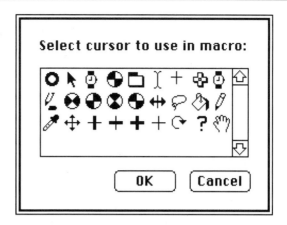

A good use of CursorWait is with the Is Not Wristwatch option chosen. These conditionals can be used to pause a Sequence while the application is working away at something—letting you know it is still alive by displaying a wristwatch. This starts up the Sequence again after the application finishes its crunching (when the wristwatch disappears).

WindowDecision

WindowDecision is the first of two very special decision QuicKeys. They allow a Sequence to branch, depending on whether or not certain conditions are met. The branching mechanism employs other QuicKeys—when a branch occurs, another QuicKey is played, then control returns to the original Sequence. You can nest several levels of decisions, resulting in very complex QuicKeys. WindowDecision is like WindowWait, except that instead of pausing a Sequence based on certain window criteria, this QuicKey chooses one of two ways for the Sequence to proceed.

If you choose WindowDecision from the Extensions submenu of the Define menu in the Sequence editor, the WindowDecision edit dialog box appears (Figure 13-15). The WindowDecision edit dialog box is identical to the WindowWait edit dialog box except for the addition of one area: the Pass/Fail QuicKey text edit boxes. You can enter the names of the QuicKeys you want WindowDecision to play (depending on whether the conditions have been met) in the Pass/Fail QuicKey text edit boxes.

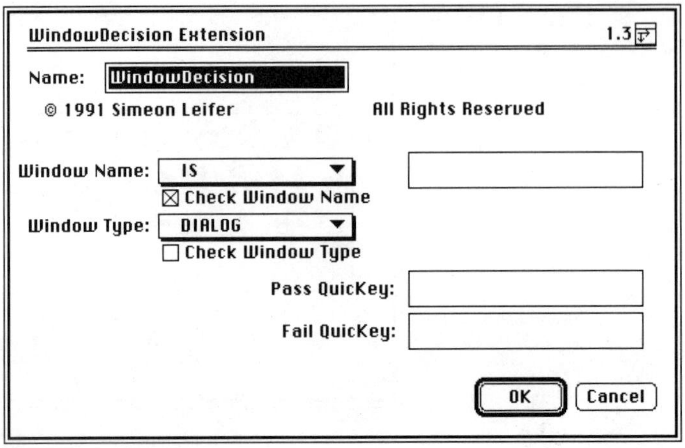

Figure 13-15
WindowDecision
edit dialog box

Because the conditionals in WindowDecision are identical to those in WindowWait, we won't discuss them again; please see the "WindowWait" section, above, for a discussion of those conditionals.

Where WindowDecision differs from WindowWait is in how it redirects the Sequence to one of two other QuicKeys, depending on whether its conditions have been met. For example, if you choose the condition that the window is a dialog box, then WindowDecision plays the Pass QuicKey if there is a dialog box active when the WindowDecision step occurs. If a dialog box is not active, WindowDecision plays the Fail QuicKey. After either of the Pass/Fail QuicKeys is played, the Sequence resumes.

Here's an example of a Sequence—an automatic-save QuicKey—created with a WindowDecision step (see Figure 13-16). It's a variation of an example given by Simeon Leifer, WindowDecision's creator. It looks deceptively simple, but there's quite a bit of functionality lurking underneath. It resides in the Microsoft Word keyset, and is activated by the timer every ten minutes. Using WindowDecision, the Sequence determines whether your active window has previously been saved or not; it then displays one of two messages, accordingly. The message boxes allow you to either cancel the subsequent save step or continue and save the active document.

Figure 13-16
The Save Sequence in
the Microsoft Word
keyset

*First step decides if the
title contains the
word "Untitled."*

*Second step (performed
after branching) saves
the document.*

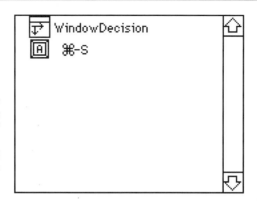

This automatic-save Sequence has two steps: a WindowDecision, and an Alias QuicKey which invokes the Save command. The WindowDecision step (Figure 13-17) asks if the document that's active contains "Untitled"—this is to check whether the document has been previously saved. If the title includes "Untitled," the conditionals have been met, so the Sequence is directed to the Pass QuicKey, a QuicKey we've named "Save Query." If the title doesn't include "Untitled," the Sequence is directed to the Fail QuicKey named "Save Warning."

Figure 13-17
WindowDecision
conditionals and
Pass/Fail QuicKeys

Window Name:	CONTAINS ▼	Untitled
	☒ Check Window Name	
Window Type:	DIALOG ▼	
	☐ Check Window Type	
	Pass QuicKey:	Save Query
	Fail QuicKey:	Save Warning

*If the document name contains "Untitled" it branches to "Save Query."
If it doesn't, it branches to "Save Warning."*

Save Query is a Message QuicKey (Figure 13-18) which states that the active document has never been saved before. It gives the options of clicking Cancel, which stops the Sequence, or OK, which allows the Sequence to continue. If you click OK, because there are no further steps in Save Query, the original Sequence picks up after the WindowDecision step, and Command-S is invoked.

Save Warning (Figure 13-19) is just like Save Query, except that the message is slightly different.

WindowDecision Considerations

All of the information in the WindowWait Considerations section, above, holds true for WindowDecision.

The names of the QuicKeys you enter into the Pass or Fail text edit boxes must be exact, except for their case. Unfortunately, you have to type them, rather than choosing them from a menu.

You don't have to branch to two QuicKeys outside the original Sequence. You may leave either the Pass or the Fail QuicKey text edit box blank. If the proper conditionals are met for a blank Pass or Fail box, the Sequence will continue on to the next step past the WindowDecision step. Essentially, you are including one branch in the original Sequence.

Figure 13-18
Save Query Message edit dialog box and resulting message

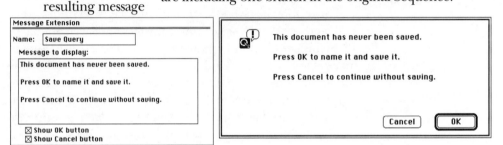

Figure 13-19
Save Warning message

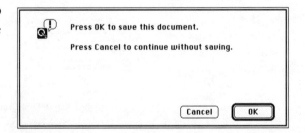

After a Pass or Fail QuicKey branch is played, the Sequence continues from the step after WindowDecision. If you don't have any steps after it, there's no problem; the Sequence just terminates after it is finished with one of the two steps. But if there are steps after WindowWait and you don't want to return to the original Sequence, you must somehow terminate (cancel) the Sequence after the branch has done its work. An easy way to do this is to create a Message QuicKey as the last step in your branch, have the Cancel option chosen, and just click Cancel in the message window.

WindowDecision Tactics

Use WindowDecision to branch a Sequence to one of two QuicKeys, depending on certain window conditions.

WindowDecision is the more important of the two branching QuicKeys available. Its window-oriented conditionals occur more often in situations where you might want to branch a Sequence. When you start to create a Sequence QuicKey with branches (you can nest conditionals several levels deep), you might want to first sketch out a flow diagram of the Sequence. This can help in determining whether you want to branch out to two QuicKeys, or to only one—with the default leading into the rest of the Sequence.

WindowDecision can come in very handy as a companion to the Repeat QuicKey. You can use WindowDecision to jump out of a Repeat-directed loop in a Sequence (see "Repeat Tactics," below).

MenuDecision

MenuDecision is to MenuWait as WindowDecision is to WindowWait. The same conditionals apply to both MenuWait and MenuDecision, except that the Pass/Fail branching mechanism is added in MenuDecision. As with WindowDecision, MenuDecision lets you nest several levels of conditional branching by building multiple QuicKeys.

You can make a MenuDecision step in a Sequence by selecting the MenuDecision item from the Define submenu in the Sequence editor. The MenuDecision edit dialog box appears (see Figure 13-20). Most of the controls in the MenuDecision edit dialog box are identical to those in MenuWait (see "MenuWait," above). The Pass/Fail QuicKey text edit boxes are for the names of the QuicKeys to which you want the Sequence to branch. The Sequence branches to the Pass QuicKey if the conditions have been met, or to the Fail QuicKey if they haven't. After either the Pass or Fail QuicKey plays, the original Sequence is played, beginning with the step after MenuDecision.

MenuDecision Considerations

All the considerations of MenuWait apply to MenuDecision (see "MenuWait Considerations," above). All WindowDecision considerations apply here, too (see "WindowDecision Considerations," above). That makes it easy, doesn't it?

Figure 13-20
MenuDecision edit
dialog box

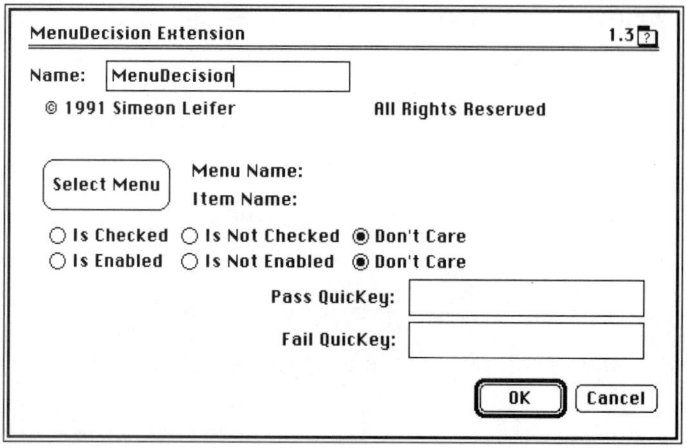

```
┌─────────────────────────────────────────────────┐
│ MenuDecision Extension                    1.3 [?] │
│                                                   │
│ Name: [MenuDecision|                    ]         │
│    © 1991 Simeon Leifer        All Rights Reserved│
│                                                   │
│   ┌───────────┐   Menu Name:                      │
│   │Select Menu│   Item Name:                       │
│   └───────────┘                                    │
│   ○ Is Checked  ○ Is Not Checked ● Don't Care      │
│   ○ Is Enabled  ○ Is Not Enabled ● Don't Care      │
│                                                    │
│              Pass QuicKey: [            ]          │
│              Fail QuicKey: [            ]          │
│                                                    │
│                        ( OK )  ( Cancel )          │
└─────────────────────────────────────────────────┘
```

MenuDecision Tactics *Use MenuDecision to branch a Sequence to one of two QuicKeys, depending on certain menu conditions.*

Just like MenuWait, we don't use MenuDecision too frequently, but we're glad it's there. If you are making a complicated branching scheme, sketch out a flow diagram for yourself; it might help you visualize where things should be.

Repeat Repeat has two roles; the most important is inside a Sequence. A Sequence Repeat allows you to loop part of a Sequence a number of times. You actually need two Repeat QuicKeys for each loop—one to start the loop, and one to end it. A Non-Sequence Repeat just plays a particular QuicKey a specified number of times. Let's get that less important role out of the way first.

Non-Sequence Repeat. You can play any QuicKey a number of times, by choosing "Repeat" from the Extensions submenu of the Define menu in the QUICKEYS management window. The Repeat edit dialog box appears with the Non-Sequence button checked in the Function options area, which causes "Non-Sequence" to be entered into the Name text edit box (see Figure 13-21).

You can play a QuicKey by entering its name in the Play the QuicKey text edit box. You can then either enter the number of times you want the QuicKey played, in the Times text edit box or check the Ask times to repeat check box. With the Ask times to repeat box checked, when you invoke the QuicKey you'll get a dialog box asking you to enter the number of times you want the QuicKey played. This Repeat dialog box has an entry that defaults to the same number as that entered in the Ask times to repeat box.

Figure 13-21
Repeat edit dialog box
for Non-Sequence

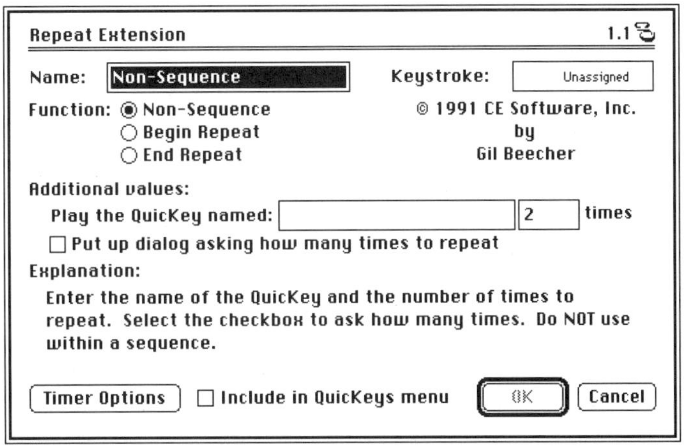

Sequence Repeat. Here's where Repeat really struts its stuff—as a device that repeatedly plays a part of a Sequence. You can add a Repeat QuicKey step to a Sequence by choosing "Repeat" from the Extensions submenu of the Define menu in the Sequence editor. You guessed it—the Repeat edit dialog box appears. Because this dialog box defaults to the Non-Sequence function, you must choose "Begin Repeat" from the Functions options to create a Begin Repeat QuicKey (Figure 13-22).

You can either preset the number of times you want Repeat to loop, by entering a number in the Repeat times text edit box, or you can have Repeat display a window prompting you for the number of times to repeat.

After beginning a repeat, you must end it, and you do so by placing an End Repeat in the Sequence somewhere after Begin Repeat. Do this by creating a Repeat step as before, but this time click "End Repeat" in the Function options.

Figure 13-22
Repeat edit dialog box
for Begin Repeat

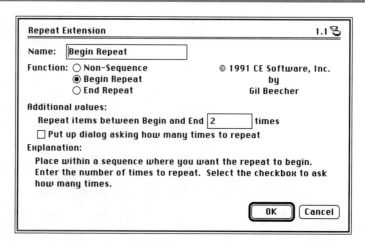

Repeat Considerations

You can't nest a Repeat loop inside another Repeat loop, and you can't put an End Repeat before a Begin Repeat. (Why would you want to?)

The maximum number of times you can have part of a Sequence repeat is 1,215,752. The number displayed in the Repeat times text edit box defaults to this number, if you enter a number that's greater.

Repeat Tactics

Use Repeat to loop part of a Sequence. Or use Repeat to play one QuicKey a number of times.

Sometimes you may want to create a Sequence QuicKey that performs a task over and over again until it is done—but you don't know how many repetitions it will take to finish the task. Unfortunately, there is no direct way to tell QuicKeys how to do that. But often you can achieve the same result by constructing a Repeat pair that will repeat part of the Sequence many more times than is necessary to get the job done (set Begin Repeat for 1,000,000 repetitions). Then branch out of the repetitions when the task is done, using a WindowDecision (or sometimes a MenuDecision) QuicKey. Here's an example.

Say you have an archive of thousands of messages from an online service. The archive is in your word-processing program (for example, Microsoft Word) and you have massaged the file so that each message constitutes its own paragraph.

You want to be able to search through your archive (let's just pretend that the entire archive consists of messages about home brewing), extract all the archives that have the word "yeast" in them, and paste them to another file.

To do this, you can build a Repeat loop in your QuicKey that loops 10,000 times (10,000 is an arbitrarily high number). You'll never get up to 10,000 repetitions because when the Word Find function gets to the end of the file, the program puts up a dialog box telling you so. You can use this change in windows to trigger a WindowDecision QuicKey, which will branch you out of the loop and tell you the Sequence is over.

Here's the Sequence (see Figure 13-23).

The WindowDecision step that gets you out of the loop watches for the Find window (see Figure 13-24). If the top window is not named "Find" (in this case, it is a message window telling you that the end of the document has been reached), then WindowDecision plays the End Sequence QuicKey, a Message QuicKey that contains a Cancel button to end the Sequence.

Figure 13-23
Sequence for culling messages

Displays message on how to start Sequence rolling

Pause allows Word Search function to find something

WindowDecision Repeat escaper

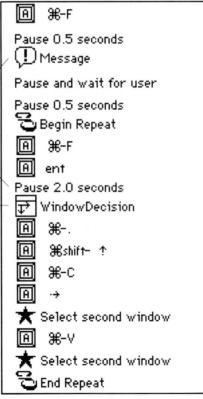

The key to making this conditional Repeat escaper is the existence of some change in a window or menu that you can pick up with Window-Decision or MenuDecision. If no such change occurs, you stay in the loop. But if one does (as they often do), you've got an out. That's one big reason that Simeon Leifer's Extensions are so valuable—and why we urge you to respond to his generous decision to distribute these Extensions on a PWYTIW (pay what you think it's worth) basis. They are available online, or direct from Simeon (See Appendix, *Resources*).

Figure 13-24
WindowDecision
conditionals

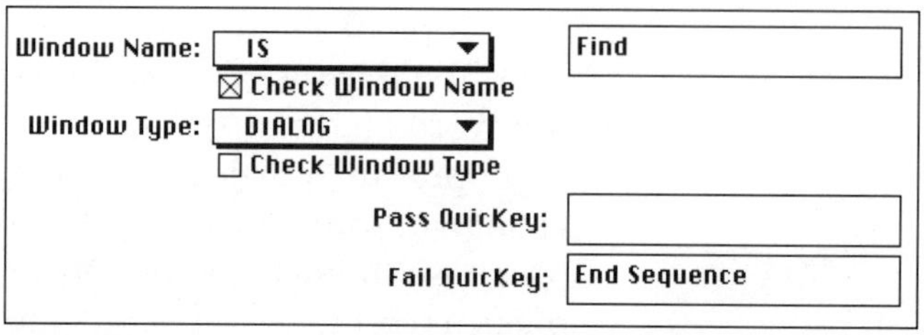

If the active window is not named "Find," WindowDecision plays the End Sequence QuicKey.

Sequence Helper QuicKeys

Message and Sound, the Sequence Helper QuicKeys, can sometimes stand outside a Sequence, but usually they are either inside a Sequence or associated with one.

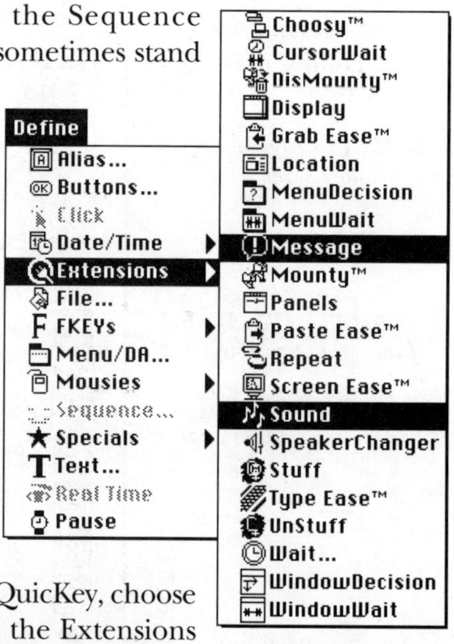

Message

A Message Extension QuicKey displays a message in a little modal window— while the window is displayed, you can't do anything else.

To create a Message QuicKey, choose the Message item from the Extensions submenu of the Define menu. The Message edit dialog box appears (Figure 13-25). The OK button on the bottom and the Show Cancel button option are dimmed, until you choose one of the two active options under the Message to display text edit window.

Figure 13-25
Message edit
dialog box

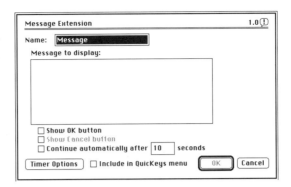

**Message Tactics
and Considerations**

Use Message QuicKeys to display information or exit from a Sequence branch.

The Message QuicKey is straightforward. Note that the Cancel button is only important if the Message QuicKey is a step in a Sequence. Clicking Cancel cancels the entire Sequence; clicking OK allows the Sequence to continue.

You can use Message to terminate a Sequence if you can branch out of the Sequence with a MenuDecision or WindowDecision step.

Sound

The Sound QuicKey plays any sound that's installed in your System. We include the Sound Extension here because you may want to make a Sound step part of a Sequence.

You can make a stand-alone Sound QuicKey or a Sound step in a Sequence by choosing "Sound" from the Extensions submenu of the Define menu. Beep! The Sound edit dialog box appears. If you press on the Play sound pop-up menu, the available sounds are displayed (Figure 13-26). Choose the sound you want to play.

**Sound Tactics
and Considerations**

Use Sound to play a sound.

You can make a stand-alone Sound QuicKey, invoked by the timer, that plays a sound every hour—just like all those watches did in movie theaters, before they drove everyone nuts. Or you can build a Sequence that plays a different sound every hour, and then repeats.

Figure 13-26
Sound edit
dialog box

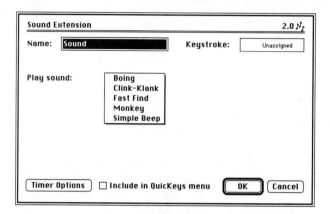

Sounds can also be used in Sequences as flags, to let you know when a Sequence gets to a particular step.

Troubleshooting

Troubleshooting is where we give you the magic—and more. This section is about playing QuicKeys with Magic's hustle, Air Jordan's bounce, and the domination of Kareem. Here's where we coach you in ducking, weaving, spinning moves that help you overcome the last vestiges of opposition on the trail to QuicKeys nirvana. Mixing our metaphors again? We don't know about you, but we can't think of anything closer to nirvana than Michael's slam-dunk. Let's hit the court!

Record More in the Middle

Here's an additional tip for maximizing your Sequence recording gain and easing the pain.

The Sequence editor's Record More button makes recording additional Sequence material a breeze—except that it is only enabled when the Insert arrow points after the last step in the Sequence window. So it seems you can't record more in the middle of an already existing Sequence.

But there is a workaround. Just go back to the QUICKEYS management window, select "Sequence" from the Define menu, and click the Record More button for this new Sequence. Record the additional steps, save this new Sequence with a recognizable name, go back to the Sequence editor of your original Sequence and import your new steps into it at the proper place (for more on that, review "Import" in Chapter 12, *The Sequence*).

Advanced Debugging and Editing

If you never make a Sequence that doesn't need editing or debugging, you aren't making many Sequences. Here are a few tricks to subduing the recalcitrant Sequence.

Finding your QuicKey in the management window. If you have a reasonably large keyset, one of the maddening properties of QUICKEYS is that whenever you open the management window, the QuicKeys window displays the beginning portion of the keyset.

So if you are in a heavy editing session on a QuicKey, you often have to scroll through your list of QuicKeys to open the right one. In some future version of QUICKEYS, we hope that CE will include a feature that opens to the editing window of the last QuicKey played. But for now, there are two ways to try to massage QUICKEYS so that your target QuicKey appears in the top screen of the management window, when it opens.

- **Use the Filter bar.** If you are editing a Sequence QuicKey, choose the Sequence icon on the Filter bar. This will probably substantially reduce the number of QuicKeys displayed. The management window retains the Filter bar settings when it closes, so your target QuicKey might show up in the top screen.
- **Rename or rekey your QuicKey.** If the first trick doesn't work, change the name or keystroke of your QuicKey so it will fall in the top screen. Remember, you can use the Sort bar to choose how your QuicKeys are sorted. Now as soon as the management window opens, you can immediately double-click to edit it.

Debugging 101—Tricks. Here are a couple of little tricks to help debug a Sequence.

- **Nip it in the bug.** If you are creating a long Sequence, it is sometimes best to build from a central core, testing as you go. This allows you to become aware of bugs after only a few additions to the Sequence, so you have a good idea of where the problem is. This is the "debug as you build" method.
- **Listen to it.** If a Sequence gets hung up, but you're not sure exactly where, you can sprinkle a few Sound QuicKeys at various points in the Sequence. If each

Sound QuicKey is set to a different sound, you'll quickly hear the silence, and know where things ran aground.

Debugging 201—The Pause. Often a Sequence goes awry because QUICKEYS tries to execute the next step in a Sequence before the active application is ready for it. You may need to add a Pause step. The key here is to remember Don Brown's philosophy of QUICKEYS: the better you use QUICKEYS, the better you know your computer, the better you use QUICKEYS. So first try to figure out what the heck your application and QUICKEYS could be fighting about. Then try Pause.

- Add Pauses one at a time, until you get things rolling. Often, these pauses can be one second or less in length, but sometimes applications require much longer times to come to their senses.
- When things start working again, you can assume the last Pause added is *probably* the only Pause step you need.
- Go back and get rid of all the extraneous Pauses.
- Reduce the time on your necessary Pause step to a workable minimum. But remember: the time it takes an application to crunch something varies, so allow for worst-case scenarios.
- See if it makes sense to replace your hard Pause with Wait, WindowWait, MenuWait, or CursorWait. All these can be more adaptable than a straight Pause step.

QuicKey Strategies

It's get-a-life, sink-or-swim, and contend-with-the-real-world time. You've reached the point where our brilliant QUICKEYS theory goes face-to-face with the realities of your computing environment. In this chapter, we test the true temper of QUICKEYS—we teach you how to manage the program so it works best for you.

There are all kinds of QuicKeys. A brief review of our keysets reveals more QuicKeys resident on our Macs than there are subspecies of birds in the Galápagos Islands. We've got everything from often-utilized QuicKeys, like the one that switches between open applications, to specific QuicKey Sequences we use to perform obscure jobs infrequently (or maybe only once). How do we organize our QuicKeys in keysets, and how do we keep track of them all?

To get the most use out of QUICKEYS, it is essential to have resident QuicKeys in appropriate keysets. Fumbling around and trying to remember the name of a macro you created to save time is counterproductive. This is especially true in net-worked offices. Offices with multiple Macs often evolve keysets and standardize them between machines.

The different strategies employed to keep track of QuicKey macros are as varied as the different types of QuicKeys. Some people use QUICKEYS sporadically, and create their invoking keystrokes arbitrarily. Others have hundreds of QuicKeys and employ a rigid nomenclature strategy (a must in bossing such a large gang of little programs). To fulfill the promise of the QUICKEYS program, you need a system which optimizes your use of it—making your overall computing environment easier to work with and more powerful.

The bottom-line questions are pretty simple.

- What QuicKeys do I need in my computing environment?
- What scheme should I use to make their keystrokes memorizable and easy to use?

This chapter investigates the first of these two questions. The next chapter, *Keystroke Strategies,* deals with the second. It turns out that these two issues are inherently linked—the types of QuicKeys you use often suggest the keystroke strategy with which you need to invoke them.

Here a QuicKey There a QuicKey

Q: What QuicKeys do I need?

A: What do you do?

A designer whose computer is networked with a hundred others uses many different QuicKeys from an author who pounds away on a single Mac. A programmer who routinely juggles fifteen applications uses many different QuicKeys from a worker bee who enters data into one. It all seems like hugger-mugger. Should we just throw planning to the wind, make up QuicKeys as we need them, name their invoking keystrokes arbitrarily, and try to keep them all in our heads? There's a simple answer: No.

We need a plan, a system, a paradigm, something to help us remember the QuicKeys we've got. Luckily, no matter what we do on the Mac, just about any QuicKey we use can be categorized as a member of a small group of functional categories. You'll probably include representatives of each of these categories in your QuicKeys quiver.

A Rough Categorization of Our QuicKeys

Here's what our QuicKeys do. In the next chapter, *Keystroke Strategies,* we discuss the actual keystrokes and keysets that we use. Note that these categories primarily consist of Universal Keyset QuicKeys. Only the last group—those QuicKeys that perform application-specific tasks—are QuicKeys that usually reside in application keysets (see Table 14-1).

Table 14-1
What our QuicKeys do

QuicKeys that:	Should go in these keysets:
Open things	
Open applications	Universal
Open documents	Universal/application
Open utility programs and desk accessories	Universal
Move to folders	Universal/application
Adjust and control things	
Adjust and control the Mac	Universal
Adjust and control windows	Universal
Press standard buttons	Universal
Change printers	Universal
Control the QUICKEYS program	Universal
Standardize shortcuts between programs	Universal/application
Perform application-specific tasks	
Press and choose controls and commands in specific applications	Application
Perform tasks in specific applications	Application
Perform tasks between applications	Application

QuicKeys That Open Things

We move around a lot through the folders and files on our computers, opening and closing lots of applications. Opening files and applications doesn't take too long, but we find ourselves doing the same things over and over again. QUICKEYS reduces these repetitive tasks to a keystroke.

Open applications. Steve and Don each have about ten applications that they use enough to warrant dedicating QuicKeys to open them. Because we want to be able to open these applications from just about any other application, we need these QuicKeys in the Universal Keyset.

Open documents. We find ourselves working on specific documents for fairly extensive periods of time. These working documents gradually change—old ones are retired and new ones take their place. We keep these in the Universal Keyset unless we have so many that we don't want to dedicate Universal keystrokes to them. They also reside in the application's keyset, if the document must be opened from within the application (for instance, with a TIFF file that was created with another program).

Open utility programs and desk accessories. You might just want to consider these as applications, especially if you use System 7. The main reason we categorize them differently is that it helps our keystroke differentiation in the busy Universal Keyset.

Move to folders. We can't think of anyone who has so few files and applications that she'd have a QuicKey to open each one of them. We have oft-visited and favorite folders to which we navigate quickly within Open and Save dialog boxes. Generally, the Universal Keyset is the place for these folder-invoking QuicKeys, although special circumstances might suggest an application keyset instead.

QuicKeys That Adjust and Control Things

We leave some adjustments on our Systems the same most of the time; others, we muck around with constantly.

Adjust and control the Mac. This category is really made up of two areas: basic Control Panel adjustments such as sound level and monitor color depth, and general housekeeping control like shutting down, dragging a file to the trash, and emptying the trash. These are usually Universal Keyset items. A QuicKey that empties the trash might be best located in the Finder's keyset, to act as a fail-safe mechanism against accidental activation.

Change printers. QuicKeys that change printers could probably also go in the previous category, but we think of them as being special enough to warrant their own listing. Besides, if you only have one printer, you don't need to worry at all about these Universal Keyset QuicKeys.

Adjust and control windows. Open, Close, Page up, Page down, and Zoom window are some of these kinds of QuicKeys. These are generally Universal Keyset items, although there may be a sprinkling of application-specific addenda to standardize all these window controls between applications (see below).

Press standard buttons. Why use a mouse to press those buttons in dialog boxes? You can use DialogKeys (which comes with your QUICKEYS program), or you can make a number of Universal Keyset Button QuicKeys that will press the most common buttons automatically.

QuicKeys That Control the QuicKeys Program

QUICKEYS has various controls that most of us want available at a keystroke. Toggling QUICKEYS on and off is a must, as is a QuicKey that opens the program (by displaying the management window). Don also has QuicKeys to start and stop Sequence recording, to start and stop Real Time recording, to pause a Sequence playback, and to create a File QuicKey.

QuicKeys That Standardize Shortcuts Between Programs

This is one of the best uses for QUICKEYS. Standardizing shortcuts between applications takes a fundamental Mac concept—Mac application-interface universality—and irons out any wrinkles that develop when theory collides with the real world. This is mostly menu-item stuff: making sure that all your applications save with with the "standard" Command-S, or setting up a non-standard menu shortcut, such as one for "Save As." Or it could be making the Page up key do its thing in all applications.

These standardization QuicKeys mostly live in the Universal Keyset, but the odd one works best in an application keyset. For example, if all of your applications (except for one) use Command-S for Save, you should put a Menu QuicKey in the rogue application's keyset to choose "Save" from its File menu with Command-S. It is more reliable to ask only one program to address QUICKEYS rather than to ask all of them.

Application-specific QuicKeys

Here's the nitty-gritty of QuicKeys. Generally, there are two types of QuicKeys that perform application-specific tasks. There are those set up permanently (for example, the QuicKey that invokes the Word Count menu item, and that hits the Count button), and those that we build for a specific, transitory task. Not surprisingly, these QuicKeys reside in application-specific keysets.

Press and choose controls and commands in specific applications. Did your application's designer leave out some keystroke shortcuts you'd love to have? Did she include some shortcuts that don't fit into your keystroke scheme? These are your permanent QuicKey fixes.

Perform tasks in specific applications. Some of these QuicKeys are permanent, some short-lived. Often they are Sequences that contain at least one command step. Want a QuicKey that sets a specific text wrap distance in PageMaker? Want one that enters specific cell note text in Excel? This is the QuicKey for you.

Perform custom tasks between applications. Some of the most powerful QuicKeys are those that mediate between programs. For example, Steve made a Sequence that took a paragraph from Word, opened PageMaker, pasted the paragraph, went back to Word and grabbed the next paragraph, went back to PageMaker, went to the top of the next page, pasted the paragraph, and so on. Although there are multiple applications involved, it is best to keep these QuicKeys in the keyset of the application in which the first function is performed.

Customize QuicKeys to Your Computing Environment

How do you go about building a QUICKEYS system? You can build a system logically, from the ground up: map out your needs, create a foundation of the basic Universal QuicKeys and application-specific QuicKeys you know you require, and then add more as your need for them becomes apparent. Or you can be like the rest of us, and make QuicKeys in a frenzied, haphazard manner like a chicken pecking for corn grits.

But there's a method to the chicken's madness and so should there be a method to our willy-nilly approach. Order becomes important when you group your QuicKeys together on the keyboard—that's the keystrokes strategy concept, which we discuss next.

Keystroke Strategies

Remember when you first used a Mac? You were probably a total vermin abuser like the rest of us. If you wanted to open a new file, you drove your little mouse up to the File menu and chose "Open." If you wanted to copy something, you made that poor rodent grab Copy from the Edit menu. Most of the time your keyboard was for entering data, and your mouse was for issuing commands.

Then you realized that you could use the keystroke shortcuts for these commands. Command-O and Command-C went through the keyboard, and the mouse got a vacation.

The keystrokes you used were mostly preset—they were hard-coded into your System and applications. If you're like us, you figured these keystrokes were determined in long sessions between programming wizards and young execs with MBAs and doctorates in Computing Science. In raucous meetings, they must have thrown reams of studies on primate behavior, human-machine interaction, and the medical aspects of keyboard and mouse design at each other, in their Herculean labors to develop the perfect keystroke system. And it was all lorded over by the gods on Olympus (read: Apple), who threw the Law of the Human Interface Guidelines down from the mountain top.

Now you can throw all that out the window. Welcome to the acme of the shortcut mountain. The keystrokes are yours.

Choosing Keystrokes

How a QuicKey is used and what keystrokes invoke it should be complementary. It eases memorization if you standardize each type's keystrokes (group them on the keyboard). For example, you don't want to have Control-W open Microsoft Word, and Control-Option-F8 open PageMaker. First you need to categorize your QuicKeys, then figure out the best way to invoke them, to help you remember where they are.

Okay, okay. If you're the kind of person who has only a few QuicKeys, and you take an oath that you'll never use any more, you can invoke them nearly arbitrarily; there'll be few enough that you'll probably remember them all. But if you're like the rest of us, it's impossible to use just one, so the best policy is to start out with a plan. That plan involves the marriage of your QuicKeys and your keyboard.

Your Keyboard Just to review, there are two types of keys on your keyboard: character keys and modifier keys. The character keys (letters, numbers, Tab, Delete, Page up, and so on) are those keys that usually do something when you press them; the modifier keys (Control, Command, Shift, Option) must be pressed in conjunction with a character key for something to happen. Caps lock is a modifier key which most applications don't use. QUICKEYS doesn't use it, so it is essentially a dead key in this discussion.

There are a bunch of different Mac keyboards. Don's first Mac keyboard (on his 128K Mac) had no keypad, no Control key, and no function keys. Don's current extended keyboard has 44 additional character keys (function keys, arrow keys, keypad keys, and so on), plus a Control key. It's a totally different environment. The Control key is so important that Steve believes it is a shoe-in for the Mac features Hall of Fame. Luckily, Apple has recognized its value, and so only a few of you out there have Macs that lack this key. But next we'll discuss you have-nots.

An aside to the basic keyboard folk. We wish that everyone who crosses a Mac with QUICKEYS also has the benefit of an extended keyboard. Basic keyboards (those that lack the Control key, function keys and so forth) severely limit the number of available keystroke combinations for QuicKeys, in two ways.

- **Keystroke combinations.** It's difficult (and a waste of time) to quantify this handicap exactly, but here's a rough sketch: Microsoft Word, the Mac application

Figure 15-1
The basic Mac
keyboard

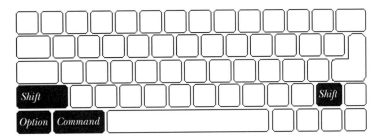

that probably hogs the most keystroke shortcuts, leaves around 1,055 combinations for you to play with when you have an extended keyboard. That number shrinks to about 129 for a basic keyboard—only 12 percent of 1,055. Still, 129 keystrokes seems like a lot of QuicKeys, except for the following.

- **Appropriateness.** You do not want to be a slave to your keystroke possibilities. You need a large, varied potential-keystroke pool to choose from, so you can define keystrokes that are easy to remember. Your keystroke paradigm might be based on geography (where the key is located), modifier combination, or something else. Limiting the number of keystroke combinations *severely* limits your ability to exploit different keystroke grouping schemes.

If you have a basic keyboard, you cannot fully utilize much of the information in the rest of this chapter. If you also have a large number of QuicKeys, you can use some of the keystroke-layout strategies we suggest, but you won't be able to exploit them fully. You may have to rely on visual devices (templates, keypad stick-ons, and so forth) to remember your invoking keystrokes (see Chapter 16, *Mechanical Memory Assist*).

Extended keyboards. Many folks who have extended keyboards don't press some of their keys very often. How many programs use the Esc (escape) key? How many support Page up, Scroll lock, and Delete? How many of your applications treat the keypad numbers differently from the standard keyboard numbers? Some of the more sophisticated applications do, sure, but do all of them? QuicKeys gives you the ability to unlock the potential keystroke combinations that lie dormant in your extended keyboard. And you can exploit this large number of combinations so that it is particularly advantageous to your setup.

Keystroke Considerations

There are some basic standards that good keystrokes meet.

They must be easy to remember. Once you get started you won't stop. You are going to have an abundance of QuicKeys if you understand how beneficial the program is, and if you spend a lot of time with your computer. Even with the best visual-aid devices in the world, you want to be able to recall your QuicKeys instantly.

They must acknowledge any keystroke shortcuts in your System and applications. You don't want to name a QuicKey "Command-S" unless it has something very fundamental to do with saving a file. Every application has keystroke shortcuts, and many of these shortcuts follow a protocol that has been developed for the Mac. You don't want to arbitrarily map over any of these with QuicKeys keystrokes, and you can take advantage of the already-laid foundation to suggest keystrokes for your QuicKeys.

They (usually) must be easy to use. Pressing Control-Option-M is relatively easy. Pressing Command-Control-Shift-Page up is relatively difficult. The ease of pressing a keystroke should be a consideration in making that keystroke part of your QuicKeys set.

Remember Mnemonics

We're experts at this. Don has been accused of not being able to remember his own name, and if his mother hadn't sewn it onto his clothes when he went to camp, he probably wouldn't have. So he's pursued memory aids with some vigor. Mnemonics are strategies that help you remember things. In theory, there can be a whole bunch of different mnemonic devices that can trigger memory, and we're sure that there are some we haven't tried at one time or another for our QuicKeys, but we've tried out a lot. We've evolved a synthesis of different keystroke strategies that use the following mnemonic devices.

The alphabet. The alphabet is an obvious choice. That's why Command-S saves, and Command-O opens. We think about our applications and utilities by name, so using the alphabet keys to represent them makes sense. So it's P for PageMaker, X for Excel, Q for QuicKeys, F for Freehand, D for DiskTop, and so on.

Of course, the problem with the alphabet is that some letters are more popular than others. P, Q, and S seem to be the fashion among whoever thinks up application names. This inherent problem with alphabet-based systems can be mitigated by a careful application of modifier keys.

Key names (and connotations). Heck, they're written right on them! No one in her right mind is going to assign the Page down key to the Line up Mousie QuicKey. Let these keys express themselves, follow their bliss, be what they want to be! These keys, at least in a minimally-modified manner, will help you remember what they are—if you play to their strengths. Help, Page up, Page down, Delete, and so on, can also be employed to trigger those tasks that can be easily associated with them in memory. For example, we use Delete plus some modifiers to shut down our Macs.

For some reason our Apple extended keyboards have "Undo," "Cut," "Copy," and "Paste" printed under the function keys F1 through F4. We don't what overworked design team came up with this one, and we don't know of any applications (except for QUICKEYS' More Universal Keyset) that support it. And why should they? It's arbitrary. Ignore it.

Geography. Location, location, location! Grouping like-minded QuicKeys together can be a great memory aid and make access very rapid. It can also be a memory-boggler to have your QuicKeys all jammed together like 1950s tract houses. In this case, it is usually advisable to have some additional stimulus to trigger your memory (see Chapter 16, *Mechanical Memory Assist*).

If you place complementary QuicKeys together (for example, Grab Ease, Paste Ease, and Type Ease), your fingers are better able to hit the successive keystrokes because they have recently hit one in the same area.

One good key in an area can influence others around it. Don uses Control-Option-Delete to shut down his Mac. He uses it at least once a day; it's his "let's get the hell out of here" keystroke. Because that connection is so strong in his mind, he's tied Control-Option-= to his his Restart QuicKey. The Equals (=) key doesn't seem to correspond to the restart function at all, but because it's adjacent to Delete, it's very easy to remember.

That's probably also the source of the standard Command-Option-. (period) QuicKey for toggling QuicKeys on and off. Command-. (period) is the key to make things stop happening on the Mac (like Control-C on IBM machines), so Command-Option-. (period) is a natural keystroke (for some people) to stop QuicKeys.

Modifiers. Using the same modifiers for the same class of QuicKeys helps keep things nicely pigeonholed, and can therefore jog the memory. Don uses specific modifier combinations to correspond to certain emotional and functional qualities of his QuicKeys. For example, his Control-Option-Command combinations connote "power"; he uses it for QuicKeys that he wants to think about before using. Control-character key signifies "application." His Control-Option-character key means "utility," and so on. We discuss this strategy in more detail in "Putting it all Together," below.

Accepted (albeit sometimes bizarre) practice. One aspect of memory is that once you've got it and you use it, it doesn't easily disappear. We could make up a very illogical, anti-mnemonic system, and you would probably memorize it if you used it repeatedly. But luckily, we don't have to invent an illogical system because someone (CE Software) already has. If you based your Universal Keyset on the default keysets that CE Software supplies as part of their package, you started out on the wrong foot.

When you install QUICKEYS for the first time, you're supplied with a little Universal Keyset (14 QuicKeys). There is also a More Universal Keyset (42 QuicKeys), which you can open to transfer additional QuicKeys. Many of the QuicKeys in these keysets are appropriate to have, but their keystrokes often leave something to be desired (see Table 15-1).

Table 15-1
Automatically Loaded
Universal QuicKeys

F1	Command-Z
F2	Command-X
F3	Command-C
F4	Command-V
Home	Home
End	End
Page up	Page up
Page down	Page down
Command-Option-Return	QuicKeys 2
Command-Option-spacebar	QuickReference Card
Command-Option-.	Toggle QuicKeys on and off
Command-Option-P	Pause
Command-Option-R	Start/Stop Real Time
Command-Option-S	Start/Stop Sequence

There are a few basic problems with the keystrokes in this keyset. Some of the keystrokes are identical to shortcuts in some applications, rendering the application's keystrokes useless. Some of them are not based on any mnemonic system. For example, what connection is there between the Spacebar and the QuickReference Card, or Return and the QUICKEYS management window? However, Steve still uses the latter because that's what he's always used, he's comfortable with it, and (in a final defense of this peculiar behavior) he says, "That's the way it came."

So we can try to be a Henry Higgins to your Eliza and clean up your act, but if you are comfortable with what you already use, you might be better off starting there, and merely adapting some aspects of our *incredibly more logical* approach.

Complements Applications and Accepted Protocols

Your QuicKey keystrokes can conflict with or complement those shortcut keystrokes already extant in most applications.

Keystroke Conflicts. What if your application uses the Command-Option-Return shortcut to make a new paragraph, but leave the cursor at the end of the old one (as Microsoft Word does)? What if your Universal Keyset has a QuicKey that uses Command-Option-Return to invoke the QUICKEYS management window? The Universal Keyset takes precedence over the application's shortcut, so you will get the management window. What if you now make an application-specific QuicKey that uses that same Command-Option-Return to do something else (for example, to enter three Returns)? The QuicKey from the application keyset takes precedence. Here's the hierarchy of keystrokes.

- The application keyset takes precedence over the Universal Keyset.
- The Universal Keyset takes precedence over the application's built-in shortcuts.

If there are duplicate (or triplicate) invoking keystrokes, only one is played, and it will be a QuicKey. Of course you can toggle QUICKEYS off, and the current application's keystroke will then take precedence.

You must consider an application's keystrokes before you assign a keystroke to a QuicKey. You should find a complete list of an application's shortcuts in its manual, or possibly within the application itself (Microsoft Word can generate a list of its keystrokes which you can print out—it's accessible through the Commands item of the Edit menu). In some circumstances, you may *want* to map over an application's keystroke. Sometimes applications have duplicate keystrokes, so you can use one of them for a QuicKey. Or sometimes the application's shortcut is active at times different from when you want your shortcut to be active, so you can often access both functions with one keystroke.

You only have a given number of keystroke areas on your keyboard-control panel. Some of them are already taken by the application. The others you must apportion to the Universal Keyset and to the application-specific keysets.

Keystroke complements. An application's shortcut keystrokes can often suggest keystrokes for your QuicKeys. Microsoft Word, like most applications, will click a default button (double-outlined) in a dialog box if you press the Return key. Steve often uses the Change dialog box (see Figure

15-2), but unfortunately its default button is Start Search and not what he usually presses, which is Change All (or Change Selection, the alternative if you have highlighted a body of text). So Steve set up Command-Return to invoke a Button QuicKey that presses Change All, which is *his* default button. He is able to remember it because of its relation to the usual keystroke in this situation (Return).

Figure 15-2
Microsoft Word's
Change dialog box

Change			
Find What:	Quark Express		
Change To:	QuarkHPress		
☐ Whole Word ☒ Match Upper/Lowercase			
Start Search	Change	Change All	Cancel

For an even more innovative solution to this Change All problem, see Chapter 17, *QuicKeys and Word*.

Ease of Use   There are physical limitations involved in spreading your fingers out over an extended keyboard. Some keystroke combinations are just easier to hit, because they naturally fit where our fingers go. Some keystroke combinations are appropriate because they are adjacent to complementary keystrokes: once our fingers have already moved to a new spot, these likely keys are close by.

Finger stretch. Have you ever had your hands so entangled while hitting three keys that you contemplate hitting the fourth key with your nose? Some modifier combinations are naturally easy to press; others are relatively difficult. You probably know what works best for you, but we came up with our own unscientific survey (see Table 15-2).

You generally choose your often-utilized keystrokes from the easy modifier combinations. However, you can make difficult keystrokes work to your advantage by making them invoke potentially dangerous QuicKeys. For example, Don uses Shift-Option-Command-Control for experimental, temporary QuicKeys. Besides being difficult to press, thereby ensuring some safety, the difficult keystroke combination is also easy to pick out in the QuicKeys management window—which aids housekeeping tasks.

Table 15-2

Keystroke difficulty—modifiers with various keys

Higher numbers indicate more difficulty.

⋀=*Control*
⧖=*Option*
⌘ =*Command*
⇧=*Shift*

	NONE	Z	F1	CLEAR
⇧	1	2	2	2
⧖	1	2	2	2
⋀	1	2	2	2
⌘	1	2	2	2
⇧⧖	1.5	2	3	3
⇧⋀	1.5	2	3	3
⇧⌘	2	3	3	3
⧖⋀	1	2	2	2
⧖⌘	1	2	2.5	2.5
⋀⌘	2	2.5	2.5	2.5
⇧⧖⋀	2	2.5	3	3
⇧⧖⌘	2	2.5	3	3
⧖⌘⋀	1	2	2	2
⇧⧖⌘⋀	2.5	2.5	3	3

Putting It All Together

Obviously, with all of these factors influencing QuicKey inclusion and keystroke designation, developing an overall QuicKeys environment is more art than science. There is often a fair amount of trial and error, experimentation and evolution that takes place in building a QuicKeys system. In this section, we'll show you the logic of our approach, and how it evolved to meet the vagaries of our work. You can borrow from our approach, and customize it to your particular situation.

We work in an office environment in which six Macs are connected within a network that also contains four printers, two scanners, and two IBM clones. Each Mac has been customized by its operator to perform best for that individual's requirements. However, since we often work on each other's machines, we've found that standardizing certain aspects of the computing environment, especially utility applications and DAs, has substantially increased productivity.

Here's how our system works. Remember—the application shortcuts, the application keyset and the Universal Keyset all have to complement each other.

Make Up Your Universal Keyset

Our Universal Keyset contains the bulk of our QuicKeys, even though we have healthy application keysets for many different applications. The Universal Keyset is a good place to start in refining your QuicKeys environment. We can retrace the list of our QuicKey functional categories that we generated in Chapter 14, *QuicKey Strategies,* and show you what we include, where their keystrokes are, and why.

Open Applications. We like to use the alphabet to remember our application keystrokes: our application-keystroke assignments tend to be permanent, and an alphabet-based mnemonic is easy to remember. We use the Control key as the modifier of choice to open applications; it is non-conflicting and easily accessible (see Figure 15-3).

Figure 15-3
Opening applications

ResEdit 2.1	ctrl-E
Aldus FreeHand 3.0	ctrl-F
PageMaker 4.0	ctrl-M
Navigator 3.0.4	ctrl-N
Adobe Photoshop™ 1.0	ctrl-P
QuarkXPress®	ctrl-Q
StupidPaint	ctrl-S
Microsoft Word	ctrl-W
Microsoft Excel	ctrl-X

Open Documents. Because we work on books divided into chapter files, we tend to have a number of documents that we want to have easily accessible on our Macs. However, these docs are rarely permanent, and often have similar names;

therefore, an alphabet system isn't appropriate. Instead we use function keys and a template device (see Chapter 16, *Mechanical Memory Assist*) to aid in their recall. Don uses Control-Shift with function keys for opening documents. When he runs out of function key combinations with Control-Shift (which often happens), he adds Control-Command.

Open utility programs and desk accessories. We think of our utility programs and desk accessories by their names (like we think of applications), so we use Control-Option with the alphabet keys to invoke them (see Figure 15-4). If you don't have too many applications or too many of these utilities, you won't find yourself running out of appropriate invoking letters, and so you can bunch this class in with the applications, using Control as the only modifier. However, if you have as many of both categories as we do, you'll find it helps to use Control-Option. It's easy to hit, and seems appropriate because we think of utilities and DAs as specialized applications.

Some of our DA invokers are actually Sequences, because they open the DA and then press an appropriate button to get into it.

Figure 15-4
Opening utilities and desk accessories

Ask AASK	opt ctrl-A
Choose-R	opt ctrl-C
Norton Utilities	opt ctrl-N
Calculator+	opt ctrl-[=]
TouchBASE	opt ctrl-B
DiskTop	opt ctrl-D
Fast Find	opt ctrl-F
GOfer™ 2.0	opt ctrl-G
BigThesaurus™	opt ctrl-I
KeyFinder	opt ctrl-K
LaserStatus	opt ctrl-L

Move to folders. Here's a QuicKey type that some people haven't discovered: the Location Extension. When you're in an Open dialog box or a Save dialog box, Location moves you to a specific folder. We'd never want to assign a File QuicKey to open each individual illustration in a book, for instance, but we often need to access the folder; hence, the value of the Location Extension.

There is some difference of opinion in our office as to the best keystroke schema for different Location QuicKeys. Don, because he relies on a template, uses Control with a function key (see Figure 15-5). Steve relies on Boomerang, a utility that includes a function very similar to Location. He invokes his folders with alphabetic keystroke schema (Command-M for his Macworld folder, Command-T for his Temp folder, and so on). Boomerang works within Open dialog boxes and Save dialog boxes, so the keystrokes are only active while the dialog box is open. If you tend to think of your folders by name, and you don't have too many of them, you could use a similar alphabetic keystroke scheme in QuicKeys, perhaps employing Control-Option-Shift as your modifiers.

Figure 15-5
Accessing folders

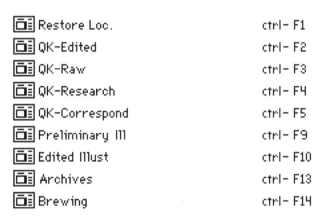

Restore Loc.	ctrl- F1
QK-Edited	ctrl- F2
QK-Raw	ctrl- F3
QK-Research	ctrl- F4
QK-Correspond	ctrl- F5
Preliminary Ill	ctrl- F9
Edited Illust	ctrl- F10
Archives	ctrl- F13
Brewing	ctrl- F14

Open anything. We can't leave this group of opening QuicKeys without mentioning one of our favorites: the Transfer Extension. Transfer launches files by displaying an Open file dialog box (for more on Transfer, see Chapter 5, *Launching and Opening*). Because Transfer is not target-specific, you only need one in your Universal Keyset. Don uses F14 (Scroll lock) to invoke Transfer, because it is easy to hit and we don't need to lock the scrolling in any of our work (see Figure 15-6). Steve doesn't think this is very mnemonic (and he's right). But we have F13, F14, and F15 reserved for System-wide tasks, and F13 and F15 perform the jobs that are printed on them, leaving F14 open.

Figure 15-6
Open anything
QuicKey

★ Transfer   F14

Adjust and control the Mac. We group these geographically, using the number keys at the top of our keyboards. Such a distribution allows us to easily mark their location on our templates. We use Control-Option as the modifier combination because we associate that combination of modifiers with utilities, which is how we think of adjustments (see Figure 15-7).

The first three QuicKeys are SpeakerChanger Extensions: the first sets the level to zero, the next two toggle the speaker up and down. Then we have a third-party freeware Extension, BitDepth, which shows the bits per pixel our monitors are currently displaying. The next two QuicKeys increase or decrease the monitor's bit level, using the Screen Ease Extension. The final two are QuicKeys Specials to turn the Mac on and off. At first their keystrokes may seem a bit weird, but they are based on Shut Down being tied to the Delete key (a fairly straightforward association). The Equals key (=), adjacent to Delete, then works well for Restart.

Figure 15-7
Adjusting the Mac

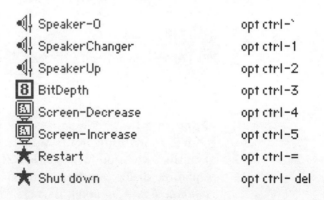

◀|⁞ Speaker-0	opt ctrl-`
◀|⁞ SpeakerChanger	opt ctrl-1
◀|⁞ SpeakerUp	opt ctrl-2
⑧ BitDepth	opt ctrl-3
▣ Screen-Decrease	opt ctrl-4
▣ Screen-Increase	opt ctrl-5
★ Restart	opt ctrl-=
★ Shut down	opt ctrl- del

Adjust and control windows. We have a large variety of window QuicKeys resident in our Universal Keyset (see Figure

15-8). Their keystrokes seem to be scattered all over the keyboard, but they actually inhabit only three areas.

Figure 15-8
Adjusting and
controlling windows

🖻	Home	home
🖻	End	end
🖻	Page up	pgup
🖻	Page down	pgdn
★	Select rear window	⌘opt- ←·
★	Select second window	⌘opt- ·→
🖻	Zoom window	opt ctrl-8
🕂	CloseZoom	opt ctrl-9
🖻	Close window	opt ctrl-0

The Page up and Page down Mousies are remapped to the correspondingly-named keys on the keyboard, as are Home and End. This serves their functional purposes, and also standardizes these functions between applications.

Zoom window and Close window use Option-Control plus numbers at the top right of the keyboard, for the same reasons we gave with the Mac adjustment QuicKeys (we think of them as utilities). Close window comes in handy sometimes, because some applications use Command-W to close a window, and some use Command-. (period). Steve uses Command-' for Close window, because it's like clicking in the upper-left corner; most applications don't use that combination.

CloseZoom is our own Mousie that clicks on the bottom-right corner of the active window (in the size box) and pulls it all the way to the top left corner, essentially shrinking the window to as small a size as it will go. The Select rear window and Select second window Specials allow you to either step through your open documents, or to toggle back and forth between the top two docs in an application.

These last two keystrokes fit snugly into the ergonomics of the Mac keyboard. It's comfortable to rest your left hand on the three lower-left corner keys (Control-Option-Command), which makes it extremely simple to press Command-Option-Right arrow to page through open docs in an application. Control-Option-Right arrow is set up to page through open applications.

Press standard buttons. We don't use these much because DialogKeys is often better, but occasionally they come in handy. Don has a bank of them—that use his utility modifiers—in his function keys (see Figure 15-9). If you want standard Button QuicKeys in your arsenal, you might want to use alphabetic keystrokes (C for Cancel, Y for Yes, and so on) with your own modifiers. And some folks swear that the Esc key (Escape) is the only key to use for a Cancel Button QuicKey.

Figure 15-9
Pressing buttons

⊙ⓚ Cancel	opt ctrl– F5
⊙ⓚ Yes	opt ctrl– F6
⊙ⓚ No	opt ctrl– F7
⊙ⓚ OK	opt ctrl– F8

Change printers. We often find ourselves switching printers, and the Choosy Extension makes it so effortless that these QuicKeys get quite a workout. Don keeps his in the function keys, where his template crib sheet jogs his memory for the less-utilized ones (see Figure 15-10). Others have found that the best way to access QuicKeys like this is by including them on the QuicKeys menu.

Figure 15-10
Changing printers

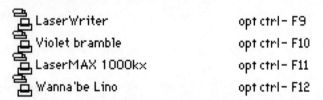

LaserWriter	opt ctrl– F9
Violet bramble	opt ctrl– F10
LaserMAX 1000kx	opt ctrl– F11
Wanna'be Lino	opt ctrl– F12

Control the QuicKeys program. We probably have more control QuicKeys than most people, but they get used a lot (see Figure 15-11). Their keystrokes break down into three areas.
- Function keys with the Control-Command-Option modifier that Don thinks of as his power modifier.
- The Pause QuicKey, which "unpauses" Sequences. We like to be able to invoke it quickly, so we use the F15 key, which has "pause" written on it.
- The other three Specials are variations on the Q key. Toggle QuicKeys on/off uses the power modifier combination because you don't want to invoke it thoughtlessly.

Figure 15-11
Controlling QUICKEYS

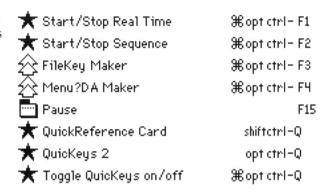

★	Start/Stop Real Time	⌘opt ctrl‑ F1
★	Start/Stop Sequence	⌘opt ctrl‑ F2
⬘	FileKey Maker	⌘opt ctrl‑ F3
⬘	Menu?DA Maker	⌘opt ctrl‑ F4
▭	Pause	F15
★	QuickReference Card	shift ctrl‑Q
★	QuicKeys 2	opt ctrl‑Q
★	Toggle QuicKeys on/off	⌘opt ctrl‑Q

A note about the QuickReference Card: we don't invoke it except when we want to puzzle over it. But some folks actually use it for its intended purpose—invoking QuicKeys—especially if they have a bushel of QuicKeys that they don't use often enough to remember their keystrokes. Since the QuicKeys on the card are "hot," you are supposed to use the QuickReference Card as an access control panel: you can invoke individual QuicKeys by clicking on them. If you often access your QuicKeys using the QuickReference Card, you will probably want to assign an easily accessible keystroke (like F14) to the QuickReference Card; or, if you use Control-Option-Q for the management window, Control-Option-R might be right for the QuickReference Card.

Standardize shortcuts between programs. This is a potpourri, because it is completely dependent on the vagaries of various programs. The category is also redundant with other categories mentioned in this section; therefore, many of the QuicKeys we list here have been seen before. Nevertheless, these QuicKeys are useful—they sweetly mollify your computing environment, taking off some of the rough edges left by the programmers (see Figure 15-12).

Page up and Page down are not supported in all applications. By assigning these Mousies to the extended keyboard keys of the same name, you guarantee the function in any application (like the QUICKEYS management window). Steve often applies Page up and Page down QuicKeys to the 9 and 3 keys on his numeric keypad, mimicking their operation in Microsoft Word on the IBM. The other standardizations consist of menu items that we employ in many programs. By using Shift-Control with an appropriate alphabetic key, we are able to recall them instantly.

The Delete forward Sequence makes your Delete forward key do what is supposed to do—in most applications. It consists of two steps: move the cursor one character to the right, then hit Delete. If you have any applications that support this feature internally (like Microsoft Word) and you want to let it operate, you can put an Alias QuicKey in the application-specific keyset that maps the Delete forward key to the Delete forward key. This preempts the Universal Keyset Sequence from occurring in that particular application.

Figure 15-12
Standardizers

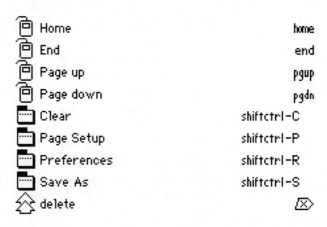

Make Up Your Application Keysets

Our application keysets are not overflowing, but the QuicKeys inside them are customized to make their applications zing. You'll find good, workhorse QuicKeys in the chapters dealing with specific applications, so we'll just provide a strategic overview here.

Press and choose controls and commands in specific applications. How do you use the application? Where do you find yourself using the mouse repeatedly? Where do you perform the same actions over and over again? These are the places for QuicKeys. See the chapters on specific applications for some good examples of this category. Using those examples as a guide, customize your applications to your work.

Set up your keystrokes to minimize hand movement. For example, working with Navigator (a communication program for CompuServe) involves a lot of screen scrolling and single-action user-defined actions. Most of our navigating through Navigator is done with our keypad; the right hand sits on it, and the right arm hardly moves through an entire session.

Perform tasks in specific applications. Most applications have tasks that beg to be performed by QuicKeys. Here's a representative example: when writing in Microsoft Word, we use many styles that are critical to our entire production process. Invoking a style in Word is done by choosing it from a pull-down menu in the ruler (awkward, especially if you have more than 40 styles, as we often do), or by pressing Command-Shift-S and then typing the style's name or its shortcut name, then pressing Return (a multi-step process guaranteed to speed the development of carpal tunnel syndrome). Don sets up his important styles on his function keys, and he reserves a few to invoke some glossary items (another multi-step process in Word). When the cursor is in the paragraph he wants to restyle, he punches the appropriate function key, and it's done.

If you work on multiple projects in one application, you can keep their respective QuicKeys in different keysets. Give the specialized keysets obvious names like "Word-QuicKeys," "Word-ComputerHealth," and "Word-DTPSurvivalGuide." When you start working with a particular project, you can open the appropriate specialized keyset, and copy its QuicKeys into your basic Word keyset. If your basic Word keyset contains any specialized QuicKeys from the most recent project, these can be deleted.

Another way to handle this is tricky, and easy to mess up: have all your project keysets named identically to the standard application keyset. These project keysets should contain both the standard application QuicKeys, and the project-specific QuicKeys. Keep each project keyset in a separate folder, to identify it. When you switch projects, remove the active application keyset from the QuicKeys folder, place it in an identifying folder, and replace it with the new project keyset. QuicKeys recognizes the application keyset by its name and location, so it will think it is the right one.

There are some specialized long Sequences (that we perform occasionally) that reside in application keysets. These can be big processing engines that search through a document, copy text, paste it in another doc, and then repeat.

Since we use these infrequently, we keep track of them with the Comments box via the QUICKEYS management window. Often these long Sequences are dangerous, so we invoke them with the Control-Command-Option modifier combination that signals, "Pay attention." If the Sequences are temporary, we add the Shift modifier to the combination which gives us the four-modifier "Hey, this is only temporary" classification.

Perform tasks between applications. These QuicKeys are often long Sequences that move text or graphics from one application to another, manipulate them, and then move them back again. They should usually reside in the keyset of the originating application. Treat them like the long Sequences described in the last section, and don't forget to use the Comments box to keep track of what they do.

Miscellaneous tasks. Here are a few screwball QuicKeys we couldn't live without (see Figure 15-13). Often, when you type on an extended keyboard, your right-hand pinky overshoots Delete and lands on Help, making some programs spin into Help mode. So we've mapped Delete to the Help key, giving us two keys that perform the Delete function (Delete and Help). We get the Help function through Command-Help.

Figure 15-13
Miscellaneous-task
QuicKeys

del		help
help		⌘-help
Trash It		⌘ opt ctrl-T
EMPTY TRASH		⌘ opt ctrl-E

Trash It is a Click QuicKey that lives in the Finder Keyset, and drags whatever is under the cursor to the trash. Don uses the last QuicKey, Empty Trash, to switch to the Finder and empty the trash, using the Special menu. Steve doesn't like emptying the trash without a more rigorous fail-safe mechanism, so his Empty trash Menu QuicKey is in the Finder keyset: you must be in the Finder for it to work, but he uses a simple Command-T, so it's pretty dangerous in its own right.

Mechanical Memory Assist

CHAPTER
16

This book would not be complete without a brief survey of the various types of mechanical memory assistance available to keep track of your QuicKeys. There are the templates that are supplied with your QuicKeys package, and additional third-party (or do-it-yourself!) keyboard enhancements available.

Template Printer

The Template Printer application that comes with QuicKeys really does do more than provide entertainment (see Chapter 2, *The Old Kit Bag*). The templates produced may be of some help to you, but they aren't the final word in QuicKeys memory-aid devices. Perhaps their biggest weakness is their difficulty in discriminating between modifier combinations using character formatting. The template is more effective if you keep the names of your QuicKeys short and descriptive.

We think there are two good ways to use Template Printer.

- Print out your keyboard template at a 400% enlargement on a laser printer. Then cut the margins off the pages and glue them all to a piece of board (like foamcore), creating a giant wall chart of your QuicKeys.
- Use the Wrap-around Extended Keyboard feature, and cut out the template that circumscribes your function keys. This template also includes notations for the top row of the lower keyboard keys—making these keys more attractive for QuicKey keystrokes.

Keyboard Enhancements

Here's a brief rundown on a few different types of memory aids. For more information, see Appendix, *Resources*.

Multicomp Keystroke Catalog

You may have received a flyer advertising this device in your QUICKEYS package. It includes the F-key Flipbook: long, thin, plastic pages—hinged at the top—for the top of your keyboard. Also supplied are two fine-line permanent markers, and an eraser that proves they're not so permanent after all.

What we like about the Flipbook is its choice of materials—they're perfectly suited for the job. The permanent inks don't smear, the plastic pages are easy to read, and the eraser expunges unwanted entries without marring the plastic surface.

What we don't like about the Flipbook is that its design doesn't really suit our computing environment. Don adapted his Flipbook to suit his own methods. He rarely flips the pages: the top page is reconfigured to allow notation of both his Universal Keyset's and Microsoft Word keyset's activating function keys. And he refers to it repeatedly, so maybe it isn't so bad, after all.

If you have extensive keysets for two or more applications, the Flipbook is probably ideal for your purposes. And you don't have to stop with the two ink colors that Multicomp supplies; you can pick up more pens from most stationery stores, for further differentiation between keystrokes.

Hooleon

Hooleon Corporation in Cornville, Arizona manufactures a passel of different keyboard-enhancement devices. Unfortunately, they are much more IBM- than Mac-oriented. Their on-the-shelf Mac arsenal include do-it-yourself keyboard labels and Dvorak keyboard labels. They also stress their custom work: imprinted snap-caps, printed keyboard labels, and the like, which might come in handy in a mega-Mac office that uses many standardized QuicKeys.

The Frugal QuicKey

If you've got the tools, some motivation, and a few hours, you can create a couple of spiffy enhancement devices yourself.

Wrap-around plastic template for the extended keyboard. Print out the function key wrap-around template, using the Template Printer. Get an Exacto knife, a metal ruler, a piece of acetate, a couple of fine-line permanent markers (in various colors), and an eraser. Oh yeah, and maybe some very thin chart tape. Anything you don't have is available at a good stationery store.

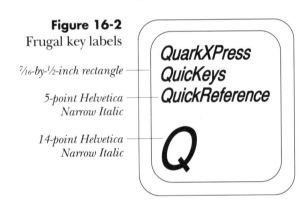

Figure 16-1
Frugal function
key template

Put the acetate over the template, and cut the acetate to conform (don't forget to cut out the long holes for the function key groups). Then use the chart tape to divide the top of your keyboard into five (or so) horizontal sections. Chuck the paper template into the alternate universe, place the acetate on the keyboard, write your most popular modifier combinations on the left and right, and then fill in your QuicKeys.

Your own keyboard labels. If you've got a steady hand, you can make your own keyboard labels with a drawing application, a laser printer, and some laser-compatible label (stickyback) paper. We'd use sheets that are already die-cut to the correct dimension ($\frac{7}{16}$ by $\frac{1}{2}$ inch) but we can't find them. As it is, we use uncut label paper and cut the little labels out. But first we cover the printed area with wide pieces of transparent tape, to protect the labels from our greasy fingers. Just set up your artwork as shown in Figure 16-2. We've found that Helvetica Narrow is the most pleasing font (it matches the type that's already on the Mac keyboard). The 5-point QuicKey names are tiny, but we can read them. Each of the three vertical positions corresponds to a different modifier combination. We use Control at the top, Control-Option in the middle, and Shift-Control at the bottom.

Figure 16-2
Frugal key labels

$\frac{7}{16}$-by-$\frac{1}{2}$-inch rectangle

*5-point Helvetica
Narrow Italic*

*14-point Helvetica
Narrow Italic*

QuicKeys and Word

CHAPTER

17

Microsoft Word has so many shortcuts, it might seem that to add more would be gilding the lily. And besides that, Word has its own built-in capability to assign keystrokes to commands and to add items to its menus, so what does it need QuicKeys for? The answer is that there are plenty of situations in Word where QuicKeys are indispensable. You can also use QuicKeys to duplicate some of Word's more popular shortcuts in other programs—standardizing these shortcuts throughout your computing environment.

You might want to change some of the Word QuicKeys discussed below (style choosers, glossary automators, and so on) from job to job. A good strategy to handle this is to reserve certain keystroke combinations for designation on a job-by-job basis. Store each job's QuicKeys in their own keyset (Word-QuicKeys Book or Word-DTP Survival Guide, for example), and just copy them to the mother keyset when you begin that job.

Choosing Styles

We work with different styles when we are putting a book together; styles are integral to our whole production process, so using them accurately is a must. Word's methods of changing styles—either choosing the style name from a menu, or pressing Shift-Command-S, typing the first few letters of the style name, and then pressing Return—are both too awkward for the high-pitched, wildly competitive, mega-post-deadline environment we work in.

You can easily assign your popular styles to keystrokes with a simple QuicKeys Sequence (see Figure 17-1). The first and the last steps of the Sequence are the same for all of these QuicKeys; the middle step changes to reflect the name of the style you want to choose. So you can create one of these Sequences (use the Literal button in the Sequence editor), copy it, paste a number of them into the same keyset in the QUICKEYS management window, and then just redefine the middle step. Give each one a different name and invoking keystroke, and you have a complete set.

Figure 17-1
Sequence for
changing to Style 1

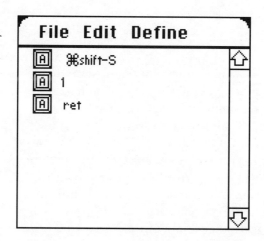

For our projects, we usually assign about four or five styles (out of around 40) to QuicKeys. Don likes to use non-modified function keys to invoke them. Just make sure your cursor is in the paragraph you want to style, press the QuicKey keystroke, and the style changes nearly instantaneously. We enter the other 35 styles in the old-fashioned way, but luckily they don't come up too often. If one did, we'd build a QuicKey shortcut for it, too.

Don't overlook the advantages of this quick restyling capability for production situations. If your writers don't style their copy (or if they style it incorrectly), you can take their files and process them on a Mac that has these style QuicKeys loaded. You can zip through the documents, restyling paragraphs with a keystroke as you go.

Sometimes our styles contain text entries. For example, we have a style named "Bullet," which begins with a bullet (•) followed by a tab. Including this bullet character with its style can be automated with a special glossary QuicKey. That's next.

Automating Glossary Use

You can invoke glossary items in Word in a manner similar to invoking styles: you press Command-Delete, type in the first few letters of the glossary item name, and then press Return. You can build a Sequence to assign a keystroke to a glossary entry. We have two types of these Sequences: one type just retrieves the glossary entry, and the other type modifies the glossary entry in some way.

Simple glossary items. Simple glossary items can be retrieved from the Glossary by making a Sequence of three Alias steps (see Figure 17-2). The middle step in the Sequence is the name (or first letter of the name) of the glossary item.

Figure 17-2
Sequence for retrieving glossary item Q

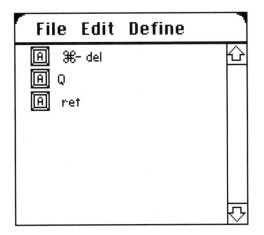

We use glossary QuicKeys for boilerplate text or commonly-used text passages. When we wrote this book, we stored the word "QUICKEYS," with its small-cap styling, as a glossary item, and invoked it with a QuicKey. The Glossary stores spaces, formatting and the like, so if you usually have a space after the glossary entry, just make that space part of the entry itself.

Modified glossary items. Sometimes you can modify or enhance the retrieval of a glossary item to benefit your particular situation. We mentioned an example at the end of the "Choosing Styles" section, above: we always begin some paragraphs with a bullet followed by a tab. So we built a QuicKey that switches to the Bullet style, and then uses a Text QuicKey to type the dingbat and the Tab (see Figure 17-3).

Figure 17-3
Changing to Style B
and typing text

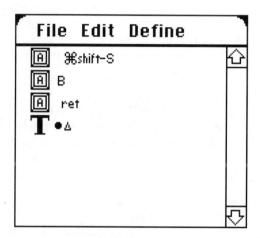

Word Count

We never write to length; *we* always let our work expand or contract to meet the needs of the material. But some of you might write to length much of the time, and so you find yourself using Word Count.

Microsoft Word's Word Count feature works just great, but you have to go through two steps to make it work: Choose "Word Count" from the Utilities menu (or use the keystroke shortcut), and then click the Count button. You can automate this operation with a two-step Sequence of a Menu QuicKey and a Button QuicKey.

Checking Out Your Open Docs

If you're like us, you open a lot of documents simultaneously in Word. If you're *really* like us, you lose track of which docs you have open. You can just press on Word's Window menu, and you'll see a list of your open docs. Or you can step through the open windows if you have the Select Rear window Special QuicKey in your Universal Keyset. But that might be too slow for some of you. Instead, especially if you are a complete anti-mouser, you can build this QuicKey. We admit it's pretty funky, but if you record it well, it works all right.

Open Docs is a Real Time QuicKey (we've included this for Don Brown) that clicks on the top of your Window menu for three seconds. We'd use a Click QuicKey to do this, but there is no way to make a Click hold down the mouse button for a predetermined length of time. The whole art of making this QuicKey (or any Real Time QuicKey) is to set up your recording mechanism and your environment for complete efficiency during the recording process. We suggest you use a Start/Stop Real Time QuicKey to initiate and terminate the recording. Have your pointer already on top of the Window menu, and let 'er rip. There's no way to edit a Real Time QuicKey, so you may have to try it a few times to get it right.

Fixing Transposed Characters

We've known a lot of different folks who have come up with this QuicKey independently of each other. That shows you how ubiquitous the need for it is.

This Sequence (see Figure 17-4) fixes common typographical errors where two characters are transposed. All you have to do is place your cursor between the two offending letters (you don't even have to click), press the invoking keystroke for the QuicKey, and watch as your typo is remade into what you intended it to be. The first step in the Sequence is the Click QuicKey, which clicks on the spot where your cursor is located (see Figure 17-5). The other steps just use Word's keyboard shortcuts to cut one letter, and paste it into its correct position.

Figure 17-4
Sequence for fixing typos

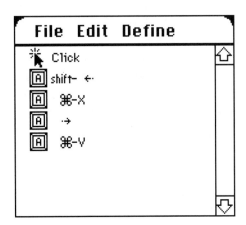

| File | Edit | Define |

Click
shift- ←·
⌘-X
→
⌘-V

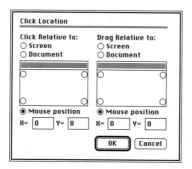

Figure 17-5
Click Location
edit dialog box

We find that we use this QuicKey often enough that we assign an unmodified function key to it, in the Word keyset.

A Smart Change All Button

In Chapter 15, *Keystroke Strategies,* we discussed a Button QuicKey that Steve created to click the Change All button in Word's Change edit dialog box—he clicks "Change All" (or "Change Selection," if he has some text selected) much more often than the default button, "Start Search" (see Figure 17-6). He's forever pressing Return and getting the next occurrence, rather than the global change he's after. So he invokes a Button QuicKey with Command-Return that clicks "Change All."

Figure 17-6
Change edit
dialog box

Change			
Find What:	Quark Express		
Change To:	QuarkHPress		
☐ **Whole Word** ☒ **Match Upper/Lowercase**			
[Start Search]	[Change]	[Change All]	[Cancel]

The problem is this: when he has text selected, the Change All button changes to read "Change Selection," so his QuicKey doesn't work. Steve solved the problem by editing the Button QuicKey so that it searches for "Change " (the word "Change," followed by a space). When he presses Command-Return, the QuicKey clicks either "Change All" or "Change Selection" in the Change dialog box.

There's another problem, though. Word has a command that gives you a new paragraph with the same style as the previous one, invoked with Command-Return. Steve's QuicKey overrides it, so when you press Command-Return and the Change dialog box isn't displayed, you just get a beep.

The solution to that takes advantage of Simon Leifer's WindowDecision Extension. First, make a Sequence like that depicted in Figure 17-7. The WindowDecision Extension is the heart of this Sequence (see Figure 17-8), which makes a decision based on the name of the active window. If the window is named "Change," the Sequence is satisfied, and so passes control to the next step (because the Pass QuicKey box is blank), in this case clicking the Change All or Change Selection button. The Fail QuicKey (if the active window is *not* named "Change") passes control to a QuicKey named "Same Style" (see Figure 17-9). The Same Style QuicKey types Command-Return, which Microsoft Word recognizes as its command to create a new paragraph with the same style as the previous one.

Figure 17-7
Change
Sequence

*Use Command-Return
as the keystroke*

Figure 17-8
The WindowDecision
edit dialog box

*If criterion is met this left
blank passes control to the
next step in the Sequence.*

*If criterion is not met this
QuicKey is played.*

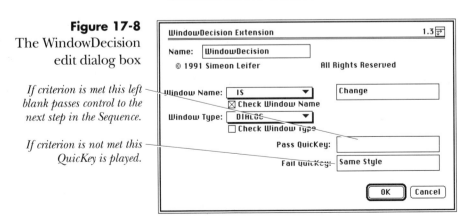

Figure 17-9
Same Style Alias
edit dialog box

*Presses Command-Return
if the active window is
not named "Change"*

```
┌──────────────────────────────────────────────────────────┐
│ Alias                                                      │
│ ┌────────────────────────────────────────────────────────┐ │
│ Name:  │ Same Style        │    Keystroke:   │ Unassigned │ │
│        └───────────────────┘                 └──────────┘ │
│                                                            │
│ Key to type:  ┌──────────────────────────┐                │
│               │              ⌘-ret        │                │
│               └──────────────────────────┘                │
│                                                            │
│                                                            │
│                                                            │
│                                                            │
│                                                            │
│                                                            │
│                                                            │
│ ┌──────────────┐  ☐ Include in QuicKeys menu  ┌────┐ ┌──────┐ │
│ │ Timer Options │                             │ OK │ │Cancel│ │
│ └──────────────┘                              └────┘ └──────┘ │
└──────────────────────────────────────────────────────────┘
```

Of course, once this is all set up, it's invisible to the user. So Steve can eat his cake and have it, too.

Choosing Fonts

Choosing fonts in Word is another change that is accomplished by either using a menu or a multistep keystroke procedure. You can automate this change easily, using Sequences similar to those for choosing glossary items and styles (see "Choosing Styles" and "Automating Glossary Use"). Set up the Sequence using Alias QuicKeys.

If your work demands that you change fonts frequently, font QuicKeys can be a big help. You might want to give them their own modifier combinations, and key their invoking keystrokes to the first letters of their names (P for Palatino, S for Symbol, C for Chicago), or to the function keys. You might also want to standardize these keystrokes throughout other applications (see "Standardizing Word's Shortcuts Throughout Your Applications," below).

Opening to a Larger Display

No matter what application you are in, there are numerous times when you may want to enlarge a document window to the full size of your display. This is especially true in Word: even if you have a big display, Word only opens its windows to a size which is narrower than a full page. You can make a QuicKey in your Universal Keyset which expands any document window to the largest size possible. Or, if you want this feature only in Word, you can include this expander

QuicKey in the Word keyset, and also make it work automatically when Word starts up and you open a new document.

This trick consists of two QuicKeys in your Word keyset. The first is a Click QuicKey which grabs the size box in the lower-right corner of the document, and pulls the document to the size you want. The second is a two-step Sequence that's activated by Command-N, the keystroke that opens a new Word document. The first step in the Sequence is an Alias QuicKey which enters Command-N, opening a new document. The second step is the Click QuicKey that expands the window—just import this into the Sequence when you build it.

Making Sequences with Word's Shortcuts

The more shortcuts you build into an application, the easier it is to create sophisticated Sequences: you have a wealth of tools available. But you have to know the keystroke shortcuts to use them. That's not easy in Word—there are around 170 standard shortcuts, plus there are many additional commands available to which you can assign Word shortcuts.

Word's built-in shortcuts. An easy way to access Word's shortcuts is to first make a list of them. Word has automated that process for you: just choose "Commands" from Word's Edit menu (if the Commands item isn't there, you must first choose "Full Menus" from the Edit menu). The Commands dialog box appears (see Figure 17-10). Click the List button on the right-hand side of this dialog box, and Word will open a new document that lists your commands.

Figure 17-10
Commands
dialog box

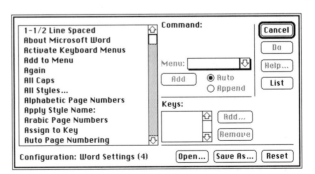

Some of the commands have keystroke shortcuts, and some do not. You can give a command a keystroke shortcut in Word by highlighting the command in the Commands dialog box. Then click the Add button in the Keys section. Word will prompt you for the keystroke, and alert you if that keystroke is already taken by another Word command. Of course, you could use QUICKEYS to assign a keystroke to a Word command; however, we feel it is good practice to use the mother application for functions that can also be performed in QUICKEYS—unless there is good reason to assign the capability only through QUICKEYS.

Sequences with Word's shortcuts. Many of Word's functions have redundant access: you can get them either from a menu, or by pressing the keystroke shortcut. We generally use the keystroke to include these functions in Sequences. It's easier because of the Literal button in the QUICKEYS Sequence editor.

Let's build a sample Sequence, to explore how Word's shortcuts come in handy. When we make up a table of contents for a book, we style lines differently, depending on their head levels (see Figure 17-11). But eventually we give all the page numbers a standard character style and point size. This Sequence uses a number of Word's shortcuts to help us do that (see Figure 17-12). To make the Sequence function, you must style the page number in the first line the same way you want all the other numbers styled, and then leave the cursor somewhere in the first line.

Figure 17-11
Partially formatted
table of contents

Word and QuicKeys   1

Choosing Styles   *1*

Automating Glossary Use   2

Simple Glossary items.   2
Modified Glossary items.   3

Word Count   4

The table-of-contents Sequence uses a Repeat QuicKey set to 100 times, to move it along. If we have more than 100 lines in the table of contents, we invoke the QuicKey again; if not, when it reaches the end of the table of contents, the Sequence beeps at us until we click the mouse button and cancel it.

Figure 17-12
Table of Contents
reformatter

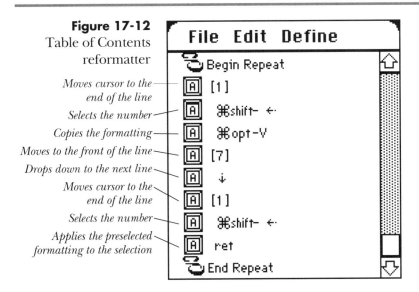

Moves cursor to the
end of the line
Selects the number
Copies the formatting
Moves to the front of the line
Drops down to the next line
Moves cursor to the
end of the line
Selects the number
Applies the preselected
formatting to the selection

File   Edit   Define

  Begin Repeat
  [1]
  ⌘shift- ←·
  ⌘opt-V
  [7]
  ↓
  [1]
  ⌘shift- ←·
  ret
  End Repeat

Standardizing Word's Shortcuts Throughout Your Applications

Because Word holds the batting title for shortcuts, if you use Word frequently you may just want to take some of its keystrokes and apply them to identical functions in your other applications (see Table 17-1). Or you can redefine your favorite Word shortcuts to other keystrokes and standardize those throughout applications.

Table 17-1
Popular Word
shortcuts

Save As	Shift-F7
Page Setup	Shift-F8
Plain Text	Shift-F9
Bold	Command-Shift-B
Italic	Command-Shift-I
Underline	Command-Shift-U
Left Justify	Command-Shift-L
Right Justify	Command-Shift-R
Center	Command-Shift-C
Go Back	Command-Option-Z
Select Paragraph	Shift-Command-Down arrow

Table 17-1 Continued	Select to the end of sentence	Shift-Command-[1] (on keyboard)
	Select to the beginning of sentence	Shift-Command-[7] (on keyboard)

How you achieve this standardization depends on what functions you want to standardize, and how they are handled in various applications. If the function is handled identically in all your applications, like a menu item in the same menu (for example, "Save As"), you can just make a Menu QuicKey in the Universal Keyset. If the function is located in different menus or dialog boxes in different applications, you may have to make a combination of a Universal QuicKey with overriding application QuicKeys for some situations.

QuicKeys and PageMaker

PageMaker 4 is not loaded with keyboard shortcuts, and the program is so versatile that there are many ways you can use QuicKeys to really speed up your page-makeup work.

Choosing Tools

If you have a smaller screen, you have to get the toolbox out of the way and select tools with keystrokes. PageMaker includes keyboard shortcuts for this—Shift-F1 through F8 (see Table 18-1). That's all well and good, but try reaching Shift-F1, much less Shift-F8.

To select this tool	You press Shift plus
Pointer	F1
Diagonal line	F2
Horizontal/vertical line	F3
Text	F4
Rectangle	F5
Rounded corner rectangle	F6
Oval	F7
Cropping	F8

Table 18-1
PageMaker's built-in tool-selection keystrokes

One solution to this finger-stretching dilemma is to choose tools using the first eight function keys, but without the Shift key. Set up eight Alias QuicKeys in the PageMaker keyset that look like those in Figure 18-1.

Figure 18-1
Alias QuicKeys for
selecting tools in
PageMaker

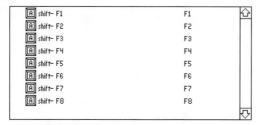

With these Alias QuicKeys set up, you can select tools without the Toolbox being visible, and without permanently stretching your left hand.

Toggling the Scroll Bars

Another way to make more space to see your publication is to turn off the scroll bars. This would be fine, since you can still get around with key-click combinations and the Option grabber hand, except that turning off the scroll bars also turns off the page number icons, which is annoying in longer documents where PageMaker's Command-Tab page-turning doesn't suffice.

So, set up a menu QuicKey to turn the scroll bars and page icons on and off (see Figure 18-2). Command-B isn't used for anything else, so it's a good keystroke for this operation.

Figure 18-2
Menu edit dialog box
for scroll-bar toggler

```
Menu

Select from menu                    Keystroke:        ⌘-B
  ● by Text:      Scroll bars            ⊠ Match exactly
  ○ by Position:  4

● Look for menu by title:  Windows
○ Search all menus
○ Only  menu

While selecting from menu, hold down:
  □ ⌘  □ Shift  □ Option  □ Control
□ Don't complain if the menu choice can't be found

( Timer Options )  □ Include in QuicKeys menu   ( OK )  ( Cancel )
```

Using Power Paste

When you copy an item and paste it again in PageMaker, it pastes the copy a bit offset from the original (if that position is visible in the window). If you hold down Option while choosing "Paste," however (or if you press Command-Option-V), the copy pastes directly on top of the original. It's called "power paste."

Move that copy, then power paste again. The second copy lands as far from the first as the first lands from the original. It's step-and-repeat duplication.

Once you've used power paste, you'll never use regular Paste again. So use an Alias QuicKey to reassign Command-V to invoke Command-Option-V—the power-paste keystroke.

Kerning with Arrows

In PageMaker 4, Command plus the Right and Left arrow keys (the ones in the inverted T shape) are positive- and negative-kerning keys. For those who use Word, this is infuriating. Command-Left arrow and Command-Right arrow should move you left and right, one word at a time (which PageMaker accomplishes with the Command key, plus either 4 or 6 from the keypad). So you go to move the cursor a word left or right, and you get kerning instead.

The solution is to set up two Alias QuicKeys, as described in Table 18-2, and to use the normal Delete key-based kerning keystrokes described in Table 18-3.

Table 18-2
Keys to move
by word

This key combination	invokes this one
Command-Left arrow	Command-[4]
Command-Right arrow	Command-[6]

Table 18-3
PageMaker's
kerning keys

This keystroke plus Delete	gives this result
Command	kern large increment left
Option	kern small increment left
Command-Shift	kern large increment right
Option-Shift	kern small increment right
Command-Option-Shift	remove all kerning

Closing Windows

If you use a Mousie QuicKey to close the currently active window, be aware that your QuicKey will close any open palettes

(Styles or Colors) before it closes the main document window. And since PageMaker remembers whether or not the palettes are open for each document, if you close a palette, then close the document window with a blazing fast double-press of your Close window QuicKey, PageMaker will ask if you want to save changes. The change it's referring to is your closing the palette.

You can get around this annoyance by instead using a Menu QuicKey to choose "Close" from the File menu. You can hide and close the palettes with PageMaker's built-in keystrokes—Command-Y for Styles, Command-K for Colors.

Expanding Palette

PageMaker's Styles palette comes up in a little tiny size that's fine if you only have a few styles. If you have a lot of styles, however, you may want the Styles palette to extend all the way down the right side of the screen, as narrow as it can be (see Figure 18-3).

Figure 18-3
PageMaker's
Styles palette

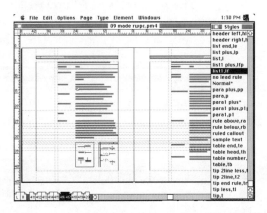

This positioning of the Styles palette covers up the right scroll bar, but cool PageMaker users never use scroll bars, anyway; they use Command-click zooming and the Option-drag grabber hand to get around the page. It also covers the window-sizing icon, but you hardly ever size the document window in PageMaker, anyway, because you can only have one document open at a time.

If you want your Styles palette to look like the one in Figure 18-3, create a Sequence QuicKey made up of the two

Click QuicKeys shown in Figure 18-4. The setup shown there works on an Apple 13-inch RGB display.

If these coordinates don't work on your monitor, create your own two-Click Sequence using the Sequence recorder. The first Click of the Sequence drags the palette to the upper-right corner of the window, the second grabs the bottom right sizing box and stretches the palette out.

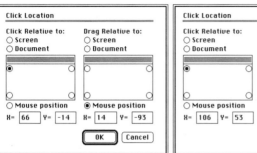
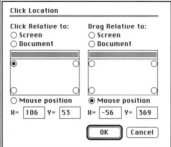

Figure 18-4
Cool Styles palette
QuicKey steps

PageMaker remembers the location of the Styles palette when you open and close the palette, but it doesn't remember the location between sessions. When you quit PageMaker, then relaunch, the Styles palette goes back to its original diminutive size; hence the necessity for this QuicKey.

Special Page Views

Two special page views (or magnifications) in PageMaker are available through the Fit in window menu item, with modifier keys held down. Pressing Option while choosing "Fit in window" (on the Page menu) changes all the pages in the publication to Fit-in-window view. Shift plus "Fit in window" changes the current page to Fit-pasteboard-in-window view—it shows the whole 17-by-22-inch pasteboard.

Use Menu QuicKeys to access these two view options with keyboard shortcuts. Try Control-Option-W to change all pages to Fit-in-window view, and Control-Shift-W to change to Fit-pasteboard-in-window view.

Reversed Type

Every type style in PageMaker has a keyboard shortcut—Command-Shift-U for Underline, Command-Shift-I for Italic, and so on. The one type style that doesn't have a shortcut is Reverse, which (besides Bold and Italic) is the one most people use the most.

It's easy enough to assign a Menu QuicKey to Reverse, but

which keystroke should you use? Command-Shift-R is already taken for Align right, so Command-Shift-V is a good choice.

Making Fractions

There's no automatic way to make fractions in PageMaker, but by putting the numerator in superscript, the denominator in subscript, replacing the slash (virgule) in between with a fraction slash (solidus), and adjusting your superscript and subscript controls, you can create a good-looking fraction. Table 18-4 shows a Sequence QuicKey to do it for you, assuming that you have the whole fraction selected, and that there's a space to the left of the fraction.

Table 18-4
Sequence for making fractions

QuicKey type	Entry	What it does
Alias	Command-T	Open the Type specs dialog box
Button	Options…	Open Type options dialog box
Text	<tab>60<tab> 30<tab>0	Enter superscript and subscript values
Alias	Option-Return	Close dialog boxes
Alias	[4]	Move cursor off fraction
Alias	[6]	Move cursor next to fraction
Alias	Shift-[6]	Select numerator
Alias	Command-Shift-=	Put numerator in superscript
Alias	[6]	Move past slash
Alias	Shift-[4]	Select slash
Alias	Shift-Option-1	Replace virgule with solidus
Alias	Command-Shift-[6]	Select denominator
Alias	Command-Shift-- (hyphen)	Put denominator in subscript
Alias	[6]	Move cursor to right of fraction

QuicKeys and Excel

By Howard Hansen

Unlike most other Mac programs, Excel has a myriad of keyboard shortcuts of its own for its most-used features. Plus, to make it work similarly to the Windows version of Excel and Lotus 1-2-3, Microsoft added the ability to access all menu commands with the keyboard by pressing the Slash key (/) followed by a sequence of letters to correspond with menus, items, buttons, etc. This means that your hands may not need to leave the keyboard at any time.

Nevertheless, as we have seen elsewhere in this book, there are many reasons to use QuicKeys. Below are those which hold true in Excel, and which this chapter will explore.

- To remap the keyboard shortcuts with more mnemonic substitutes
- To create shortcuts left out by Microsoft
- To create editing Sequences

Since you can do almost everything in Excel from the keyboard, the best way to get started is to practice. Turn the Command Underline feature on (see Figure 19-1) and begin to use it. Instead of mousing to "Save As" on the File menu, type /FA; or to use "Replace," type /RE instead of choosing "Replace" from the Formula menu.

Excel's Menu Keys

Figure 19-1
Accessing Excel menus from the keyboard

&#63743;	**File**	**Edit**	**Formula**	**Format**	**Data**	**Options**	**Macro**	**Window**	

The Excel menu changes when you have "Command Underline" turned on.

To turn on "Command Underline," select "Workspace" from the Options menu (see Figure 19-2) and click "Command Underline" on. This lets you see what keys to press to activate menus. Even if you don't use the the Slash key technique much initially, you're likely to learn the keys by osmosis.

Figure 19-2
Excel's Workspace
dialog box

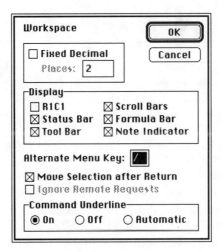

So once again, why use QuicKeys? Consistency is one reason. You can build QuicKeys to align cell entries, for example (see below), using easy-to-remember keystrokes. Before we get to that, though, a little philosophy.

Keystroke Guidelines

My keystroke strategies vary somewhat from Don and Steve's. Choosing which keystroke to use can be especially difficult with Excel, since it has so many shortcuts of its own. Here are my rules of thumb.

- **Use the Control key.** For compatibility with Windows Excel, Mac Excel often treats it as the equivalent of the Command key.
- **Try to be consistent.** Use standards set by other programs (like Word), and stick with those models.
- **Use Shift for opposites.** If you create a QuicKey to perform an action and another to do the opposite, use the same keystroke except with Shift added for the opposite command. (For example, Tab moves you one cell to the right, and Shift-Tab moves you one cell to the left.)

- **Be kind.** If other people will be using your computer, don't replace commonly used keyboard shortcuts with your own QuicKeys.

Print Preview

Print Preview is so often used that it really deserves a more straightforward keyboard shortcut than /FV. Control-P is a great keystroke for a Print Preview Menu QuicKey.

Paging and Scrolling Up and Down

In Excel, you move the position of the current selection when you use the Page up, Page down, Up arrow, and Down arrow keys. If you want to move your view without moving the selection point (to Shift-select a range of cells, for instance), and you don't want to use the scroll bars, you can use Page up, Page down, Line up, and Line down QuicKeys (Figure 19-3).

Figure 19-3
Some movement QuicKeys

Line down	⌘- ↓
Line up	⌘- ↑
Page down	⌘-pgdn
Page up	⌘-pgup

I use these Command-modified keystrokes to move around the worksheet without resorting to the scroll bars.

Aligning Text

To center text in a cell, you normally type /TAC and then press Return—not exactly what you'd expect. How about remapping the command so Word's standard Command-Shift-C centers cells (by clicking the center alignment button on the tool bar)? See Figure 19-4.

Figure 19-4
Click to center a cell in Excel

Click
Name: Center Click   Keystroke: ⌘shift-C
Click: From:(284,30) on screen / To:(0,0) from current location
Window: Any Window
Control area: None
Click [1] time(s)
Hold down: ☐⌘ ☐Shift ☐Option ☐Control
Timer Options ☐ Include in QuicKeys menu   OK   Cancel

To create shortcuts for right- and left -aligning cells, copy this Click and paste it back into your keyset twice. Double-click on each new QuicKey, and change the names and click definitions as shown in Table 19-1.

Table 19-1
Text alignment
QuicKeys

Alignment	Keystroke	x=	y=
Left	Command-Shift-L	268	30
Center	Command-Shift-C	284	30
Right	Command-Shift-R	305	30

Paste Function

It's impossible to remember all of Excel's myriad functions. With the Paste Function command, you don't need to—Excel presents you with a list of all available functions, along with their arguments. Unfortunately, there is no keyboard shortcut for Paste Function. This is an excellent place to use a Menu QuicKey—assign Paste Function a keyboard command.

Make a menu QuicKey for Paste Function with a keystroke of Command-F. This can now be used at any time, even when editing in the formula bar, to bring up the Paste Function dialog box and insert a function with all its arguments.

Comment/ Uncomment

Excel won't let you enter an incorrect formula. This is good policy to minimize errors, but it means you need to type each formula exactly right before leaving the editing line. This is not realistic, since people don't always have the information needed to do it correctly. To store a temporary formula, we "fool" Excel into thinking of the formula as text by typing a character in front of the equal sign which starts every formula. Adding and deleting this extra comment character requires some attentive mousing, but creating two small QuicKey Sequences to comment and uncomment is quite simple. For our comment character, we prefer the bullet (Option-8), because it shouts, "Comment," to us whenever we see it.

To add the bullet as your comment character, your Sequence should include the following steps.

1. A Click step that clicks at the far left side of the formula bar (the flashing insertion pointer will appear in front of the equal sign). Figure 19-5 shows you the Click Location dialog box for this Formula Start Click step.

Figure 19-5
Clicking at the
beginning of the
formula

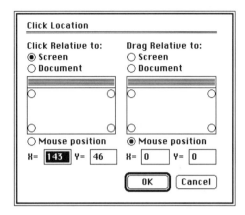

2. A Text step that types the bullet character in front of the formula.
3. An Alias step that presses Enter to accept the change.

To create a Sequence that uncomments the formula, copy the Comment Sequence and make a few changes.

1. Again, begin with the Formula Start Click.
2. Include an Option-Right arrow Alias step to move the insertion pointer in the formula bar between the first and second characters.
3. Make another Alias step that deletes the extra character.
4. Use the same Alias step as before to type Enter to accept the change.

Figure 19-6
Uncommenting
a formula

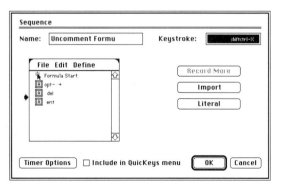

These two Sequences, or modifications of them, are excellent in macros to skip certain cells containing commands you may not always want executed; for instance, the =STEP() command for debugging.

Repetitive Editing

QuicKeys for sophisticated editing within cells? You bet. Say you've got a list of names in a column and you want to split the first and last names into separate cells. Hours of repetitive editing? *Au contraire*, one QuicKey.

If we remember that the formula bar in Excel is a little word-processing area that acts a lot like Word, things will be easier. Here's what the Sequence should do.

1. Type Command-U. This activates the formula bar and places the insertion pointer at the end of the formula (a name, in this case).
2. Type Command-Shift-Left arrow. As in Word, this selects the word to the left of the insertion pointer (the last name).
3. Type Command-X to cut the last name.
4. Press Delete to remove the space between the first and last names.
5. Press Tab to move one cell to the right. The first name is now in the original cell.
6. Type Command-V to paste the last name into the current cell.
7. Press Return to accept the entry and move down one row.
8. Press Left arrow to move to the next cell to be processed.

Figure 19-7
Name splitting

240

If you really want to automate this process, place a Repeat QuicKey at the beginning and end of the Sequence. QUICKEYS will keep fixing up those names until you tell it to stop. For more on using Repeat, see Chapter 13, *Sequence QuicKeys.*

Now it's true that this same maneuver can be done a lot faster using Excel's text functions, but you may be able to create the QuicKey and run it faster than you can figure out how to use those Excel functions.

Day and Time Stamp

Use this Sequence to put the current day and time into a given cell (see Figure 19-8).

Figure 19-8
Entering date and time

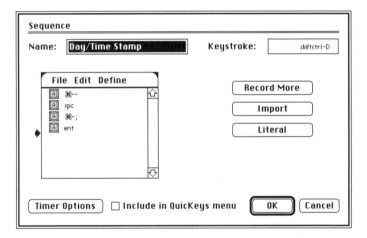

1. Type Command-- (hyphen) to enter the current date.
2. Type a space to separate day from time.
3. Type Command-; to enter the current time.
4. Press Enter to accept the entry.

Pasting Values and Formats

The Paste Special command is one I use constantly. First you copy some cells containing formulas, and then you paste only the formulas, values, or formats (see Figure 19-9).

I use these functions so often that I've created QuicKey Sequences for the four most common Paste Special setups, as show in Table 19-2.

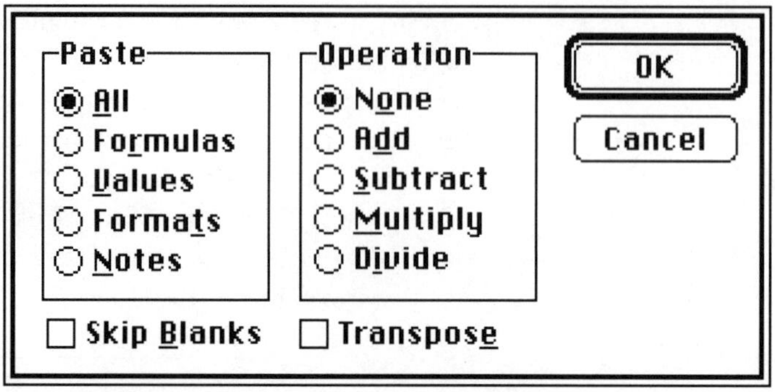

Figure 19-9
The Paste Special
dialog box

```
┌─Paste──────┐  ┌─Operation───┐   ╭──────────╮
│ ◉ All      │  │ ◉ None      │   │    OK    │
│ ○ Formulas │  │ ○ Add       │   ╰──────────╯
│ ○ Values   │  │ ○ Subtract  │   ╭──────────╮
│ ○ Formats  │  │ ○ Multiply  │   │  Cancel  │
│ ○ Notes    │  │ ○ Divide    │   ╰──────────╯
│            │  │             │
│  ☐ Skip Blanks   ☐ Transpose │
└──────────────────────────────┘
```

Table 19-2
Paste Special
QuicKeys

Keystroke	What's pasted
Control-Option-R	Formulas
Control-Option-V	Values
Control-Option-T	Formats
Control-Option-N	Notes

These Paste Special Sequences consist of three steps each—select Paste Special, type a keystroke shortcut that selects the appropriate radio button option (Button QuicKeys don't seem to work in this dialog box), and then press Enter.

Format Broadcaster

Sometimes we have spiffy formatting for a cell, which we want to apply to other areas within the spreadsheet. The usual method for doing this is to copy the cell, select the target cells to be formatted, and then apply a format-only Paste Special. We've already shown you how to speed up this process by creating a format-only Paste Special QuicKey. Now here's a way to use another Sequence QuicKey to make things even faster.

This Sequence copies the formatting of a cell (or cells) you've highlighted and pauses for you to select a target cell (or cells). Then that target is given the same format as the original cell. We made this Sequence by importing the three steps of our format-only Paste Special QuicKey into the new Sequence (see Figure 19-10).

The Pause step that is built into this Sequence is a little tricky. It would be nice just to pause for a short period of time (five seconds, for example) while you select the target cells. But you can't do a timed Pause step, because you usually drag the mouse to select the target cells, and clicking the mouse during a Sequence interrupts the Sequence.

Figure 19-10
Importing into our
format broadcaster
Sequence

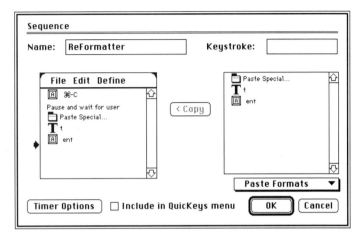

Instead, you must include a Pause and wait for user step, which means that the Sequence must be manually "unpaused" to get it to perform the rest of the Sequence. The easy way to do that is to have a pause/unpause QuicKey (the Pause Special) in your Universal Keyset that you can invoke after you select the target cells.

Howard Hansen is a senior partner with The Oasis Group, a Macintosh business consulting firm which specializes in Microsoft Excel programming, training, and consulting. If you have any questions or comments about the information contained in this chapter, or about Excel or QuicKeys, please don't hesitate to contact him at The Oasis Group, 1818 Westlake Avenue North, Suite 128, Seattle, WA 98109, 206-282-6255.

QuicKeys and FileMaker

CHAPTER

20

By Joe Kroeger

QUICKEYS is a useful adjunct to FileMaker in a variety of ways. Simple Aliases for keyboard navigation within the program are handy, especially for users familiar enough with menu items to be able to use the keyboard instead of a mouse. More complex macros can save a lot of time when you're processing database information, especially record-to-record data. In the range between the simple and the complex, there are various utility operations that make data entry and manipulation more efficient. Many of the general QUICKEYS ideas discussed elsewhere in this book work well in FileMaker. It's nice, for example, to use one QuicKeys keystroke to type a phrase or a paragraph into a field.

Mapping Function Keys

There are plenty of different ways to allocate the 15 function keys on an extended keyboard, using Menu QuicKeys. (Don't be confused by the FKEY option inside QUICKEYS—here we are simply assigning a keyboard function key to a menu item.) My scheme for assigning QuicKeys on an extended keyboard for use with FileMaker is a little different from that used by Steve and Don.

Assign F1 through F4 to the conventional Undo, Cut, Copy, and Paste commands. You may want to put these QuicKeys in the Universal Keyset instead of FileMaker's, so that they can be used anywhere.

I don't make much use of the Undo function, so instead of the conventional approach, I assign "Select All" to F1. Further, since in FileMaker "Select All" is often used in conjunction with Cut, Copy, and Paste, it's nice to have it near those keys. While it's easy to remember the Command-key combinations for Cut, Copy, and Paste, I find that a single function key is a little faster for me.

I then assign F9 through F15 to seven frequently used Apple-menu items. For me, this usually means the key assignments shown in Table 20-1.

Table 20-1
Menu item
QuicKeys

Key	Menu Item
F9	Calculator
F10	Chooser
F11	Scrapbook
F12	Finder
F13	Image Grabber
F14	Control Panel
F15	Fast Find

Figure 20-1
The FileMaker Pro
Select menu

```
Select
✓ Browse        ⌘B
  Find          ⌘F
  Layout        ⌘L
  Preview       ⌘U
..............................
  Find All      ⌘J
  Refind        ⌘R
  Omit          ⌘M
  Omit Multiple... ⇧⌘M
  Find Omitted
..............................
  Define Fields... ⇧⌘D
  Sort...       ⌘S
..............................
  View as List
```

That leaves F5 through F8, which I use for FileMaker menu items. One of the nice things about FileMaker is that you manage basic navigation—moving into different modes—via a single menu: Select (see Figure 20-1). You use the Browse, Find, Sort, Omit, and Layout operations, or modes, so frequently that the built-in FileMaker shortcuts (simple, mnemonic Command-key equivalents) come readily to mind. Even moderately active users know these keyboard shortcuts already, so a function is not necessary.

I find that with other Select menu items that I don't use as often, and/or which have awkward built-in keyboard shortcuts, I maximize efficiency by assigning them the F5 through F8 slots. Naturally, your needs will determine your specific F5-F8 selections, and with QuicKeys, it's very easy to make new designations as circumstances change. I often use the four shown in Table 20-2.

Table 20-2
F5–F8 Keys

Key	Menu Item
F5	Define Fields
F6	Omit Multiple
F7	Preview
F8	Find All

The View as List and Find Omitted commands are usually best left as menu selections only.

Paging Through the FileMaker Book Icon

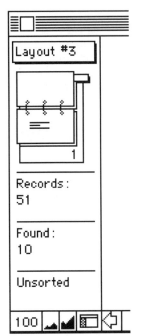

Figure 20-2
Moving through records and layouts

The book metaphor is used by FileMaker to move from record to record (in Browse mode) or from layout to layout (in Layout mode). See Figure 20-2.

FileMaker has built-in key commands for moving through the book as an alternative to mousing through it. Command-Tab moves to the next record (or page) and Command-Shift-Tab moves to the previous. But many users want to avoid mental confusion and save all tabbing for moving between fields rather than records. Plus, with the Page up and Page down keys available and so logically associated with the book icon, it makes sense to create QuicKeys that move up and down through the book. I use Alias QuicKeys to substitute for the existing built-in shortcuts. These particular QuicKeys are great not only for manual movement through the book, but they can also be integrated into a complex macro that picks up information from an adjacent record.

Another standard keyboard key is the Home key, located above the four arrow keys. It is useful in conjunction with the book icon for taking the database to the first record in the currently found set of records. FileMaker has no menu items or keyboard equivalents for moving to the top of the book; however, it does have a button option that performs such a task (unfortunately, there is no similar "go to end" function).

I discuss creating the Home button below. Once it's in place, it's a simple matter to make a QuicKey that clicks the button. For such a QuicKey to work with multiple layouts, the location of the button on each layout must be the same. The upper-right corner is often available, but any convenient location is fine. The figures that follow use the upper-left corner.

Don't worry about putting such a button on a layout intended for printing—a FileMaker button can be made nonprinting for use on report layouts.

What we are going to do is create a button within File-Maker Pro that moves to the first "page" of the book icon. Here is the procedure.

1. Enter Layout mode and locate a layout where the Home button will appear.
2. Create a graphic, or a text block, or both, which will be used for the button object. You might make it quite small in order to use less layout space.
3. Select the button object (click on it once) and select "Define Button" from the Scripts menu. In the resulting dialog box, se-lect the Perform a Com-

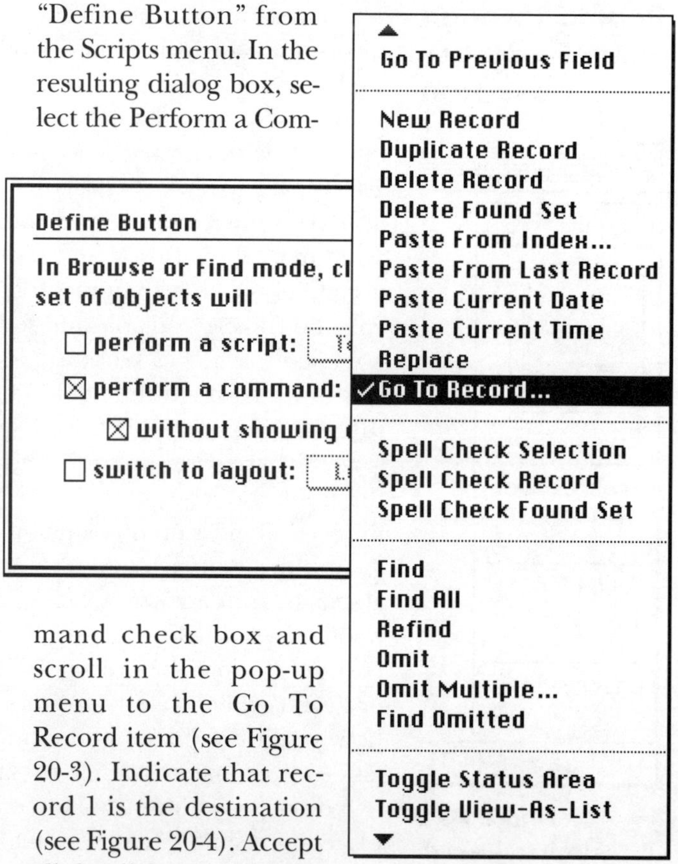

Figure 20-3
Go To Record item

Go To Previous Field

New Record
Duplicate Record
Delete Record
Delete Found Set
Paste From Index...
Paste From Last Record
Paste Current Date
Paste Current Time
Replace
✓**Go To Record...**

Spell Check Selection
Spell Check Record
Spell Check Found Set

Find
Find All
Refind
Omit
Omit Multiple...
Find Omitted

Toggle Status Area
Toggle View-As-List

Define Button

In Browse or Find mode, cl
set of objects will

☐ perform a script:

☒ perform a command:

☒ without showing

☐ switch to layout:

mand check box and scroll in the pop-up menu to the Go To Record item (see Figure 20-3). Indicate that rec-ord 1 is the destination (see Figure 20-4). Accept all the dialog boxes until you are back to the layout. Move to the Browse mode.

Figure 20-4
Go to record
text edit box

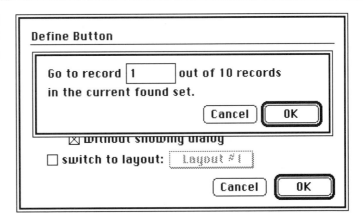

4. Create a Click QuicKey that clicks on the button you've created in FileMaker (see Figure 20-5). The click should be relative to the upper-right or upper-left corner of the window. Give this Click QuicKey a name and specify the Home key as the activating key. Save the result.

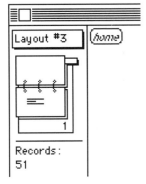

Figure 20-5
Home button

Now whenever you press the Home key, the button will be clicked, and FileMaker will move the book slider all the way to the top of the currently found set. Once you have defined the button on a given layout, you can copy it to the Clipboard and paste into any other layouts that need it. (Be sure to put it into the same location on all layouts where it is used.) When you copy a FileMaker button, FileMaker carries with it the associated command that you have specified, so no additional button or QuicKeys work need be done. You can even paste the button from the Clipboard into another FileMaker file.

Working with Addresses

There are many types of repetitive actions that are performed in typical address-processing operations that can be automated with QuicKeys. The need to locate pairs or sets of records with duplicate last name entries, duplicate telephone numbers, or duplicate serial numbers occurs often. FileMaker is good at locating *all* records that have, say, duplicate last names. But then what? In some cases, it is necessary to go through the entire found set, record by record, and examine the individual duplicates to see if one should be deleted. Here is a QuicKeys procedure which solves that problem.

1. Use FileMaker to find all the records that have duplicate entries in the field of interest. Assume we're interested in the Last Name field, for example. (It may be more effective to create a field for this purpose, often called a NameCode or MatchCode field. But that's another discussion.)
2. Since locating all the duplicates in a file can take quite some time, and it's necessary to access them again and again, mark the found set resulting from the FileMaker duplicate find with, say, an "A" in the Temp field of all found records. This makes it easy to locate the rest of the duplicates after dealing with one set of them.
3. Find all records with "A" in the Temp field.
4. Initiate a Sequence QuicKey (described below) that finds all records containing the same last name as the last name in the first record marked "A" in its Temp field.
5. Examine the resulting set of records and decide on their disposition. Mark an "X" in the Temp field of those that will be deleted later, and remove the "A" from the keepers.
6. Perform Steps 3 through 6 until all the "A" records have been processed.

The Sequence QuicKey used in Step 4 above performs the following series of operations. The number of discrete QuicKey steps in this sequence will depend on your particular file design. If you record it, you will not need to be concerned with the type of QuicKey used for each step.

1. Tab into the Last Name field. Click in it if you have to, but tabbing is usually more reliable, especially when you'll be using this Sequence with several files. Save time by using the FileMaker Tab Order command (in the Arrange menu) to minimize the number of tabs it takes to move into the Last Name field.
2. Select All.
3. Copy.
4. Tab into the Last Name field. (Be careful: this may be a different number of tabs than in the first step, since the Find mode is active.)
5. Type =. This step assures that FileMaker locates only whole-word duplicates of the pasted text. If you are

looking for duplicates of the name "Bar," you don't want to find "Barber" and "Barker" as well.

6. Paste.
7. Press Enter.

Any key assignment that you can remember will work well for this macro—Command-Option-L, for example ("L" for last name).

A similar QuicKey helps process duplicate phone numbers using a similar procedure. (Duplicate phone numbers are sometimes good clues for locating multiple entries in an address database.) Step 5 is not required in the case of phone numbers, but it is vital that all phone numbers be formatted in the same way. Don't mix 408-555-1234 with 408/555-4321 with 555-5678. Command-Option-T (for "Telephone") is a convenient assignment for such a Sequence QuicKey.

Note that when you are deleting A's and entering X's in this procedure, you can take advantage of another QuicKey or two. When you have decided which one to mark for deletion, a Sequence QuicKey, perhaps initiated with Option-Command-X, can highlight the Temp field and insert an "X" there. Here are the steps.

1. Tab to the Temp field. I keep mine very early in the tab order so it is easy to get to.
2. Select All.
3. Type X.

Similarly, another QuicKey could highlight the Temp field and clear it, perhaps using Option-Command-Space. In fact, in some cases where the order of the records to be deleted and saved is the same, you can combine both actions. If the combined QuicKey is always initiated when the second record of the pair is active, and when it is the second record that is to be deleted (other arrangements are possible), you would need the following steps in your Sequence.

1. Tab to the Temp field.
2. Select All.
3. Type X.
4. Page up to the previous record (if you have implemented the Page up QuicKey).
5. Select All. The cursor should still be in the Temp field.
6. Press Delete.

Other variations are possible. In some cases, it will be convenient (although more dangerous) to replace the record-marking steps with a Delete Record command. You may find that you want to transfer some information into the keeper record from the record to be deleted before it's erased.

Perhaps you keep Last Order Date information in this database, and the duplicate record has been imported from an order entry file in order to update the order history for this customer. QuicKeys can copy from the Last Order Date field, mark the record for deletion, move to the previous record, tab to the Last Order Date field, highlight and paste, and then clear the Temp field. This Sequence makes a very effective macro.

If you need to transfer several items from one record to another (perhaps the address needs updating), QuicKeys is very good at taking advantage of the FileMaker Paste Ditto function, which can paste from one record to another without repetitive movements back and forth.

Filling in Forms

You can use QUICKEYS effectively for completing repetitive forms or orders. FileMaker is quite good at providing automatic and semi-automatic field fill-in with auto-entry, lookups, and popups. Even so, there are many cases when QuicKeys can, with one initiating keystroke, type for us a series of entries in a series of fields. Even the tabs that move the cursor between fields can be included in the QuicKeys Sequence. Data entered by QuicKeys can go on to trigger subsequent FileMaker lookups.

The key to efficient use of such macros is to realize that while individual records may be quite distinct overall, nonetheless, sometimes there are subsets of information that tend to be entered together. In an order-entry form, it may be that most customers who buy item 1023 usually also buy items 2204 and 2310, so it makes sense to enter all three with a Sequence QuicKey, even if once in a while it is necessary to go back and change or delete an item. On a personnel form perhaps, once a new employee is designated as an engineer, she automatically becomes "salaried" and "first shift" and an "E" is used to begin her employee number. QUICKEYS can enter all this for you.

Entering Fax Numbers

We quite often, these days, need to enter a fax phone number in addition to a voice phone number. Quite often the fax number will have the same area code and the same prefix as the voice phone, and it is a shame to enter the same stuff again. FileMaker has many aids to data entry, but not something easy that helps with the fax number. A simple Sequence QuicKey can highlight the voice number, copy it, tab to the Fax field, and paste. It can even backspace a couple of digits, in preparation for the revised numbers to be entered manually.

Working with Stacks

In FileMaker, it is sometimes handy to treat a set of repeating fields as a 'stack' of information. QuicKeys can help manage the stack. While it is usually better to design such a stack as an "add-on" stack (where new data is put into the first empty slot as you move down the repeating field), a "push-down" stack is sometimes used.

In order to put new data into a push-down stack, existing information must all be moved down. QUICKEYS does this nicely. Assume the tab order is the order of the numbers, and assume that the cursor is already located in position 6. Follows these steps to push the stack. See Figure 20-6 to compare a pair of repeating fields before and after manipulation.

Figure 20-6
Stack manipulation

Serial Num	Mail Date	Mail Item
10731	8/25/91	Catalog
10732	5/4/91	Brochure3
10733	1/8/91	Brochure4
10734	11/29/90	Sample
10735		
10736		

Before

Serial Num	Mail Date	Mail Item
10731		
10732	8/25/91	Catalog
10733	5/4/91	Brochure3
10734	1/8/91	Brochure4
10735	11/29/90	Sample
10736		

After—ready for the new entry

1. Shift-Tab to move back to position 5.
2. Select All.
3. Cut.
4. Tab to 6.
5. Select All.
6. Paste.
7. Shift-Tab twice to move back to 4.
8. Select All. Repeat Steps 1–8 as necessary.

Temporary QuicKeys

In addition to fixtures like those described above, there always seem to be recurring data-editing situations where a QuicKey or two can be created just for a specific short-term task, and then disposed of. Since recording a QuicKey is now so easy, temporary tasks invite temporary macros, even strange and convoluted ones.

For example, in imported addresses from an outside source, some data may appear in a wrong field. The source may have mixed up the Title and the Organization fields. They can be rearranged easily using FileMaker equations if the reversed ones can be identified all at once. Otherwise, a little QuicKey can be activated selectively as you encounter a reversed situation during manual scanning.

To make a temporary QuicKey easy to identify later for deletion, you can use a unique naming scheme (like putting "X" in front of each one) or a unique key combination. Steve and Don suggest using Command-Control-Option-Shift, which makes it easy to edit out later. Even just Command-Control-Option (all lined up) will work nicely.

Lots of database problems can be solved within FileMaker, and it's challenging to discover the procedures that make it efficient to use. QUICKEYS is a nice supplementary tool—it plus FileMaker equal a synergistic combination.

Joe Kroeger is editor of The FileMaker Report, *a journal for File-Maker users. Box 1300, Freedom, CA 95019; 408-761-5466.*

QuicKeys and QuarkXPress

The first thing to know about using QUICKEYS with QuarkXPress is this: in order for Menu QuicKeys to work, you almost always need to select the Search all Menus option in the Menu QuicKey editing dialog box. Otherwise (we don't know why), QUICKEYS can't find the menu items.

Bring to Front and Send to Back

The most important keystroke shortcuts missing from QuarkXPress are those to invoke the Bring to Front and Send to Back commands. Unfortunately, the obvious Command-F and Command-B keystrokes are already taken (for the Find and Frame commands).

We believe that the Bring to Front and Send to Back commands are so important (especially in QuarkXPress, which is forever making boxes opaque) that they need single-modifier Command keystrokes—like Command-F and Command-B. So using Alias QuicKeys we redefine the keystrokes for Find (to Command-H, as in change) and Frame (to Command-E, as in edge), neither of which is used for anything else in QuarkXPress. Then we use Command-F and Command-B for the Bring to Front and Send to Back commands.

Alternately, you can get around the problem by using the shortcuts used in Adobe Illustrator—Command-+ and Command-- (hyphen).

QuarkXPress 3.1 also has Bring Forward and Send Back commands, which move the item one layer forward or back. You access these commands by holding down Option while selecting the menu item. The obvious QUICKEY keyboard shortcuts are to add Option to the Bring to Front and Send to Back commands. Remember to select the Option check box in the Menu edit dialog box so QUICKEYS holds it down when making the menu selection.

Styles and No Style

XPress lets you assign keystrokes to styles, but you can only use certain keys—the function keys (F1 through F15) and the numeric keypad keys, with any combination of modifiers. If you want to use a more mnemonic keyboard combination, use a Menu QuicKey to choose the style from the Style Sheets submenu off the Style menu.

You absolutely must assign a QuicKey to No Style, because QuarkXPress doesn't let you assign one. We use Command-Option-N (and we use it all the time).

Section

Section, under the Page menu, is where you set the starting page numbers for sections. Since we use this command at least once per document, we've assigned the keystroke Command-Option-S.

Fractions

QuarkFreebies gives QuarkXPress 3.0 the ability to make fractions, and the feature is standard in QuarkXPress 3.1. You'll find it hidden away on the Type Style submenu off the Style menu, but you won't find a keyboard shortcut. We think it needs one, so we use a Menu QuicKey with the invoking keystroke Command-Option-F.

Clone in Place

One thing we *always* want to do in XPress is clone an item—make an exact duplicate of the object right on top of the original. Figure 21-1 shows a Sequence you can build that does just that.

This Sequence only works if you have an item or items selected (if you don't, you get an alert box which tells you it can't find the Step and Repeat menu item). When you invoke this Sequence, it calls XPress' Step and Repeat command, enters "1" for the number of copies and "0" for the two offsets, and then presses Return. You can replace all the Aliases with a single Text QuicKey, if you want.

Figure 21-1
Sequence to clone
an item in place

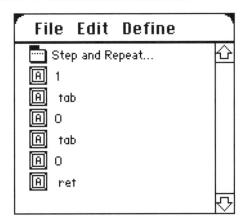

File   Edit   Define

Step and Repeat...
1
 tab
0
 tab
0
 ret

We use Command-= for this QuicKey, since that's the clone command shortcut in Aldus FreeHand (and it's Free-Hand that made us want this command in QuarkXPress).

Use the Numeric Keypad

We grew up using Microsoft Word on the IBM, so the numeric keypad cursor movement keys from that program are second nature to us. We've set up Alias QuicKeys to make the numeric keypad work as we like (see Figure 21-2).

Figure 21-2
Numeric keypad
Alias QuicKeys

pgdn		[3]
⌘-pgdn		⌘-[3]
pgup		[9]
⌘-pgup		⌘-[9]

Selecting Tools

Okay, XPress fans. Here's the one you've been waiting for—the tip worth the whole price of the book.

Ever since XPress 3 came out, QuicKeys/XPress users have been complaining that they can't select tools from the tool palette with QuicKeys. Weird things happen, as you'll see if you try to define a Click QuicKey that selects a tool. We won't explain why these weird things happen (we're not completely sure). Let's just say that they do.

But we finally figured out a workaround—Real Time QuicKeys. Create one Real Time QuicKey to click on each tool in the tool palette. Steve uses F1 through F13 for the 13 tools.

There's one trick to creating the Real Time QuicKeys: you want them to execute quickly, without the mouse touring around the screen before and after clicking. To avoid it, follow these steps.

1. Build a Start/Stop Real Time QuicKey. This Specials QuicKey starts and stops your Real Time recording. The trick is to assign your Start/Stop Real Time QuicKey a keystroke you can press easily with one hand. You'll see why in a moment.
2. Position the mouse cursor over the Item tool (the first tool in the palette), and execute the next three steps as fast as you can. (It sometimes helps to do this with a friend. The potential of the following as a party game has not escaped our attention.)
3. Press the Start/Stop Real Time QuicKey.
4. Click the mouse.
5. Press the Start/Stop Real Time QuicKey.

You've just created a Real Time QuicKey that selects the Item tool. Assign a keystroke (like F1), and go on about creating the other tool-selection Real Time QuicKeys. When you've finished creating them, you can get rid of the Start/Stop Real Time QuicKey (or just change its keystrokes).

Moving Through the Tools

Okay, what if you're used to the standard Command-Tab and Command-Shift-Tab to move down and up through the tools? That's great (especially for toggling between the Item and Content tools), but Command-Shift-Tab is a lot of keys. So how about Command-` for moving up through the menus? It's intuitive, because it's right above the Tab key. Steve likes to use Command-' to close windows, though, so he uses the F1 through F13 keys to choose tools, and the standards, Command-Tab and Command-Shift-Tab, less frequently.

Changing Page Views

QuarkXPress' keyboard-click combinations are the best ways to zoom in and out on pages, but there are times when you want to just press a key to go to a certain magnification. QuarkXPress has shortcuts for "100%" and "Fit in Window," but not for its other menu zoom items. So we created shortcuts (see Figure 21-3)

Figure 21-3
Zooming QuicKeys

📄	200%	⌘-2
📄	50%	⌘-5
📄	75%	⌘-7
📄	Thumbnails	⌘-N

The percentage QuicKeys all use the keys at the top of the keyboard, leaving the numeric keypad keys free for other things. Thumbnails uses "N" because it's about the only key left that's included in that word.

The only conflict in this set of keys is Command-2, which normally inserts a Previous page # token in text. We've remapped this to Command-Option-2 using an Alias QuicKey.

Typing a Zoom Percentage

We haven't figured out a way to consistently type a number in the percentage box in the bottom left of document windows. You never know how many palettes are going to be up in front of the document window, and unless you never open more than one document, you never know the window's position. The only workaround is to position the pointer over the box, then invoke a Sequence that clicks at the mouse position, types in a number, and presses Return.

If you figure out a better way, let us know.

APPENDIX

Resources

Aladdin Systems, Inc.
StuffIt Deluxe
Deer Park Center
Suite 23A-171
Aptos, CA 95003
408-685-9175

Aldus Corporation
PageMaker
411 First Ave. S.
Suite 200
Seattle, WA 98104
206-622-5500

CE Software
QuicKeys
DiskTop
Box 65580
West Des Moines, IA
50265
515-224-1995

Claris Corporation
FileMaker Pro
5201 Patrick Henry Dr.
Santa Clara, CA 95052
408-987-7000

CompuServe Information Service
5000 Arlington
Centre Blvd.
Box 20212
Columbus, OH 43220
614-457-8600

Hooleon Corporation
Keyboard enhancements
Box 230
Cornville, AZ 86325
602-634-7515

Simeon Leifer
MenuWait, WindowWait,
CursorWait, MenuDecision, WindowDecision
1134 Oak St. S.
Pasadena, CA 91030
CompuServe: 71131,3555
   Simeon asks that if you use the US mail, include a SASE and disk, or $5 for postage and disk, besides the pay-what-you-think-it's-worth amount.

Microsoft Corporation
Microsoft Word
Microsoft Excel
One Microsoft Way
Redmond, WA 98052
206-882-8080

Multicomp, Inc.
F-Key Flipbook
Keystroke Catalog
Box 2761
Abilene, TX 79604
915-676-0844

Quantum Computer Services, Inc.
America Online
8619 Westwood Center Dr.
Vienna, VA 22182
703-448-8700

Quark Inc.
QuarkXPress
300 S. Jackson, Suite 100
Denver, CO 80209
303-934-2211
800-356-9363

Index

More from Peachpit Press...

CANNED ART: CLIP ART FOR THE MACINTOSH

▲ *Erfert Fenton and Christine Morrissett*

A fully indexed sample book showing over 15,000 pieces of clip art available from 35 different companies. Includes coupons for over $1,000 in discounts on commercial clip art. The two optional All Star Sample Disks contain 61 pieces of clip art. *(825 pp)*

CANVAS 3:0: THE BOOK

▲ *Deke McClelland*

The first guide to Deneba's newly enhanced drawing and painting program, officially endorsed by Deneba Software. *(373 pp)*

DATABASE 101

▲ *Guy Kawasaki*

An elementary introduction to Mac databases by the author of *The Macintosh Way*. Includes a disk with test-drive versions of TouchBASE and FileMaker Pro. (176 pp plus disk)

DESKTOP PUBLISHER'S SURVIVAL KIT

▲ *David Blatner*

Essential tips and tools for setting up a Mac desktop publishing system. Includes a disk containing 12 great desktop publishing utilities, two PostScript fonts, and 450K of clip art. *(426 pp plus disk)*

LEARNING POSTSCRIPT: A VISUAL APPROACH

▲ *Ross Smith*

An easy show-and-tell tutorial on the PostScript page description language. Each left-facing page introduces a PostScript concept, including a short demonstration program; each right-facing page shows the printed result. *(426 pp)*

THE LITTLE MAC BOOK, 2nd Edition

▲ *Robin Williams and Kay Nelson*

Peachpit's bestselling beginner's guide to the Macintosh, updated for System 7. *(184 pp)*

THE LITTLE SYSTEM 7 BOOK

▲ *Kay Yarborough Nelson*

Teach yourself the essentials of System 7 and skip the technical mumbo jumbo! (160 pp)

THE MACINTOSH FONT BOOK, 2nd Edition

▲ *Erfert Fenton*

Long acknowledged as the definitive guide to Macintosh fonts, this book is now revised for TrueType and System 7. Everything from font basics to resolving ID conflicts. (348 pp)

THE MAC IS NOT A TYPEWRITER

▲ *Robin Williams*

Twenty easy tips for producing beautiful typography with a Mac and a laser printer. Winner of the Benjamin Franklin Award. *(72 pp)*

PAGEMAKER 4: AN EASY DESK REFERENCE
▲ *Robin Williams*

Written by the author of *The Little Mac Book* and *The Mac is not a typewriter*, this comprehensive reference book is designed both for beginners and advanced PageMaker users. The unique format lets you look up information about PageMaker according to the problem or task at hand. *(784 pp)*

PAGEMAKER 4: VISUAL QUICKSTART GUIDE
▲ *Webster & Associates*

This book relies on pictures rather than lengthy explanations to quickly get you up and running in PageMaker 4. *(166 pp)*

THE PUBLISH BOOK OF TIPS
▲ *Robin Eckhardt, Bob Weibel, and Ted Nace*

Hundreds of the best desktop publishing tips gleaned from five years of *Publish* Magazine. The book covers both Macintosh and IBM software and hardware, including PageMaker, Ventura, QuarkXPress, FreeHand, Illustrator, clip art, PostScript, fonts, laser printers, file formats, and imagesetting. (640 pp)

THE QUARKXPRESS BOOK, 2nd Edition
▲ *David Blatner and Keith Stimely*

Peachpit's bestselling, comprehensive guide to QuarkXPress and XTensions, now updated for version 3.1. Tim Gill, the founder of Quark, wrote, "This is not a good book on XPress. It is a great book." While still appropriate for version 3.0, this second edition provides an extensive section on the new features of version 3.1, along with full-color illustrations showing Quark's new color capabilities.

THE QUARKXPRESS POSTER
▲ *David Blatner*

This 17-by-22-inch chart has every QuarkXPress keystroke laid out in an easy-to-see and easy-to-use format, so you don't have to waste time or brain space trying to remember the darn things. Works with QuarkXPress version 3.0 or 3.1.

REAL WORLD FREEHAND 3
▲ *Olav Martin Kvern*

The ultimate insider's guide to the latest release of this popular Mac drawing program. After laying out the basics, the book concentrates on advanced techniques and delves into how to fine-tune FreeHand, how to work with color, how to overcome printing problems, and how to create special effects. *(474 pp)*

REAL WORLD FREEHAND DISK
▲ *Olav Martin Kvern*

This disk contains all the PostScript lines and fills shown in *Real World FreeHand 3*, plus additional lines and fills not shown in the book. Besides that, you'll find FHX3 files for supercharging your copy of FreeHand, ColorMaker (an application for generating color libraries), several useful color libraries, ResEdit templates for creating your own FHX3 files, FreeHand templates containing tiling and latticework patterns, and more tips and tricks.

Order Form

phone: 800/283-9444 or 510/548-4393
fax: 510/548-5991

Quantity	Title	Price	Total
	Canned Art: Clip Art for the Macintosh (book only)	29.95	
	Canned Art: Clip Art for the Macintosh (book and disks)	39.95	
	Canvas 3.0: The Book	21.95	
	Database 101 (book and disk)	18.95	
	Desktop Publisher's Survival Kit	22.95	
	Learning PostScript: A Visual Approach	22.95	
	The Little Mac Book, 2nd Edition	14.95	
	The Little QuicKeys Book	18.95	
	The Little System 7 Book	12.95	
	The Macintosh Font Book, 2nd Edition	23.95	
	The Mac is not a typewriter	9.95	
	PageMaker 4: An Easy Desk Reference (Mac edition)	29.95	
	PageMaker 4: Visual QuickStart Guide (Mac edition)	12.95	
	The Publish Book of Tips	24.95	
	The QuarkXPress Book, 2nd Edition	27.95	
	The QuarkXPress Poster	9.95	
	Real World FreeHand 3	27.95	
	Real World FreeHand Disk	20.00	

Tax of 8.25% applies to California residents only.	**Subtotal**	
UPS ground shipping: $4 for first item, $1 each additional.	**8.25% Tax (CA only)**	
UPS 2nd day air: $7 for first item, $2 each additional.		
Air mail to Canada: $6 first item, $4 each additional.	**Shipping**	
Air mail overseas: $14 each item.	**TOTAL**	

Name

Company

Address

City

State   Zip

Phone

☐ Check enclosed   ☐ Visa   ☐ MasterCard

☐ Company Purchase Order #

Credit Card Number

Expiration Date

Peachpit Press, Inc. ▲ 2414 Sixth St. ▲ Berkeley, CA 94710
Satisfaction is unconditionally guaranteed or your money will be cheerfully refunded!